SPECIAL DEVOTION

TO THE

HOLY GHOST

A MANUAL

FOR THE USE OF SEMINARIANS, PRIESTS, RELIGIOUS AND
THE CHRISTIAN PEOPLE, BY THE

VERY REVEREND
Dr. OTTO ZARDETTI, V. G.

With a letter of introduction by the

Rt. Rev. John Keane, D.D.,

Bishop of Richmond.

Imprimatur.

✠ Michael Heiss,

Archiepiscopus Milwaukiensis.

Milwauklue, die 25. Sept. 1888.

"Postremo, quum frustra speraretur fore, ut qui in apostolicum ministerium assumuntur, sanctae suae vocationi respondeant nisi spiritum ecclesiasticum, qui est abundans quaedam seu copiosa participatio spiritus Christi, in se habeant, de eo vivant, ab eo moveantur et per eum operentur, sedulo ac ferventer colatur in seminariis devotio in Spiritum Sanctum, ut ille Spiritus Christi, Summi Sacerdotis, veniat in clericos, apud eos maneat, in eisque operetur; quem in finem commendamus Confraternitatis Spiritus Sancti propagationem in seminariis, quae confraternitas a S. Sede jam approbata est."

Conc. Balt. III. Tit. 5. C. II. n. 165.

IN SPIRITU ET VERITATE

PROVIDENCE, R. I., July 22d, 1888.

My Dear Dr. Zardetti:

Your request that I should write a few lines in regard to your forthcoming work on "Devotion to God the Holy Ghost," finds me in the midst of labors, which more than sufficiently occupy my time and tax my strength. But He who is "*In labore requies*" must enable me to comply with your request.

I am deeply convinced that the object of your work is entirely in accord with the yearnings of the Sacred Heart of our Divine Lord. He who told his disciples that it was expedient for them that He should leave them in order that the Paraclete should come to them, assuredly yearns to see that Holy Spirit appreciated as He ought to be. The special direction towards devotion to God the Holy Ghost, which His Providence is now giving to innumerable souls throughout the church, may well be considered one of the greatest graces vouchsafed to our generation.

The Third Plenary Council, whose name will forever be associated with the foundation of the Catholic University of America, will also be renowned for its declaration that a great devotion to God the Holy Ghost ought to reign in the heart of every priest, and that its assiduous cultivation in aspirants to the holy priesthood should form a notable part of their ecclesiastical training. Most appropriately do these two decrees emanate together from that venerable assemblage of all the Bishops of our country In vain would we strive for the bestowal of the highest learning on our priests and our people, unless the Holy Spirit of Truth and of Love were its light and its life. If only we can pour that highest light and highest love into our country's mind and heart, then what can there be too great and noble for her attainment?

We are pioneers in a grand work. The finger of God and of His church points it out to us ; we feel that we must be up and doing the best we can. Others will call our work rude and rough. We acknowledge beforehand that they are right in the criticism, and none will rejoice more heartily than we when they surpass us. Meanwhile, let us press on.

May God abundantly bless your look, and may it serve to bring forth the Fruits of the Holy Ghost in innumerable souls.

Your friend in Christ,

JOHN J. KEANE,

Bishop of Richmond.

Preface.

THE usual object of a preface is to solicit the reader's interest for a book, or his indulgence for its defects, or his better understanding of it through explanations of its plan and disposition. Whilst now this mode-t little volume which we present to the public, bears its own justification on the front page by reproducing the solemn and-authoritative words of the Fathers of the last Plenary Council of Baltimore with reference to the Devotion to God, the Holy Ghost, we have but to say a few words on its general plan and above all, to crave the indulgence of the reader, both for the boldness of our attempt and the many defects necessarily and unavoidably resulting from our inability for so noble and sublime a task. In his letter to the Rt. Rev. Mgr. O'Connell, D. D., Rector of the American College at Rome, His Eminence, Cardinal Manning, says: " *You have done well in making the devotion of the Holy Ghost the devotion of the American College, and the Bishops of America have set us all an example in their forwardness to promote this adoration of the Sanctifier.*" It was in reflecting upon these words that we thought that our "forwardness" could also be kindly excused.

For years we have looked upon this devotion as the most efficacious means that could be used to awaken in us the consciousness of the presence and indwelling of the Holy Ghost, not only in the Church as a whole, but also in each one of us, and to neutralize the peril of the day, the unspirituality of man and the revival of naturalism in the world. Since, however, those have spoken, whose voice we

are bound to revere as the voice of God, and since
the most solemn assembly of Bishops that ever met
on American soil under the guidance of the Holy
Spirit and with the confirmation of the Vicar of
Christ has laid it down as a most emphatic desire
that this devotion should be fervently practiced and
earnestly promoted and cultivated, especially in
our Colleges and Seminaries, by the aspirants to
the holy priesthood who are to be the future priests
of our country, it would be superfluous were we to
say more of the legitimacy of our object in view.
Our little volume consequently aims at providing
simply an humble aid in carrying out the wish of our
apostolic Fathers, the Bishops of the Church in this
country, towards cultivating and furthering this
devotion. We shall scarcely be contradicted in
saying that this devotion, so essentially christian
and so eminently practical, is hardly known and
practiced enough even among the devout people.
There have indeed appeared books of recent date
treating on this subject, yet whilst the golden books
of Cardinal Manning, the apostle of this devotion,
are not within the reach of all and are even beyond
the grasp of mind of some, the so-called " Little
books of the Holy Ghost," published some years
ago in London, seem to us inadequate to fully
answer the urgent demand of a substantial, practical, comprehensive manual of this devotion. Our
intention, therefore, in composing this volume was
exactly this : To gather into *one* volume as far
as possible, all that could and should be said of
this devotion and to give into the hands of the
devout " servants of the Holy Ghost "—whose
number may ever increase—inside and outside of
our seminaries a little counsellor imparting a
devotional instruction and making devotion in-
structive.

In the first part we tried the best we could, to
throw light on the various relations of this devotion and show its peculiar fitness for our time, age,
country and state, thus enlarging upon Cardinal

Manning's words : " *How, then, is it that this truth, which is like the luminous ether of the church, has been so slightly and seldom practiced by private devotion?.. Is not this, then, the devotion for bishops and priests? Are not Christians the anointed, and is it not the devotion for all Christians?* " We have in a special chapter, we think sufficiently, treated of the relations of this devotion to others, principally to the devotion to the most Sacred Heart of Jesus and on the often objected mystical or impractical character of this devotion.

Part the second deals with all the formalities, as we may call them, of this devotion and of its concrete form, the Confraternity of the Servants of the Holy Ghost. This part was absolutely required to make this volume a practical manual for the use of our seminarians and priests. We thought it proper, to add, *in extenso*, the two official letters of Cardinal Manning and of Rt. Rev. Bishop Keane of Richmond.

Part the third might seem to some not to occupy the right place. They may think, that the exposition of the office of the Holy Ghost should precede all explanations of the devotion to Him. In making, however, the chapter on "the Office of the Holy Ghost " the third part of this volume and by it immediately introducing the fourth part containing prayers and devotional exercises, we were led by another motive. Cardinal Manning has in his book, " The glories of the Sacred Heart," a most luminous chapter under the heading : " Dogma the source of devotion." A true, correct, deep and comprehensive understanding of the truths of revelation is the only source of truly deep devotion and most surely a deep and fervent devotion to the Third Person in the Trinity must needs result from a comprehensive view of this transcendent office and the all embracing relations to the works of salvation of God the Holy Ghost. We, therefore, in the third part did not so much endeavor to say all that could be said of the " Theology of the Holy

Spirit "– a task by far beyond our purpose—as to show in logical cohesion all His operations and consequently to set in the right light the transcendency of His working. This, we thought, should immediately prepare the mind of the faithful for actual devotion. Our expositions may seem defective to many as to completeness, but they will, we think, be found correct and sound. To make the brief instructions of each chapter directly melt into devotion, we have always added a corresponding "aspiration" and given an appropriate intention of prayer. Thus the reading of these chapters for the members of the Confraternity could be so disposed, that beginning with chapter the first on the Friday after Ascension, the first day of the Novena, previous to Pentecost, the whole part could be gone through at the end of the Octave.

Part the fourth, then, contains a selection of prayers and hymns with some theological introductions, which may prove acceptable to those who are mindful of the words of the Apostle, that our faith and worship be " reasonable service, " (Rom. XII, I). and that it most especially becomes a Servant of the Holy Ghost to adore God in the spirit and the truth.

It would be needless to say from what sources we have, or rather from which main source we have principally and continually drawn. The mottoes on all the title pages of the four parts of this volume, as well as the numerous quotations interwoven in our text, must at once show that we not only drew from the truly apostolic writings of Cardinal Manning, but that we directly strove to make this great man speak, and in doing so we simply borrowed the views, ideas and expressions of the man to whom we owe in sincerest gratitude all the little of our devotion to the Holy Spirit. Not only do we confess that what this volume contains, apart from its great defects due to our littleness, is but a reproduction of ideas stored up in our mind by an uninterrupted and reverential reading of the works of our great Cardinal, but we glory in that and shall be happy if our endeavors have at least not obscured the luminous rays of his teaching. To any attentive observer it must appear most striking how the light of the Pentecostal sun is reflected upon every page of Cardinal Manning's works, books and sermons, so that he must be truly recognized and styled the Apostle of the Holy Spirit. The " Kindly light" led him from the twilight of a fragmentary Christianity to the noonday revelation in the Church of Christ. What he writes : *" The Apostolic preaching shows that we are under the dispensation of the Spirit. The presence and office of the Holy Ghost pervade all the Apostles wrote. The writings of the Fathers are full of the Holy Ghost. They wrote as in the light of the day of Pentecost ; especially St. Thomas, St. Augustin, St. Basil, St. Dydimus, St. Gregory of Nazianzum, and St. Athanasius. The Person, the Presence, and the Office of the Holy Ghost pervade their writings also in continuity with the writings of the Apostles,"*—is true of; Cardinal Manning himself. It is the dazzling light of the noonday sun of Pentecost that sheds forth its rays from our Cardinal's writings and sayings as, for instance, when he says : *"It is this devotion that illuminates and infuses the light of all dogmas of the faith. As all things are visible in the light of the sun, so all truths, from the Holy Trinity to Extreme Unction, are made manifest by devotion to the Holy Ghost. If we were pleni Spiritu Sancto, we should understand the divine tradition of the Church and the Summa of St. Thomas by a kindred intuition."* Besides, then the writings of Cardinal *Manning*, the Theology of Cardinal *Franzelin*, the most valuable book of the Very Rev. *Hecker*, "The Church and the Age," the devotional books of Mgr. *Preston*, V. G.. " The Divine Paraclete " and the " Little Books of the Holy Ghost " have repeatedly been used and quoted.

It is our intention to have, in case of a good circulation of this volume, at least three others of the same size, following it at intervals, so as to form a little series of books to further the devotion and to make it more practical and popular. Of these eventually forthcoming volumes the next will have the title " *Pentecost* " and accordingly contain all about Pentecost of the old and the new law, its history, meaning, liturgy and so forth. Our former conversation with seminarians in the Provincial Seminary, of Milwaukee, to whom also as a token of remembrance and affection we especially present this little book, strengthens us moreover in the hope that our explanations in this and following volumes of the same object may prove useful to the priests in their pastoral work and in the discharge of the apostolic office of breaking the bread of life to the faithful people in short and solid instructions.

We have reason to plead once more for indulgence on account of the many imperfections of this publication. Not only must they be ascribed to our imperfect knowledge of the English idiom, which is not our mother tongue, but also to the many difficulties for literary work, that are involved in a condition such as ours at present, where the duties of practical administration allow a man to give but interrupted leisure moments or evening hours to such work. Whilst these circumstances must surely plead excuse for many shortcomings of our writing, we on the other hand, must say that it was always a sweet recreation to turn from the labors of the day to this little work and that we somewhat at least realized the beautiful saying of St. Francis of Sales in his preface to the book, " The Love of God " : " *As those who engrave or cut precious stones, having their sight tired by keeping it constantly fixed upon the small lines of their work, are glad to keep before them some fair emerald that by beholding it from time to time they may be recreated with its greenness and restore their weakened sight to its natural condition—so in the press of business which my office daily draws upon me I have ever little projects of some treatise of piety, which I look at when I can, to revive and un-weary my mind."* (Engl. Translat. by Father Mackey, O. S.B., page 10).

Most special thanks are due and herewith tendered for the great kindness and ability with which the Reverend Father *Redmond*, Rector of the Church of the Sacred Heart of Jesus in Yankton, Dak., has willingly given time and trouble to peruse and correct our manuscript. Likewise we wish to express our thankfulness to the Reverend Fathers *Thomas L. Rabsteinek* and *Anthony O'Hara* of this Vicariate, who, whilst students in the Bishop's house, have rendered us most kindly their valuable services in selecting and copying the many quotations, prayers, hymns, etc. We humbly hope that this little volume may, in divine mercy, aid the members of the Confraternity in their devotion to the Divine Spirit and be a means of exciting new and more intelligent piety in many hearts. With the knowledge of the Holy Ghost, the Spiritual life will deepen and the love of God grow stronger in our souls. Thus this devotion, though by no means new, will nevertheless produce a revival of true faith and sincere piety. We conclude by quoting the words of our great Cardinal in his letter to Dr. O'Connell: *"May the Holy Ghost make you all Apostles of Jesus Christ in your great and noble land!"*

YANKTON, Dakota, on Whitsunday, 1888.

THE AUTHOR.

Contents.

I. *Decree of the III. Council of Baltimore* 3.

II. *Preface* .. 6.

III. *Contents* .... .13.

PART I.

𝕿𝖍𝖊 𝕯𝖊𝖛𝖔𝖙𝖎𝖔𝖓 𝖙𝖔 𝕲𝖔𝖉 𝖙𝖍𝖊 𝕳𝖔𝖑𝖞 𝕲𝖍𝖔𝖘𝖙.

1. The Devotion to the third Person in the Most Holy Trinity.................. 19
2. The Devotion to God, the Holy Ghost, called by St. Paul "The Ministration of the Spirit," the Devotion of the period.. 30
3. The Devotion of our time and age......... 41
4. The Devotion of this country............. 57
5. The Devotion of the priests... 71
6. The Devotion in its relations to other devotions and confraternities,.............. 86
7. The Devotion and the fruits it is expected to bear..... 104

PART II.

𝕿𝖍𝖊 𝕮𝖔𝖓𝖋𝖗𝖆𝖙𝖊𝖗𝖓𝖎𝖙𝖞 𝖔𝖋 𝖙𝖍𝖊 𝕾𝖊𝖗𝖛𝖆𝖓𝖙𝖘 𝖔𝖋 𝖙𝖍𝖊 𝕳𝖔𝖑𝖞 𝕲𝖍𝖔𝖘𝖙.

1. Origin of the Confraternity.................135
2. Object, Rules and Obligations of the Confraternity of the Servants of the Holy Ghost.................................151

3. Privileges of the Confraternity of the Servants of the Holy Ghost..................161
4. The Arch-Confraternity of the Servants of the Holy Ghost..... 166

PART III.

The Office of God the Holy Ghost.

1. The Holy Ghost in the Most Holy Trinity..191
2. The Holy Ghost and the Creation.........199
3. The Holy Ghost and the Creation of Man..202
4. The Holy Ghost and His universal operation after the fall of man....................208
5. The Holy Ghost and the people elect.......214
6. The Holy Ghost and the Promise of the Father by the mouth of the prophets 219
7. The Holy Ghost and the Mother of God....224
8. The Holy Ghost and the Word Incarnate...232
9. The Holy Ghost and the Promise of the Son.237
10. The Holy Ghost and "His Advent on Pentecost"...................................242
11. The Holy Ghost and the Mystical Body of Christ......... 249
12. The Holy Ghost and the properties and notes of the Church......................255
13. The Holy Ghost and the Authority in the Church.... 271
14. The Holy Ghost and the Fountains of Revelation................. 284
15. The Holy Ghost and Separation from the Church......... 294
16. The Holy Ghost and the Sanctification of Individuals...........................300
17. The Holy Ghost and His gifts and fruits in the faithful soul....................312

18. The Holy Ghost and the sin against Him...326
19. The Holy Ghost and the Consummation of
    all things.... 346
20. Conclusion.................................. 354

PART IV.

Daily Devotion to God the Holy Ghost.

I.

Daily Prayers to the Holy Ghost.

1. Acts of Faith, Hope, Charity and Contrition.366
2. First prayer to God the Holy Ghost 369
   Second "   "   "   "   "   " 370
   Third "   "   "   "   "   " 370
   Fourth "   "   "   "   "   "   ... 371
3. Short prayers to God the Holy Ghost 372
4. Two Hymns to God the Holy Ghost 374

II.

The Holy Ghost and the Sacrament of Penance.

1. Considerations to excite Contrition. 380
2. The Miserere............... 382

III.

The Holy Ghost and the Sacrament of the Most Holy Eucharist.

1. Orations before Holy Mass.................388
2. Some Orations in Latin for Priests........392
2. A Mass of the Holy Ghost.................396

IV.

Prayers to the Holy Ghost for Extraordinary Occasions.

1. Prayers for the seven gifts of the Holy Spirit..426
2. Acts of Adoration.......................................430
3. Little Office of the Holy Ghost...... 433
4. Litany of the Holy Ghost......... 440
5. Prayer for our Country.................. .446

V.

Hymns to the Holy Ghost.

1. To the Holy Ghost; God over all Blessed forever.................................449
2. A Hymn of the Servants of the Holy Ghost to their Loved One......................451
3. Nunc Sancte nobis Spiritus.................462
4. O Fons Amoris Spiritus....................463
5. Sancti Spiritus adsit nobis gratia..........463
6. O Ignis Spiritus Paracliti...... 467
7. Amor Patris et Filii.......................469
8. Veni Creator Spiritus, Spiritus Recreator..470
9. Veni, Summe Consolator...................471
10. Simplex in essentia........................474
11. Part of a Hymn of Hugo of St. Victor....476
12. Spiritus Sancte, Pie Paraclite.............478

PART I.

The Devotion to God, the Holy Ghost.

"You have done well in making the devotion to the Holy Ghost the devotion of the American College, and the Bishops of America have set us an example in their forwardness to promote this adoration of the Sanctifier."

Cardinal Manning in his letter to Doctor O'Connell, the Rector of the American College, 1887.

I.

The Devotion to the Third Person of the Most Holy Trinity.

WHEN in the last Plenary Council of Baltimore the Bishops of these United States, *"congregati in Spiritu Sancto"* were consulting how to further the education and the training of the future clergy of this country, they did not confine their advice, admonitions, and decrees, merely to the cultivation of science and the advancement in ecclesiastical learning. Knowing full well, that "knowledge puffeth up," (I. Cor. 8, 1.) "but the Spirit quickeneth," (II. Col. 3, 7.), they laid special stress on the "spiritus ecclesiasticus" which the Candidates for the holy Priesthood, should above all others, acquire and exercise both in the seminary and afterwards in the practice of the holy ministry. Pointing, therefore, to the very best means, by which the true clerical spirit could be acquired, the Bishops "whom the Holy Ghost has placed, to rule the church of God," (Act. 20, 28.) most emphatically commended the Devotion to God the Holy Ghost in the beautiful expressions, given in the first page of this volume.

The word of authority has thus been spoken. The Confirmation of the Council by the Holy Father has put the final seal on the various decrees. The sole fact, that "it seemeu good to the Holy Ghost" and to the Bishops, (Act. 15, 28.) to speak so profusely and impressively of this Devotion must be sufficient evidence to us, both of the importance of the advice and of the ardent desire on the part of the Most Reverend Fathers, to see their suggestions complied with. The seed of the apostolic sowers has thus been planted, but it will be our duty, to prove, that it has fallen on good ground, and that we are the ones who, in a good and very good heart, hearing the word, keep it, and bring forth fruit in patience." (S. Luk. 4, 15.) The idea has been suggested and a most ardent desire of our ecclesiastical superiors has been made known to us. We know the decree, but we also know from holy Writ, that "the letter killeth, but the Spirit quickeneth" (II. Cor. 3, 6), and we must consequently do our best to make the idea take shape, the word bring fruit and the action of our bishops call forth our corresponding activity and devotion.

" Devotion, or worship, or adoration is the love and veneration with which we regard God and His Divine Truth. There can be no Divine Truth which ought not to be an object of love and veneration. Every truth that God has revealed is the word of God; it is the mind of Jesus Christ—it comes to us from a divine voice. How is it possible that we can do otherwise than love and venerate every such divine declaration? If, when a divine truth is declared to us, our hearts do not turn to it, as the eye turns to the light; if there be not in us an instinctive yearning, which makes us promptly turn to the sound of the divine voice, the fault is in our hearts; for just in proportion as we know the truth we shall be drawn towards it.

We may therefore understand the relation between dogma and devotion to be simply this, that without knowledge we cannot have either a love or a veneration for truth. Our Lord said, ' You adore that which you know not;' and because they knew it not they could not 'adore in spirit and in truth.' S. Paul found some of the disciples who did not even know that the Holy Ghost existed. Could they have had any love and veneration for the Third Person of the Blessed Trinity, of whose coming, nay, of whose existence, they never heard? We may, indeed, love a person whom we have never seen, because S. Peter says of our Divine Lord, 'Whom not having seen you love;' but we cannot love anybody whom we do not know. Therefore it is a law of our nature that we can will nothing and can love nothing unless we first know it. The intellect is said in philosophy to carry a light before the will. What is called dogma, or divine truth, must go before all devotion; and in the proportion in which we have the light to know the objects of faith, in that proportion, if we be faithful, devotion will spring up in our hearts."

The Devotion to God, the Holy Ghost, has in its very nature something more mystical than other devotions and is partly for this reason also less popular, than others. More than other devotions it is therefore the devotion of those: "to whom it is given to know the mystery of the kingdom of God" (S. Mark. 4. 11.); it is peculiarly the devotion of priests, and only through them will it spread to the faithful. For the Pentecostal effusion of the Holy Spirit in all its fulness has first been bestowed upon the Apostles and God has ordained "that through them and their successors the Holy Spirit should be given to the faithful" (Pontificale Rom. in ritu

Confirmationis.) Hence this devotion, even more than others, must be preached and communicated to the people by the priest.

Now the Latin adage has it: "*nil volitum, nisi prius cognitum*." Nothing will be highly appreciated, unless it be first fully known in its value and thoroughly understood in its meaning and importance. Hence the following brief explanations aim at nothing, but to impress upon the reader of this little volume the special characteristics of this Devotion to God the Holy Ghost.

"It seeks," says the Cardinal, "to awaken in us a consciousness of the presence and indwelling of the Holy Ghost, not only in the Church as a whole, but in each one of us. St. Augustine says that those who saw the miracle of the loaves in the wilderness wondered; but that they had no wonder at the daily miracles of the natural world, because by habit they had become unconscious of them. So we are unconscious of the internal presence of the Spirit of God. We speak of grace, but we forget the divine Person whose presence and power confer grace upon us. The object, then, of this Devotion is to awaken our consciousness with a personal love, with fidelity of conscience and with the fervor of punctual and exact obedience." With the knowledge of the

Holy Ghost, the spiritual life will deepen and the love of God grow stronger in our souls.

Devotion springs as necessarily forth from a living faith, as heat and light beam forth from a sparkling flame. Devotion is the perfume and flavor of the flower, if faith is its root. Hence it is, that true devotion supposes the true faith, and a devotion is the more essential, deep, sublime, salutary and commendable, the more essential in the christian revelation the specific truth is that forms its main object.

Now we cannot say anything more than this to throw the full daylight upon the importance of this our devotion. Christian revelation has it as its first and cardinal article of faith, that we believe in and profess *one* God in *three* divine persons, and Catholic Theology tells us, that these two truths of the most holy Trinity and of the Incarnation of our Lord are truths which must be believed "*necessitate medii*" by all who wish to be saved. So all-important and so necessary to salvation is faith in the Most Holy Trinity, that the Church, in commending a departing soul to the mercy of God, she lays most solemn stress on the fact, that, although this soul has often sinned and offended God, yet it never denied and ever believed and professed the triune God, the Father, the Son and the Holy Ghost. (Preces Commendationis animae in Breviario Romano.)

Whenever we say the Credo we solemnly profess: *"And I believe in the Holy Ghost, the Lord and Lifegiver, who proceedeth from the Father and Son, who together with the Father and the Son is adored and glorified."*

Whenever alone or in communion with others we repeat the ancient doxology: *" Glory be to the Father and to the Son and to the Holy Ghost,"* we practice a special devotion towards the Three Divine Persons.

In adoring with a special devotion the Third Person of the Most Holy Trinity, we do not by any means exclude from our worship the other two Persons. Thus adoring One God and paying the tribute of a special and distinct devotion to the Divine Person of the Holy Ghost we only in practice express, what Catholic doctrine in the Athanasian Creed teaches us, saying: *" This is the Catholic faith that we adore one God in Trinity, and the Trinity in unity, neither confusing the Persons nor separating the substance. One is the person of the Father, another that of the Son and another that of the Holy Spirit. But one is the divinity of the Father, the Son, and the Holy Spirit; the glory is equal and*

the majesty is co-eternal."   Hence our Devotion
towards the Third Person of the Godhead is
only the realization of the old and un-
changeable truth, the bringing into clearer
light and action That which is essential to
our Christian confession and spiritual life.

The Holy Catholic Church has under
the guidance of this Spirit, dwelling and
acting in her, always given the most solemn
and public expression to the truth of the
Nicean Creed: "I believe in the Holy
Ghost, the Lord and Lifegiver, who proceedeth from the Father and Son, ... *who together with the Father and the Son is adored and
glorified.*"   The same must likewise be
granted with reference to the faithful in general, since they, following the lead of the
Church, ever and everywhere have recourse
to the Holy Spirit, invoke His coming, implore His illumining and strenghtening
assistance.   Nevertheless we must say with
our Cardinal: "It has always seemed to me
both strange and wonderful that whereas we
worship   the   ever   blessed   Trinity—the
Father, the Son, and the Holy Ghost—in
con-substantial unity; and whereas we worship the Person of the Father with a special
and daily oration every time we say the
Lord's Prayer, and whereas we worship the
Person of the Son by concluding all our

prayers through His Name, and by adoring Him in the ever blessed sacrament; nevertheless, we rarely worship and adore with a distinct and special adoration the Person of God the Holy Ghost. Why is this? I believe it to be for this reason. The conception of the fatherhood of God and of our filial relation to Him is a conception altogether natural to our hearts. We learn it in our home from our earliest consciousness in the relation we bear to our earthly father. The incarnation of the Son of God brings Him also within the sphere and range of our intelligence and heart; so that we conceive Him as Man incarnate, visible upon earth, and invested with all our sympathies, and with the love of His sacred Heart full of compassion for us. These two conceptions are, I may say, within the range of nature. They come to us at once. But the Holy Ghost is a Spirit that has never been seen, has never been incarnate, is always inscrutable, present everywhere, never manifest except by the operations of His power—this is a reality, like the motion of the earth, which we know in our reason, but cannot detect by any sense, or it is like the circulation of the blood, which we know as a fact, but never perceive all day long. So the indwelling and the work of the Holy Ghost (both in the Church

as a body and in the individual soul) is a
divine truth, so inscrutable, so impalpable,
so insensible, that we are oblivious of its existence. Therefore it is that we do not so
often adore the Author and Giver of all
grace with a special worship." To make
up, therefore, for such deficiencies, in the
past, Devotion to God, the Holy Ghost tends to
bring home to our mind the Personality and
Office of the Third Person of the Most Holy
Trinity. This it does by calling to our
memory and consciousness the majesty and
transcendent operation of the Holy Ghost in
the entire plan of salvation and by arousing
in our souls the spirit of prayer, by which
alone the " Paraclete " is drawn down upon
us and thus a larger effusion of this Divine
Spirit is communicated to the souls of those,
who participate in the devotion. " The
glory of His Person " is consequently the
first reason for this devotion. " The titles of
the Holy Ghost declare his divine glory.
He is the Term, or the Complement, of the
Holy Trinity, because the Son is begotten of
the Father, and the Holy Ghost proceeds
from the Father and the Son ; but there the
Holy Trinity rests complete. No divine
Person proceeds from the Holy Ghost. He
is the last of the three divine Persons, and
therefore he is the Complement, the Per-

fecter, and the Term of the ever blessed Three. He is, so to speak, the Bound of the boundless nature, which is unlimited. Again He is called the Perfecter for this reason: God the Father is uncreated being, God the Son uncreated intelligence, and God the Holy Ghost is uncreated love; and the uncreated being, intelligence, and love of God, are God. God without intelligence would not be perfect; and God without love would not be perfect; and as we can conceive nothing beyond being, intelligence and love, God the Holy Ghost who is the love of the Father and the Son, perfects the mystery of the ever blessed Trinity. But, in as much as He is the Term of the divine Persons, and after Him and beyond Him there is no other divine Personality, it is He, who is in immediate contact with all creatures." This leads us to the following consideration.

2.

The Devotion to God, the Holy Ghost, called by St. Paul "the Ministration of the Spirit," is the Devotion of the period.

In our contemplation of God and the divine Persons we may reverently look at the Deity within itself and at the Deity in its outward action upon things created. The Office of the Holy Ghost in and towards created things is called his outward work, though, strictly speaking, there is nothing *without* the Trinity and all outward work is common to all the three divine Persons. Connecting therefore the relation, which God the Holy Ghost has within the Trinity to the other divine Persons, with the relation we especially appropriate to him without the Trinity, "*ad extra*" Cardinal Manning so beautifully says: "In the Holy Ghost the infinite nature of God has its fulness and by him the finite nature of creatures begins to exist." Speaking of the Holy Ghost's relations towards things created we speak of an action appropriated only to the Third Person. These are relations and operations common, indeed, to the three Persons, but *appropriate* to the Holy Ghost and in this office of appropriation, and in these appropriate relations, we can and ought to adore, to honor, to venerate, and to invoke the Holy Ghost, without excluding from this distinct worship the Father and Son. Now the appropriate mission and Office of the Holy Ghost is that of the Spirit of Truth, or of the Illuminator and the Sanctifier, both of the Church as a whole, and of the single individual soul. This is according to Holy Scripture, saying: " The charity of God is poured out into our hearts by the Holy Ghost, who is given to us." This appropriation, however, arises from two distinct reasons : the one is that the communication of sanctity has a special affinity to the Holy Ghost ; and the other, that as the Son had a special mission into the world to redeem mankind, so the Holy Ghost has a special mission into the world to sanctify those who are faithful to the Redeemer. Of this appropriate Office of the Holy Ghost we now speak, mentioning the " *Ministration of the Spirit* " as the time and period of his more special and more prominent operation among men.

Upon our first father Adam the Holy
Ghost descended, and then "was he made
into a living soul" and constituted in original sanctity.   Never since, not even after the
fall of man, has His merciful operation been
interrupted.   He sanctified those who were
saved in virtue of Christ's redemption anticipated; He dwelt in the just ones of the
Old Covenant; He finally descended in
visible form upon the Messiah whilst being
baptized in the Jordan, to consecrate Him
into His messianic work and to rest upon
Him.

Why then speak of a special mission of
the Holy Ghost assigned to our time?
Which is this most especial, "*Ministration of
the Spirit*" or "dispensation of the Holy
Ghost?"   Why do we, so to speak, stand
in a more immediate relation to this Third
divine Person than those who lived before
or even at the time of Christ?   Under the
guidance of the Church we ascribe the creation especially to God the Father.   To God
the Son we ascribe the redemption, as He
alone took to Himself human nature and
was incarnate.   To God the Holy Ghost,
however, we in accordance with Holy
Writ, the Fathers and constant Theological
doctrine ascribe the work of sanctification
by the application of Christ's redemption

to mankind in all succeeding generations. According to the Father's will and the Son's emphatic promise, the Spirit should complete the work and mission of the Son on earth and hence the saying of Christ: "It is expedient for you that I go, for if I go not, the Paraclete will not come to you : but if I go, I will send him to you." (St. John XVI; 7, 13.) St. John says furthermore: "As yet the Spirit was not given, because Jesus was not yet glorified" (St. John. VII. 39); for in order to send the Holy Ghost and make him start His own special mission on earth, the Son had first to accomplish His. The Spirit who vice versa would "glorify" the Son (St. John XVI. 7) would only come, when the Son "ascending above all the heavens, was sitting at the right hand of the Father" (Praefatio in die Pentecostes). And he came at the allotted time. This "Promise of the Father" was poured down upon the Apostles on the great day of Pentecost. Then the "Ministration of the Spirit" began, to continue throughout the course of centuries up to the day, when the Son, "whom they had seen taken up into heaven shall so come as (they) have seen him going into heaven." (Act. I, 11.)

On this "Ministration of the Spirit" in the new law in contrast to the dispensation of the Spirit in the old, the Apostle of the Gentiles enlarges in his second Epistle to the Corinthians, saying: "Being manifested, that you are the epistle of Christ, ministered by us, and written not with ink, but with the Spirit of the living God: not in tables of stone, but in the fleshy tables of the Heart (III. 4).—"Who also hath made us fit ministers of the New Testament, not in the letter, but in the Spirit: for the letter killeth, but the Spirit quickeneth." (III. 6.) — "Now if the ministration of death, engraven with letters upon stones, was glorious, so that the children of Israel could not steadfastly behold the face of Moses, for the glory of his countenance, which is made void: How shall not the ministration of the Spirit be rather in glory? For if the ministration of condemnation be glory: much more the ministration of justice aboundeth in glory. For even that, which was glorious in that part was not glorified, by reason of the glory that excelleth. For if that which is done away was glorious; much more that which remaineth is in glory .... Now the Lord is a Spirit: and where the Spirit of the Lord is, there is liberty. But we all beholding the glory of the Lord with open face, are transformed into the same image from glory to glory, as by the Spirit of the Lord" (III. 6—12, 17, 18).

Of this " Ministration of the Spirit," that is, of the administration of the plenitude of "grace and truth " as it was in Christ Jesus and is given us by the Pentecostal mission of the Paraclete, the Apostle speaks *ex professo* in his first Epistle to the Corinthians, saying : " My speech and my preaching was not in the persuasive words of human wisdom, but in showing of spirit and power : that your faith might not stand on the wisdom of men, but on the power of God ... But we speak the wisdom of God in a mystery, a wisdom which is hidden, which God had ordained before the world unto our glory. Which none of the princes of this world knew : for if they had known it, they would never have crucified the Lord of glory. But, as it is written : That eye had not seen, nor ear heard, neither had it entered into the heart of man, what things God had prepared for them, that love him : But to us God had revealed them by his Spirit : For the Spirit searched all things, yea the deep things of God. For what man knoweth the things of a man, but the spirit of a man that is in him ? So the things also that are of God, no man knoweth but the Spirit of God. Now we have received not the spirit of this world, but the Spirit that is of God ; that we may know the things that are given us from God : which things also we speak, not in the learned words of human wisdom, but in the doctrine of the Spirit comparing spiritual things with spiritual. But the sensual man perceiveth not these things that are of the Spirit of God: for it is foolishness to him and he cannot understand: because it is spiritually examined. But the spiritual man judgeth all things: and he himself is judged of no man. For who had known the mind of the Lord, that he may instruct him? But we have the mind of Christ." (I. Cor. II, 4—16.)

Of this "Ministration of the Spirit" or the Pentecostal mission of the Holy Ghost, under the immediate influence of which we all stand, our Cardinal again so forcibly speaks, saying: "Saint Paul declares to the Galatians, that "when the fulness of the time was come, God sent forth His Son, made of a woman, made under the law, that we might receive the adoption of Sons;" that is to say, all the prophecies of the Old Testament were a prelude to the advent of the Son of God into the world: in like manner I may say that all the prophecies of the Son of God when He came were especially pointed to-the advent of the Holy Ghost. He said: "It is expedient for you that I go; but if I go not, the Paraclete will not come to you; but if I go, I will send Him unto you." "I will ask the Father, and He will send you another Paraclete, that He may abide with you for ever." And on the day of Pentecost, as we read in the Acts, that prophecy was fulfilled: the advent of the Holy Ghost was accomplished. And Saint Augustine calls the day of Pentecost *Dies Natalis Spiritus Sancti*—the nativity of the Holy Ghost, parallel to the nativity of the Son. Saint Paul draws out the contrast between the dispensation of the Old Testament and the dispensation of the New in this manner: He calls the Old Testament the Ministry of the Letter, and he calls the New Testament the Dispensation of the Spirit. We are, therefore, under the dispensation of the Spirit, that is under the dispensation of the Holy Ghost. And yet, with the New Testament in our hands, many are still unconscious, as I said before, of the intimate relation in which we stand to the Third Person of the ever-blessed Trinity, under whose immediate action we are for our sanctification, and by whose divine voice we are guided in our faith. I can easily understand, that a man ignorant of the Scripture history might travel through the Holy Land, and pass through the sacred places, without being conscious of where he was or of the supernatural history attaching to anything he saw. Another man, whose mind was full of the thought of Jesus of Nazareth, and to whom the sacred land consecrated by the footsteps of the Savior, was familiar, in going through Judea and Samaria, would see memorials and admonitions of our Divine Saviour on every side.   In like manner, any man who takes the New Testament into his hands, without the realization of the personality and pres- ence of the Holy Ghost, would perhaps read it from end to end and not perceive the special relation in which we stand to the Holy Ghost.   But any one who will read the New Testament, bearing this truth in mind, cannot fail to perceive what I call the foot- steps, the traces, and the marks of the com- ing and of the working of the Holy Spirit in the church and in our souls.   He will find the New Testament to be full of this main idea of the Gospel—namely, that through the Incarnation of the Son of God, the Holy Ghost has come, by a special mission and with a special office, to dwell personally in the midst of us."

Now these words: " With the New Testa- ment in our hands, many are still uncon- scious, as I said before, of the intimate personal relation in which we stand to the Third Per- son of the ever-blessed Trinity, under whose immediate action we are for our sanctification, and by whose divine voice we are guided in our faith "—are most certainly golden words and expressive of the state of mind of the majority of the faithful. We speak of the Church, of the teaching Authority in the Church, of Holy Scripture as the word of God, of grace and supernatural gifts, but as a rule we are not sufficiently alive to the fact, that the living soul of the Church, the source of the authority and infallibility of the teaching Church, the Inspirer and Interpreter of Scripture, the Author of grace and immediate Distributor of all gifts, consequently the One, under whose Ministration and dispensation we are placed, is the Third Person of Holy Trinity, God, the Holy Ghost. No doubt the exceedingly great merit of our Cardinal's sublime writings and especially of his two incomparable books on "The Temporal Mission of the Holy Ghost" and on "The Internal Mission of the Holy Ghost" chiefly consists in this that, in writing of revelation, the Church, and the dispensation of supernatural grace, he always, unlike those that wrote before him, traces the divine operations to their last source, from which they spring,—to God the Illuminator and Sanctifier both of the Church and the individual soul, to God, the Holy Ghost.

The devotion to God the Holy Ghost con-

sequently commends itself to us living in
"*the Ministration of the Spirit*" by the very
character of this period, as the period, I
might say, of the Holy Ghost par excellence.
To remind us of this fact, to bring home to
our mind the continued effusion of the Pentecostal Spirit and to make us Spiritual, as
the character of the time in which we live
requires us to be, is the principal end of this
Devotion. This again induces us to view our
Devotion from a still more special standpoint.

3.

The Devotion to God the Holy Ghost as the Devotion of our Time and Age.

The period, called by St. Paul the " Ministration of the Spirit," embraces all the time from the day of Pentecost to the second coming of Christ at the end. Dividing, however, again into ages the thousand and more years, that according to St. Peter's saying are " with the Lord as one day " (II. Petr. III, 8), we have special reasons to call our age in a yet fuller sense that of " the Ministration of the Spirit." If, as the Very Reverend Father Hecker beautifully remarks " the history of civilization, since the moment of the Churches' institution on the day of Pentecost is nothing else than a record of the several steps of progress of society, under the guidance of the Catholic Church," there are unmistakable signs, that the members of the Church have in our days entered upon a deeper and more spiritual life than they ever did before.

Our Lord sometime upbraided the Pharisees that they knowing how to discern the
face of the sky did not know the signs of the
times." (Math. XVI, 4.) We can and should
then according to our Lord's hint, watch the
signs of the times and understand the peculiarities of the age in which we live.   Now to any
close observer of our present time it must be
obvious, at first sight, that two contrary movements mould the character of the age: an
ever developing apostasy from church and
faith, and an ever increasing reaction and
revival within the church itself.   Both these
movements call for a new effusion of the
Spirit.   Both these tendencies of our days
are evidence enough that more than ever
before, we stand in need of the Spirit of
strength to resist, and of the Spirit of life, to
prove equal to our task.   Let us have a glance
at these two characteristics of our present
time and we will more vividly perceive the
fitness and expediency of our Devotion.

Nobody can deny that "the mystery of iniquity" has in our days almost reached its
pitch and climax. A new paganism, worse
than the first, because the curse of apostasy
weighs upon it, is spreading far and wide.
The nations are falling away; "sensual men,
not having the Spirit, separate themselves;"

(S. Jud. 19.) "truths are decayed from among
the children of men;" Psalm XI, 1.) and a
daily more increasing darkness that weighs
upon the people sometimes urges upon us the
saying of our Lord, so full of anxiety: "But
yet the Son of man, when he cometh, shall
he find, think you, faith on earth?" (Luk.
XVIII, 8.) "No one" says our Cardinal, "can
read the history of Christendom without discerning the same law of decline and deterio-
ration, which has from the beginning obtained among mankind, prevailing not over the
Church, as it is a work of the Divine presence,
but over the moral, intellectual, social conditions of nations professing Christianity."
Since the so-called Reformation has split the
unity not of the Church but of Christendom,
the spirit of dissolution has done its work
and the stone of authority against which the
Reformers struck, has ground their foundations to powder and to atoms of ever multi-
plying sects. The prodigal son of the six-
teenth century, who refused obedience, left
his father's house, went into the far-off country, has squandered all he had taken along of
his father's fortune. "Look at those who, three
hundred year's ago, rejected the principle of
faith, and adopted in its stead the theories of
criticism, of private judgment, of private interpretation. The Christianity of these sepa-

rated brethren is like a tree that is dying. If
the trunk stands, the branches are bare; or
if there be leaves, they are withered long ago.
National religions are gradually drying up.
The tree is returning to the dust, falling in
upon its own roots. In a little while the
place thereof shall know it no more. Because
men refused to believe the Divine Teacher,
they have lost, first the divine certainty of
revelation; next, the fulness of truth; then
the certain interpretation of Holy Scripture;
and lastly, the inspiration and canon of Scripture itself, together with the consciousness
that faith is a grace infused into the soul,
whereby we live in a supernatural order."
This consciousness of a supernatural order is
especially the great truth decayed amongst
"the children of men" in the present age,
and because it is with most of them a sinful
blindness, veiling their eyes, the words of
St. Paul to the Romans have found again a
fulfillment in our days, as they scarcely did
when first put down by the inspired writer,
saying: "As they liked not to have God in
their knowledge: God delivered them up to
a reprobate sense: to do those things which
are not convenient, being filled with all iniquity, malice, fornication, avarice, wickedness;
full of envy, murder, contention, deceit, ma-
lignity; whisperers, detractors, hateful to

God, contumelious, proud, haughty, invent-
ors of evil things, disobedient to parents, fool-
ish, dissolute, without affection, without fidelity, without mercy, who having known the
justice of God, did not understand that they
who do such things are worthy of death."
(Rom. I, 28–32.) Nor can we say, that the
spread of apostasy and iniquity has not also
its dangerous and ruinous influence on the
children of election and the members of God's
holy Church. We all breathe the same spiritual atmosphere impregnated with false principles and theories; we all are exposed to
the same epidemic poison of iniquity, and our
corrupt nature makes us liable to succumb;
the circumstances in which we live combine
to make one great and most dangerous temptation, that calls to our mind the words of our
divine Saviour: "Because iniquity hath
abounded, the charity of many shall grow
cold." (Math. XXIV, 12.) What then shall
be the remedy against so many actual and
possible evils? What shall break the spell
of the bad spirit of the age and give us
strength to resist "in the evil day"? Will it
not be the going back to the source of truth
which man had deserted, and in consequence
of his desertion is perishing miserably?

When St. Judas Thadeus spoke of "the
sensual men, who separate themselves, hav-

ing not the Spirit," he at once, turning to the faithful, placed in such severe trials, exhorted them, saying : "But you, my beloved, building yourselves upon your most holy faith, *praying in the Holy Ghost*, keep yourselves in the love of God, waiting for the mercy of our Lord Jesus Christ unto life everlasting." (St. Jude Ap. I, 21.) The Apostle thus emphatically mentioning the "prayer in the Holy Ghost," as the best means to resist the seduction of those "who have not the Spirit" and to "keep ourselves in the love of God," is furthermore seconded by St. Paul whose constant doctrine it is that in the spirit alone we shall conquer the flesh. "Walk in the spirit," he says to the Galatians, "and you shall not fulfil the lusts of the flesh. For the flesh lusteth against the spirit and the spirit against the flesh : for these are contrary one to another : so that you do not the things that you would .... They that are Christ's have crucified their flesh with the vices and concupiscences. If we live in the spirit, let us also walk in spirit." (Gal. V, 17). As flesh and spirit are fierce antagonists so also, in the end, will there be a striking contrast between the followers of the one and the other, for : "he that soweth in the flesh will reap corruption of the flesh; but he that soweth in the

spirit will of the spirit reap life everlasting."
(Gal., VI. 8). "In this age then" we sum
up with the impressive appeal of Bishop
Keane, of Richmond, "when the spirit of
error is trying to make men believe that
their life is only like that of the beasts of
the field, the Church, guided ever by the
hand of God, turns the attention of her
children, perhaps more specially than at any
previous time, to the interior and supernatural life of their souls, of which the Holy
Ghost is the Author. The Devotion to the
Holy Ghost, together with the teaching concerning our spiritual life with which that
Devotion is inseparably connected, is unquestionably the best antidote for the materialistic and degrading tendencies of our
times." (Pastoral letter of 1879.)

This ever increasing apostasy from faith
and christian morals is, however, but one of
the characteristic features of our time. There
is another one, more bright and more consoling, to which now we shall turn our
attention. This again, as we shall readily
observe, is a potent appeal to the Christians
of our days to urge the Father and to con-
jure the Son to pour upon us a larger
effusion of the Spirit. It is equally true,
that as those "who separate, not having the
Spirit," are stronger and more numerous

than ever, so also the members of the Church "that keep the unity of the Spirit in the bond of peace" (Ephes. III.) are more than ever "one body and one Spirit," (v. 4.) and a revival and reaction within the Church ever since the Council of Trent went apace with the dissolution of faith and discipline without.

The Church bereft of all, which time and the world and the princes thereof had in the course of centuries bestowed upon her, honours, wealth and privileges, has fallen back on her proper and essential strength which is the "power of the Spirit." "When the civil society of man refuses any longer to be guided and upheld by the sanctifying grace and the sovereignty of God, the Church shakes off the dust from her feet, and goes back to her apostolic work of saving men one by one. She is at this time doing this work and will do it; and in doing it the Church becomes more free, more independent, more separate from all contacts and embarrassments of this world. She may be indeed persecuted; perhaps she may become less in numbers, because nations and races go out from her. But she becomes once more what she was in the beginning, a society of individuals, vigorous, pure, living, and life giving." (Card. Manning. Fourfold Sovereignty

of God, p. 159.) This is a graphic description of the period on which the Church has
entered. The Church in the present and in
the near future will be more and more
like the Church in England and in the
United States, the great world wide and
world embracing Church, but not so much
the Church of the nations as the church of
individuals, or "devout men out of every
nation under heaven" (Act. II, 5,) as she was
on the first Pentecost day. The Church of
God, being conscious of her immortal life
and divine inherent power can afford to be
deserted by the princes of power, science
and wealth, because the Lord whispers into
the ear of his spouse in these hours of de-
reliction the word: "Not with an army, nor
by might; but by My Spirit," (Zach. IV, 6.)
and the princes may see, whether they can
afford to be without her or whether in them
shall be fulfilled the Spirit's verdict: "The
nation and the Kingdom that will not serve
thee shall perish." This re-action within the
Church started, we may say, with the Council of Trent. It has triumphed over the
universal rebellion of infidelity and "the
pride of life," in our days, and reached its
fullest evolution in the Council of the Vatican. Hence it is, that, again to speak with
our Cardinal: "the development of error

has constrained the Church to treat especially of the third and last clause of the Apostles' Creed, " I believe in the Holy Ghost, the
Holy Catholic Church, the Communion of
Saints." The Definitions of the Immaculate
Conception of the Mother of God, of the Infallibility of the Vicar of Christ, bring out
into distinct relief the twofold Office of the
Holy Ghost, of which one part is His perpetual assistance in the church, the other His
sanctification of the soul, of which the Immaculate Conception is the first fruits and the
perfect exemplar." (Preface to Intern. Miss.
of the H. G.; X.) The very tornado of opposition, aroused by the Vatican definition,
proved the malady of our age, the uncon-
sciousness of the supernatural element in the
Church and the so-called " Old-Catholics "
" professing to desire to bring about a more
perfect reign of the Holy Spirit in the
Church, by their opposition rejected, so far
as in them lay, the very means of bringing
it about. Blessed fruit, purchased at the
price of so hard a struggle, but which has
gained for the faithful and increased divine
illumination and force, and thereby the renewal of the whole face of the world." " The
Definition of the Infallibility having rendered
the supreme authority of the Church more explicit and complete, has prepared the way for

the faithful to follow, with greater safety and liberty, the inspirations of the Holy Spirit." (Hecker, "The Church and the Age," page 29.) To Pius IX was given the providential mission to separate light and darkness; to lead the elect people out of the captivity; to rouse the dormant energies of the Church and as a second Moses to point to the land of promise, the new Age to come. Leo XIII, as a second Josue, "filled with the Spirit of wisdom" (Deuteron. XXXIV. 9.) followed him, entered upon this new age, rallied again what seems capable of salvation and in his own mission, compared to the one of his great predecessor verified the adage "*Per crucem ad Lucem.*" If the restraining influence of Pius IX was necessary to purify the atmosphere, the expansive and reconciliatory action of Leo XIII will bring about cheerful co-operation. "Are not all these but so many preparatory steps to a Pentecostal effusion of the Holy Spirit on the Church, an effusion, if not equal in intensity to that of the apostolic days, at least greater than it in universality? If at no epoch of the Evangelical ages the reign of Satan was so generally welcome as in our days, the action of the Holy Spirit will have to clothe itself with the characteristics of an exceptional extension and force." (The Church and the Age, pag. 31.)

A certain indefinable presentiment of such a coming effusion of the Holy Spirit for the actual world exists, but the importance of this presentiment ought not to be exaggerated; yet it would be rash to make no account of it. "Is not this the meaning of the presentiment of Pius IX, saying: "Since we have nothing, or next to nothing, to expect from men, let us place our confidence more and more in God, whose heart is preparing, as it seems. to me, to accomplish, in the moment chosen by himself, a great prodigy which will fill the whole earth with astonishment." Was not the same presentiment before the mind of De Maistre, when he penned the following lines: We are on the eve of the greatest of religious epochs . . It appears to me that every true philosopher must choose between two hypotheses, either that a new religion is about to be formed, or that Christianity will be renewed in some extraordinary manner." Did not such a presentiment strike even the philosophical genius of Schlegel in Germany to make him say: "We are about to see a new exposition of Christianity, which will unite all Christians and even bring back the infidels themselves." (The Church and the Age, pag. 40.)

Far be it from us to prophecy or to venture an exact prediction of what character

such a new effusion of the Spirit will be.
"It is not for us (them) to know the times or
moments which the Father had put in his
own power," (Act. I, 7) but the signs of the
time and the existence of such a universal
presentiment are to us evidence enough,
that in this or in another way "we shall
receive the power of the Holy Ghost coming
upon us." (Act. I, 8.) The future of Pius
IX becomes indeed actually present by the
providential enlightenment of Leo XIII, and
we understand daily more the great appeal
of Cardinal Manning to the Catholics of our
present day: "It is towards evening and
the day is far spent .. The foundations of
Christendom—not of the Church—are dis-
appearing, and modern legislation has
removed itself from the basis of revealed
truth to the state of natural society. What
is then our duty?—not to lament the past
nor to dream of the future, but to accept the
present. Dreams and lamentations weaken
the sinews of action: and it is by action
alone that the state of the world can be
maintained . . . The hand has moved onward on the dial and all our miscalculations
and regrets will not stay its shadow . A
new task, then, is before us. The Church
has not longer to deal with parliaments and
princes, but with the masses and with the

people.   Whether we will or no, this is our
work.   And for this work we need *a new
spirit and a new law of life.*   The refined,
gentle, shrinking character of calm and
sheltered days will not stand the brunt of
modern democracy."   (Charge of the Clergy
of the Arch-deaconry of Chichester, 1849.)

At what we rejoice at more than all else
is, that without exception all connect the
expectation of this new age, with the Holy
Spirit.   It is already a valuable gain, that
the consciousness of being in need of and
dependent on the Holy Spirit is more
and more gaining ground and makes the
faithful turn in expectation and in prayer to
"this power from on high "—God the Holy
Ghost.   Let us then welcome this special devotion as the best means to make ourselves
spiritual and prove equal to the task before
us.   We cannot conclude these reflections
without quoting the splendid passage from
Father Hecker's book on the men our age requires.   It is a delight to observe, that especially in England and in America the faithful
are exhorted by the very leaders of the people
to turn towards the Holy Spirit in order to
bring about a better future.   The passage,
"The Men the Age demands," runs as follows :   "The age, we are told, calls for men
worthy of that name.   Who are those worthy

to be called men? Men, assuredly, whose intelligences and wills are divinely illuminated and fortified. This is precisely what is produced by the gifts of Holy Ghost; they enlarge all the faculties of the soul at once.

The age is superficial; it needs the gift of Wisdom, which enables the soul to contemplate truth in its ultimate causes. The age is materialistic; it needs the gift of Intelligence, by the light of which the intellect penetrates into the essence of things. The age is captivated by a false and onesided science; it needs the gift of Science by the light of which is seen each order of truth in its true relations to other orders and in a divine unity. The age is in disorder, and is ignorant of the way to true progress; it needs the gift of Counsel, which teaches how to choose the proper means to attain an object. The age is impious; it needs the gift of Piety, which leads the soul to God as the Heavenly Father, and to adore Him with feelings of filial affection and love. The age is sensual and effeminate; it needs the gift of Fortitude, which imparts to the will the strength to endure the greatest burdens, and to prosecute the greatest enterprises with ease and heroism. The age has lost and almost forgotten God; it needs the gift of Fear, to bring the soul again to God, and make it feel conscious of its responsibility and of its destiny.

Men endowed with these gifts are the men for whom, if it but knew it, the age calls. Men whose minds are enlightened and whose wills are strengthened by an increased action of the Holy Spirit. Men whose souls are actuated by the gifts of the Holy Spirit. Men whose countenances are lit up with heavenly joy, who breathe an air of inward peace, and act with a holy liberty and a resistless energy. One such soul does more to advance the kingdom of God than tens of thousands without these gifts. These are the men and this is the way, if the age could only be made to see and believe it, to universal restoration, universal reconciliation, and universal progress, as far as such boons are attainable."

4.

The Devotion to God, the Holy Ghost, the Special devotion for this Country.

Time and country constitute the main environments of a man's life. Quoting in our foregoing consideration the statement of Cardinal Manning, that the Church is daily becoming more the Church of individuals, and that in the present and future we will not have to deal so much with princes and parliaments, as with the masses, we are led by this great man to consider also the relations of this Devotion to our glorious country. What the Church will probably be more or less everywhere in the world, she is at present in America, a vigorous, free, independent Church of individuals. Princes and parliaments the church has not to deal with here, being exclusively based upon the people in the land of the brave and the free. For the solution of the great problems of the future, divine Providence seems to gather portions " from every nation under heaven" (Act. II, 5,) on this new stage of the new world, for

" Westward the course of empire takes its way,
    The first four acts already pa st,
The fifth shall close the drama with the day,
    Time's noblest offspring is the last."

I deem it no exaggeration or gratuitous assumption to call the Devotion to God the Holy Ghost the devotion especially adapted to the peculiarities and needs of this our new country. I have already alluded to the striking fact that this Devotion has been transplanted to American soil from England; that consequently the land by the apostasy of which the fathers of this country have forfeited the unity of faith has also given us the most potent means to regain this unity; and that this Devotion has more than in other countries taken root and spread amongst the English speaking people. What, then, are the motives for the cultivation of this devotion in this country? What are the reasons justifying my assertion? Methinks that they can hardly escape the eye of the most superficial observer.

We all believe in a divine Providence "playing in the world" (Prov. VIII, 31), "reaching from end to end mightily and ordering all things sweetly." (Wisdom VIII, 1.)

The Devotion to God the Holy Ghost is indeed, as we have shown, the Devotion of the coming age of our times, of the present and next period of God's Holy Church. Why then must it not also in a special sense be the Devotion of this country in which a task of incalculable importance awaits the Church of God? If the greatness of the old Roman empire so seized upon the mind of Cicero, that he saw in it a direct disposition of the Gods, to what other conclusion must we come viewing the immensity, prosperity, and future of a country washed by two oceans, awaiting millions to settle on its almost boundless lands and developing with a rapidity that challenges all the past records and baffles our imagination. When Christendom was on the eve of being split asunder, when a new era had dawned upon the old world, and when Providence wanted to have the stage ready whereon to perform a new act of divine wisdom, the gates of this new country were flung open and Europe listened to the mysterious voice:

"Lo! I uncover a land
Which I hid of old time in the West,
As the sculptor uncovers his statue
When he has wrought its best."

By the unsearchable designs of Providence the first founders of our institutions did not

belong to the one true Church of Christ.
The mustard-seed of divine truth was first
sown in a field all covered with the
cockle of heresy.   Nowhere, as far as history
goes, has the parable of our Lord been more
truly verified: "The kingdom of heaven is
like to a grain of mustard-seed, which a man
took and sowed in his field : which is the
least of all seeds indeed, but when it is
grown up, it is greater than all herbs, and
becometh a tree, so that the birds of the air
come, and dwell in the branches thereof."
(Matth. XIII. 30—32.) The first beginnings
of the Church in this country were indeed
like " the least of all the seeds."   Now she is
the strongest and best organized of all de-
nominations, truly a "tree greater than all
herbs."   Her roots spreading far and wide,
her trunk standing firm and immovable,
her mighty crown waving in the air of
liberty, the Church of God, grown up in
virtue of her innate vital power of the
Spirit, shows and proves herself to be truly
the plantation of the heavenly Father.

Leonard Calvert, the brother of Lord
Baltimore and the leader of the Catholic
colony, having sailed from England in the
Ark and the *Dove*, reached his destination on
the Potomac in March 1634, and the first
mass attended by the first settlers of the first

Catholic colony of Maryland was celebrated by Father White, S. J., on the 25th of March, the day, on which "overshadowed by the Holy Ghost" the Blessed Virgin became the Mother of God. The Immaculate Conception of Mary, this "first fruits and perfect exemplar" of the working of the Holy Ghost, the Sanctifier, in individual souls, as Cardinal Manning calls it, has been unanimously chosen by the Bishops of this country and solemnly been given by the Holy See as the patronal mystery of the Church in these United States. It consequently seems to us not only casual but highly significative, that our Cardinal and present Archbishop of the mother-see in the Union has chosen, as we are told, for his Cardinalitial coat of arms the "Dove hanging over the continent", brooding, as it were, over the process of social evolution and ecclesiastical formation. God is a God of order. The Church is the first and great object of God's divine solicitude and providence on earth. Hence there can be no doubt, that, whatever may be the drawbacks, whatever may be our own shortcomings, whatever the pessimist may fear for the Church in this country, God has His most signal plans for the Church of his Son in this new world of the future and through the Church for the country itself.

"For myself, as a citizen of the United
States, and without closing my eyes to our
shortcomings as a nation, I say with a deep
sense of gratitude and pride that I belong to
a country where the civil government holds
over us the ægis of its protection, without
interfering with us in the legitimate exercise
of our sublime mission as ministers of the
Gospel of Christ." These are the words of
the highest church Dignitary of this new
world in the oldest and eternal city of the
old world, at Rome, when taking possession
of Santa Maria in Trastevere, his Titular
Church, as Cardinal.

"The moral power of Christianity which
has received the homages of the greatest
nations of the past, receives now, through our
most worthy President, the tribute of a free
and independent people, of the freest and
most progressive people in the world. They
are naturally Christians, brave, just, generous,
and such they will be in the future as in the
past history of the nation." Thus spoke Archbishop Ryan, of Phildelphia, in the throne
hall of the Vatican at Rome, at the time of
Leo XIII.'s golden Jubilee, presenting to His
Holiness the gift of Grover Cleveland, President of the United States, the gorgeously
bound copy of our Constitution.

"As the head of the Church I owe my

duty, love and solicitude to every part of the Church, but towards America I bear especial love. Your government is free, your future full of hope,"—this was the greeting tendered to our nation from the august throne of the present Vicar of Christ on earth, Pope Leo XIII.

These authoritative words, uttered on the most solemn occasions, certainly prove, that in believing in a great and providential mission of the Church in this country, we do not show ourselves over-enthusiastic or entertain any too sanguine hopes. Spanning the immense tract of land and the ever increasing multitude of this nation, "naturally Christians," as Archbishop Ryan says, we must needs be mindful of our divine Lord's address to his apostles: "Lift up your eyes and see the countries, for they are white already to harvest." (St. John IV, 35.) Scripture says: "Where is the Spirit of the Lord, there is liberty" (II. Cor. III, 17), and so may we also safely hope, that true liberty will help more efficaciously the growth and development of the true Church, than "the armies and might" of monarchical Europe ever did, according to Holy Writ: "Not with an army nor by might; but by my Spirit: said the Lord of hosts." (Zach. IV, 6).

America is not a country of revolutionists,

as it is sometimes falsely represented by Europeans. "What Franklin maintained was that we were not in rebellion; the American colonies were not guilty of that kind of revolution which is a crime. They were fighting for principles which had always been an Englishman's birthright, and, part of the inheritance of all Catholic people. The Americans never intended to be rebels; they were not rebels. Nowhere in their fundamental law will you find rebellion erected into a principle." (The Church and the Age, 104.) Again, the American state is not indifferent to religion, as another calumny runs. "They accuse us of having a theory of government which ignores the moral precepts of the natural law and the Gospel. Such is not the case and never has been from the beginning. That is a false interpretation of the American state. By ecclesiastical affairs we mean that organic embodiment of Christianity which the Church is in her creeds, her hierarchy, and her polity. The American state says in reference to all this, I have no manner of right to meddle with you, I have no jurisdiction." (Same, page 113.) What an influence upon the entire civilized world America is destined to wield in no distant future, Archbishop Ireland has recently exposed in one of his masterpieces of eloquence, concluding his sermon at the consecration of Bishop Burke in the Cathedral of Chicago, as follows : " In America do we more than men do elsewhere breathe the spirit of the age, do we touch with our hands its workings. In America more than elsewhere are all the great living questions pressing for replies. America leads in modern movements and as she thinks and acts so will the world think and act. Hence in our own country the most glorious mission opens to the Church, the most hopeful field invites our labor. Great are the responsibilities of Catholics in America. It is our prayer, that they fail not in their duty."

Here we strike the right note. It is not so much our part to espy the future for the mere sake of knowing it or arousing enthusiasm, but it becomes our part to realize our responsibilities and to pray that we do not fail in our duties. In order to hold our own, to spread the true religion, to propagate the true Church, to make her spirit the leaven of our public life, to correspond on our part with God's designs, we stand in need of a supernatural assistance, we must have recourse to the Spirit Creator, who renews the face of the world and we must, in a fervent Devotion to God the Holy Ghost, repeat the solemn prayer, recited by our Cardinal at the opening of the centennial celebration of our Constitution, in Philadelphia: "We pray Thee, O God of Might, wisdom and justice, assist us with thy Holy Spirit of wisdom, counsel and fortitude." (Prayer of Card. Gibbons.)

Christian, as America claims to be, the nation is still in danger of losing gradually those remnants of the Christian faith which its fathers have saved from the common shipwreck of a so called Reformation, unless Christ's only true Church, the bulwark and rampart of Christianity will rally more and more those, who being of good will are yet "like children tossed to and fro, and carried about with every wind of doctrine by the wickedness of men, by cunning craftiness." (Ephes. IV, 14.)   "This eternal life that they may know Thee the only true God: and Jesus Christ whom Thou hast sent," is the summing up of all that Christianity teaches, for as the rays of the sun concentrate in the focus, so all primeval and imperishable revelations of God from the beginning concentrate and are perfected in the personality and revelation of the Godman, according to holy Writ: "God, who commandeth the light to shine out of darkness, had shineth into our hearts, to give the light of the knowledge of the glory of God in the face of

Jesus Christ." (II Cor. IV, 6.) This historical and perfect Christianity however, is
Catholicity, nor can the faith in the Incarnate God be full, perfect and secure outside of
this Church, the logical consequence, expansion, prolongation and perpetuation of the
Incarnation. "To say that Christianity is
Catholicism and Catholicism is Christianity,
is to utter a truism. There cannot be two
Christianities, neither can a fragment be
mistaken for the whole. The mountain has
filled the earth, and the drift and the detri-
tus which fall from it cannot be taken, by
any illusion, to be the mountain ... When
I say Catholicity, I mean perfect Christianity, undiminished, full-orbed, illuminating
all nations, as S. Irenaeus says, like the sun,
one and the same in every place.

Free and prospering as America is, it must
still be on guard lest the slavery of passion,
only removable in the power and strength
of the true religion and supernatural grace,
will destroy in its very essence our noblest
national privilege, freedom and independence, or that these prerogatives degenerate
into licentiousness and lawlessness. Where
the Spirit of the Lord is there is liberty
(II. Cor. III, 17); but liberty in the spirit and
in the truth will not, and cannot be where the
Spirit of the Lord is not and where in willful

blindness men refuse to believe the divine
Teacher witnessing to Jesus Christ in and
through his Church—the Holy Ghost.
Great and bright as our future seems, it will
depend principally on our moral virtues, on
the victory of the spirit over encroaching
materialism, and above all, on the minor
and greater illumining, sanctifying and restraining influence of God's true revelation
in Christ's true and only Church.

Why then should not the Devotion to
God the Holy Ghost be eminently the Devotion for this country? Are not the foregoing reflections so many urgent notices to address ourselves in our own behalf and in
that of our brethren to the Spirit of truth and
unity? Who but the "Spirit of God moving
over the waters" in the creation (Gen. I, 1)
and "renewing the face of the earth" (Pslm.
104, 30.) will and can bring order and unity
and harmony out of the religious chaos on
this side of the ocean? The Holy Spirit
leads to the Son, as the Son leads to the
Father, and his chief mission is to glorify,
make known and loved God Incarnate, for
"by this is the Spirit of God known: every
spirit, which confesseth that Jesus Christ is
come in the flesh, is of God. And every
spirit, that dissolves Jesus, is not of God,
and this is the Antichrist, of whom you

have heard that he cometh and he is now already in the world." (I. S. John. IV. 2.) The Holy Spirit it is, that "when He is come" upon a man, upon a generation, upon a people, "will convince the world of sin, and of justice, and of judgment. Of Sin, because they believed not in Me; of Justice, because I go to the Father and you shall see Me no longer; and of judgment, because the prince of this world is already judged." (S. John. XVI. 8, 9, 10.) The Holy Spirit must dawn upon our people "that they may receive the sight and be filled with the Holy Ghost. And immediately there will fall from their eyes, as it were, scales, (Act. IX, 18) and "receiving the unction from the Holy one, they will know all things." (I. St. John. II, 20.)

But first of all, we, the children of light, must be illumined by this "kindly light from above." First we, the seed of election in this country, must be proof against the spirit of materialism and sensuality, for, the peril of the day is unspirituality of men and the revival of naturalism in the world." This, however, cannot be met by a more diametrical and supreme antagonism, than by devoting ourselves to the special worship of God the Holy Ghost. Towards our fellowmen yet sitting in the shadow and darkness of death, our efforts to save them, to draw them near to Christ and His church, to convert them, will prove vain and void without Him, by whose indwelling we are spiritual and supernatural and so capable to draw souls to Him by His own light and power. "Let no one suppose," says Gregory the Great, "that learning comes to man from the mouth of a teacher, for unless the eternal teacher is within, the master will labor in vain." (Cardinal Manning's letter.) The dove then, must hang with outspread wings over this continent, and by a special devotion to God the Holy Ghost we will bestow upon our country and nation the greatest benefit by procuring it a larger effusion of the Holy Spirit. If in cultivating this Devotion to God the Holy Ghost, the Pentacostal flame would burn, rest, sparkle on our head, we could do wonders for our brethren as the Apostles did for the Gentile world, when they had received "the power from on high." As Catholics, and still more as Priests of God, let us in view of our nation say and pray with the Apostle of the gentile world: "*That we should be ministers of Christ Jesus among the gentiles: sanctifying the Gospel of God, that the oblation of the gentiles be made acceptable and sanctified in the Holy Ghost.*" (Rom. XV, 16.)

5.

The Devotion to God the Holy Ghost, the special Devotion for the Priests and Candidates of the holy Priesthood.

" Ministers of Christ Jesus," as the Apostle calls himself, "among the Gentiles: sanctifying the Gospel of God (Rom. XV, 16,) are in the word's fullest sense those, who have been elected, ordained, set apart and sent out to preach the Gospel of Christ—the Priests of God. The Council of Baltimore in commending this Devotion to the Candidates of the holy ministry, speaks of it almost exclusively as the Devotion for Seminarians and Priests. The same is the mind of our Cardinal who wishing all the faithful to have a share in the blessings of this Devotion, nevertheless says: "I rejoice all the more in this (the establishment of the Confraternity), because I believe that Devotion to the Holy Ghost ought to be the special Devotion of Priests. We are consecrated and anointed by Him, and our whole priestly work and pastoral office depends on Him." (Letter to V. Rev. Rawes, 1879.)

It is a general truth that, as a rule, the blessings of heaven are bestowed upon the flock by the ministration, prayer and merits of the pastor, and that he who is set to be "a pattern of the flock from the heart" (I. Petr. V, 3) will chiefly be instrumental in making the faithful, committed to his solicitude, partakers of the various graces, blessings, and devotions of Holy Church. As it has pleased Almighty God to save mankind in one man, "who is mediator between God and men, the man Christ Jesus, who gave Himself a redemption for all" (I. Tim. II, 5), so has God in His inscrutable wisdom again ordained, that, as a rule, man should be saved by man's instrumentality and the visible work of redemption performed by the Godman, should be continued by men divinely called, divinely ordained, divinely constituted and therefore truly "men of God," according to the Apostle (I. Tim. VI, 11). Hence it was that forseeing this inseparable co-operation of His invisible Spirit in the visible ministry of apostolic men, our Lord said: "But when the Paraclete cometh whom I will send you from the Father, the

Spirit of truth, who proceedeth from the Father, He shall give testimony of Me: and you shall give testimony " (St. John XV, 27).

With regard to this Devotion, however, the truth, that the benefit of redemption flows from the priest over to the people, seems to assume a more striking character. As Christ after His resurrection did not appear to "all the people, but to witnesses preordained by God" (Act. XI, 41), so also, though the Holy Ghost came on Pentecost day upon the entire congregation in the "upper room" in Jerusalem, He came with a most special mission and plenitude to the Apostles, so that they were then not only made partakers of the Spirit in communion with the faithful, but also the Spirit's elect organs, whose duty it would be to communicate the Holy Ghost to others. "In Christ," says Holy Writ, "you are all built together into an habitation of God in the Spirit" (Ephes. II, 22), and the organic nature of this mystical structure, the Church, requires that the Spirit especially, principally and prominently dwells and works in the higher life-giving and life-preserving organs of this body—the Priests.

It seems but a matter of course for us to say, that not as all other devotions, but more than all other devotions, the Devotion to the

Holy Ghost ought to be first the Devotion of the Priests. To us, to the exclusion of the faithful, has been given in holy Ordination the Spirit, whom the Son had breathed upon the Apostles, saying : " Receive ye the Holy Ghost; as the Father had sent me, I also send you " (St. John XX, 22), and we should consequently be so full of the Spirit, that our very word, action and person would again breathe this Spirit upon all that come in contact with us. We have indeed but to realize, what the innermost nature of the priestly ministry is and the singular importance of a Devotion to the Holy Ghost must needs seize upon our mind.

The analogy between the constitution of the Son of God as redeemer of the world and the mystical constitution of the Priest is perfect. Both constitutions are the work of the Holy Spirit par excellence. As all the facts, words and deeds of our divine Saviour reveal to us the co-operation of the Holy Spirit, so is the priesthood of Christ in his ministers both created and perfected " co-operante Spiritu Sancto." The Spirit in the holy men of the old law prepared the Incarnation of " the Holy One," so, too, priestly calling, priestly training, and priestly education in the new law is pre-eminently the Spirit's grace and work, and accordingly we read in the life of St. Ambrose, that while yet a boy, still "a Spiritu Sancto nutriebatur ad Sacerdotium." "The Holy Ghost shall come upon thee and the power of the most High shall overshadow thee" (S. Luk. 1, 35), said the angel to Mary, when the mystery of the Incarnation was about to be accomplished, and it is the same Spirit, who comes over the elect ones of the Lord, overshadows them, creates in their souls the character of the priesthood of Christ and makes them "in the moment of ordination, Priests forever according to the order of Melchisedec," (Psm. 109).

Again the Spirit from above descended visibly on our Lord in the moment of entering upon His public life, on Him He rested all the days of His ministry and in the Holy Ghost "Christ offered Himself unspotted unto God" (Heb. IX, 14); in like manner must He rest upon us all the days of our ministry as a shining, burning and sparkling flame, and thus verify the prophet's saying of the ministers of Christ: "The Spirit of the Lord God is upon me, because the Lord had anointed me to preach the Gospel to the poor, He has sent me, to heal the contrite of heart, to preach deliverance to the captives, and give sight to the blind, to set at liberty them that are bruised, to preach the acceptable

year of the Lord and the day of reward."
(S. Luk. IV, 18, 19.)

It is true, that the sacramental power of
the Spirit will work in and through even the
wordly, nay the sinful priest, as far as his
sacerdotal power is independent of the personal faith and sanctity of the minister.
With the sacerdotal power, however, the
priest receives in holy Ordination the special
grace of the sacrament, to enable him to perform his duties worthily and successfully
and unless this sacramental grace work con-
comitantly with the sacerdotal power, his
power, his ministry, to say the least, will be
barren and void of the blessing and unction
that should go forth from him, "even from
the hem of his garment," (Matth. IX, 20.)
that is from the least of his sacerdotal functions.   To make us "not neglect the grace
that is in us (thee,) which was given us (thee)
with the imposition of the hands of the
priesthood," (I. Tim. IV, 14.) and to make us
"stir up the grace of God" that is the "cha-
risma" of the sacerdotal character, of the
sacerdotal power, of the sacerdotal grace
(II. Tim. I, 6), no better means could
be devised than a tender and fervent
Devotion to God the Holy Ghost.   The two
texts just quoted, are indeed a compendium
and summary of all that Catholic Theolog

teaches of the sublime sacrament of Holy Ordination. It has always seemed to me, that this treatise is not sufficiently inquired into, during the years of seminary life and that consequently only a few have a deeper, more perfect and coherent realization of the great mystery wrought in their very souls, when the hands of the ordaining bishop overshadow them. Whilst in religious orders the anniversary of profession is usually celebrated with a preceding retreat and many circumstances calculated to bring home to the individual a full realization of the profession made to God, the anniversary of our ordination and consecration to God which was sublimely effected by the Almighty's own divine interference and action in impressing upon our soul the sacred character of Christ the High Priest, passes unobserved, without even a serious thought as to the momentous effect produced in our soul on that day.

What the Apostles were, although constituted Apostles by Christ before the advent of the Holy Spirit, we are even after our ordination without the quickening and stirring power of the Spirit,—slow to believe, weak in virtue, timid in our ministry, left to our natural resources which are extremely poor and unequal to the task before us. What the Apostles became, when the power of the Holy Ghost overshadowed them, we may, at least in part, become, illumined by supernatural light, strengthened by divine power, changed into other men, fortified by the seven gifts of the Spirit, nay, even endowed with those extraordinary gifts which are by no means altogether withdrawn from the Church, but granted in various forms and degrees to those who are "full of the Holy Spirit."

The effusion of the Holy Ghost on Pentecost day may be divided into the effusion first of the author of all gifts, the "*donum altissimi Dei*" God, the Holy Ghost Himself; secondly into the effusion of the ordinary gifts of the Holy Ghost, given to all in proportion to their merit or position in the Church of Christ; and thirdly into the effusion of those "*carismata*" or extraordinary manifestations of the indwelling Spirit which were so common in the Apostolic age, and though rarer since, have never been denied to the Church of God as a whole and have ever been signally shown in the lives and works of the various Saints and Elect. "The manifestation of the Spirit is given every man unto profit" (I. Cor. XII, 7), but especially to those, to whom is committed the " ministry of reconciliation." "There are diversities of graces, but the same Spirit" (I. Cor. XII, 4), and He "working all these things, dividing to every one according to His will (v. 11,) most certainly will favor those with His signal privileges that work for the building up of the body of Christ, His Church. As then "in one Spirit we have all been baptized into one body" (v. 13,) we the ministers of Christ, should also "drink in one Spirit" that is live in and act under the perpetual and vivifying influence of this Spirit. "The working of miracles" or "prophecy" or "diverse kinds of tongues" may not be given to us, but "the word of wisdom," "the word of knowledge," and "faith in the same Spirit" (v. 8, 9.) will not be refused to those who pray and praying induce the Spirit from on high to come upon them. There are many gifts akin to those before mentioned or rather differing from them in degree and we need them to live up to the high standard of our vocation. Taste for religious exercises, application to sacred studies, understanding of things divine, pleasure in spiritual reading, intelligence of the scriptures, discerning of spirits, unction in speech, prudence in action, zeal in the ministry, success in the apostolic work,—all these are also diversified gifts of the same Spirit and He will bestow them upon His servants,

clients and worshipers.   True it is, that only
a rich effusion of the Holy Spirit will complete the work of God in us and through us
in others, and without having Him co-operating with us we could never say to the faithful under our care and jurisdiction, what St.
Paul said and a truly apostolic man must be
able to say again :   "And I, Brethren, when
I came to you, came not in loftiness of speech
or of wisdom, declaring unto you the testimony of Christ. And I was with you in weakness and in fear, and in much trembling;
and my speech and my preaching was not
in the persuasive words of human wisdom,
but in showing of the Spirit and power: that
your faith might not stand on the wisdom of
men, but on the power of God" (I Cor. II, 1–4).

The priest must first of all know "the
mystery of the Kingdom of God," that he
may be able to make "the counsel of God"
known to others. The Spirit only will give
this taste for and understanding of spiritual
things, "for the sensual man perceiveth not
these things that are of the Spirit of God:
for it is foolishness to him and he cannot
understand." (I. Cor. II, 14.) The Spirit
will "stir up" the grace of God that is in us,
as the passing wind stirs up the dying
embers, but without this vivifying Spirit the
words of St. Paul to Timothy and through

him to all vested with the apostolic office
may strike the eye or the ear but will not sink
into the heart and become fact and reality;
"Meditate upon these things, be wholly, in
these things, that thy profiting be manifest to all, take heed to thyself, and to doctrine; be earnest in them. For in doing
this, thou shalt both save thyself and those
that hear thee. (I Tim. IV, 16.) The Spirit,
fervently implored and humbly besought to
enable us to realize the great mystery of our
own priesthood, will fill us with the consoling, happy idea, that we are consecrated
"ministers of Christ and dispensators of the
mysteries of God" (I. Cor. IV, 1); for "having received the Spirit that is of God, we
may know the things that are given us from
God." (I. Cor. II, 12.) Furthermore, the
priest must not only know the divine mysteries, but he must preach the Gospel, instruct the people, and be powerful in word
and speech. The "sword of the Spirit" is
the word of God, and only this sword will
conquer the world. Without the power of
the Spirit, our rhetoric may strike the ear
and win the praise of men, but it will not
strike the conscience, captivate the mind,
conquer the heart, and convert our hearers,
it will prove void and useless. Those only,
who are filled with the Spirit, without whom

it is impossible to speak the name of Jesus, much less to preach Jesus crucified with supernatural fruit, will be enabled to comply with the exhortation of Cardinal Manning, given in his preface to the book, (" The Temporal Mission of the Holy Ghost"), " Speak, as none other can, with the authority of God and his infallible Church: Preach as the Apostles preached, and as the rule enjoins; with a *sancta et virilis simplicitas*," with a holy and manly simplicity.   Contend with men, as a loved and honored friend has said of the Apostles, " they argued not, but they preached; and conscience did the rest."   The priest exposed to all the dangers of this wicked world and himself denied the pleasures thereof must have some compensation, to keep up strength of will and serenity of mind in all adversities and trials.   The Spirit alone affords him a compensation exceeding great in his holy joy " *Gaudium in Spiritu sancto*," "joy in the Holy Spirit," which is the principal characteristic of his indwelling in a soul.   And as the Spirit of God made Saint Lucia " an immovable column " when her enemies tried to conduct her to the place of shame and sin, so will the power of the Holy Spirit make us an immovable column to defy all the agressions, and persecutions of the prince of this world and we shall prove in the highest sense "*rectores ecclesiae inamovibiles.*

"Receive ye the Holy Ghost" was said to us, and we did not receive "the spirit of fear, but of power, and of love, and sobriety" (II. Tim. I, 7.) The latent energies, bestowed upon us, when the sacerdotal character was indelibly impressed upon our souls, must be stirred up, called forth and brought into activity. Devotion and prayer to the Spirit alone will effect, "that we become fit ministers of the new testament, not in the letter, but in the Spirit." (II. Cor. III, 6.) "And for this cause we must pray that the Holy Ghost will descend in the unction of truth and the unction of sanctity upon the Bishops, and Pastors and Priests of the Church throughout the world. They were the first fruits of the Holy Ghost. To them our divine Lord said, when he breathed upon them—"Receive ye the Holy Ghost; on them He descended: they were baptized with the Holy Ghost and with fire," that they might be to the end of the world, the salt of the earth, the light of the world, the image of our Lord's own perfection as the Great High Priest, and the Great Shepherd of the sheep. As they are, so will be the flock, if the salt lose its savor, the people will corrupt; if the light burn dimly, the people will wander in darkness. Pray then, for the Bishops who were set by the Holy Ghost to rule the Church of God, which He purchased with His precious blood. Pray for the Pastors that, in charity and courage, they may feed the flock, and if need be, lay down their lives for the sheep. If the seven Gifts rest upon them, their intellect will be guided, they will be strong; they will be holy, humble, undefiled, and separate from sinners, and when Priests are holy the people will be uncontaminated by the spirit of the world. (The Cardinal in his oration on June 5, 1879.)

Why then should not this Devotion to God the Holy Ghost be at once recognized as the special Devotion of the clergy, and be warmly welcomed by them and by all candidates for the holy priesthood? I may add that the Devotion especially commends itself as being the characteristic Devotion of the secular or the pastoral clergy, who in the closest union with the episcopacy constitute the ordinary organ of apostolic ministration and power. Religious bound by their holy rules and consecrated to God by their vows have usually their own, appropriate devotions and means of sanctification. So, too, we, the secular priesthood, having our lasting consecration in the indelible character of ordination and being, therefore, likewise in the state of perfection inseparable from the pastoral office, should by all means have our modes of sanctification : and pre-eminently, the best is a warm devotion to God the Holy Ghost, who has thus set us to bear the heat, the burden of the day in God's vineyard.

The feast of the Immaculate Conception of Mary, the Spouse of the Holy Spirit, is the national feast of the Catholic Church in the United States. It seems to be the desire of the Most Reverend Fathers of the Council of Baltimore that the great solemnity of Pentecost should, by our own singular Devotion to God the Holy Ghost, become the special feast of our seminaries and the clergy. Thus the bond of the Spirit would form a unit of the present and the future generations of the Priesthood in this country and keep fresh the sacred unction of " the Holy one " in us. Then the beautiful oration would meet with its fulfilment. " *Deus, qui facis angelos tuos spiritus et ministros Tuos flammam ignis, emitte Spiritum Tuum et rennova faciem cleri, ut de regno Tuo tollant omnia scandala et ignem, quem venisti mittere in terram, in omnium cordibus vehementer accendant. Amen.*"

6.

The Devotion to God the Holy Ghost in its relation to other devotions and Confraternities.

Devotion is the natural outgrowth of faith. Faith is the root, and devotion is the flower's perfume. Where there is true Faith, a genuine devotion will necessarily spring forth. This will undoubtedly prove true, if we consider devotion in its full and general import. Devotion to some particular object, truth, or mystery of revelation is again the consequence of the special sway with which some particular mystery, more than others, seizes upon our mind and heart and soul. Hence, because there are many mysteries in God's holy revelation, many dispositions of mind in the faithful and many distributions of graces from on high, although there is but one Spirit, dividing to every one according as He will (I. Cor. XII. 11), we can count and distinguish many devotions existent in God's Holy Church.

Devotions, then, are as so many flowers of variegated hues, which, under the prolific rays of the Holy Ghost, the sun of the supernatural world, spring forth from the seed sown by the Son of God in the ever growing and flourishing garden of His Church.

They appear according to supernatural laws in due season; spring forth in various places, spread more or less, last a longer or shorter while, become more or less prominent, thrive, flourish, wither again, and for a time die away like a fading flower.

Devotions in the Church of God are as various as the flowers in a well-stocked garden. Hence, as each individual has a different taste and not every one takes a fancy to the same blossom, so, too, every member of the Church is free to choose and cultivate whatever devotion suits his cast of mind, his spiritual need or position in life. Too many flowers clustering together in one bed, spoil beauty of design and check growth and development; in like manner, too, many devotions cultivated by individuals tend to lessen fervor in each, and finally degenerate into mere formalities and external professions without the interior life-giving spirit.

Here we have reached the very point upon

which we have yet to enlarge. According
to rhetorical rules demonstration should precede the refutation of objections. Having
therefore endeavored to the utmost of our
ability to advance the various motives for a
special devotion to God the Holy Ghost, we
now deem it timely to answer, some at least,
of the objections usually made against this
devotion in particular and the multiplication
of devotions in general. Why, it may be
asked, add a new devotion to the many
already existing, and wielding a most salutary influence amongst the faithful? Is not
the devotion to the most Sacred Heart of our
Divine Redeemer the special devotion of our
time and also of priests? Is not the devotion to the Holy Ghost of a nature too mystical, little bearing upon and entirely too
impractical for every day life?

These objections, have been actually
made and are still advanced by not a
few whose positions and relation to matters
spiritual make the surprise the greater. The
reflection that they are already engaged in
many devotions will, doubtless, have no little
tendency to keep not a few persons, otherwise well disposed, from placing their names
on the roll of the servants of God the Holy
Ghost, whilst others again will find an excuse
in a pretended over-delicate fear, if I dare

say so, of rousing competition between the honor due to the Sacred Heart of God the Son and the honor due to God the Holy Ghost.

This objection I should like to meet first. Far be it from us to call in question or obscure the prominency, the universality, the striking influence in our time of the devotion to the Sacred Heart of our Savior. It is not only the devotion of our day, but has been designed and sanctioned as such by our Lord Himself in His apparition to Blessed Margaret. All that from the very start we will gladly grant. Whilst St. Teresa had a most singular devotion to the Holy Ghost, she was at the same time jealously watchful against any devotion not centering in the Incarnation and deriving therefrom truth and grace. This jealousy was but a natural sequence of the truth she held that through the Incarnate Son we receive the spirit of adoption. Hence, it is not so much my purpose at present, to refute the notion that this devotion to the Holy Ghost tends in any way to obscure or impede the devotion to the Sacred Heart, as to show lucidly, and if possible, impressively that devotion to the Holy Ghost, and to the Sacred Heart of Jesus are most closely united and helpful to one another. Roots so cognate become not aliens in their shoots, flowers and fruits. Closer relation it is impossible to conceive than that which exists between the Son and the Holy Ghost even apart from their unity of God-head, so, closer relation cannot exist between devotions than that which unites these two; and what theory advances, practice will ever confirm.

Certainly no man ever loved the Sacred Heart of our Lord more ardently, practically and enthusiastically than St. Paul, who in the excess of his burning love exclaimed: " I am sure that neither death, nor life, nor angels, nor principalities, nor powers, nor things present, nor things to come, nor might, nor height, nor depth, nor any other creature shall be able to separate us from the love of God which is in Christ Jesus our Lord." (Rom. VIII., 39.) The very beginning of St. Paul's wonderful life and career is described by Holy Writ as being "filled with the Holy Ghost." Ananias, sent to baptize him, expressly connects the co-operation of the Lord Jesus and the Holy Ghost: "Brother Saul," said he, "the Lord Jesus hath sent me, He that appeareth to thee in the way as thou camest, that thou mayst receive the sight and be filled with the Holy Ghost." (Act. IX, 17.) The same apostle whose enthusiastic love for Christ makes him utter the terrible verdict: "If any man love not our Lord Jesus Christ, let him be anathema, maranatha," (I. Cor. XVI, 22) also tells us that "no man, speaking in the Spirit of God, says anathema to Jesus. And no man can say, the Lord Jesus, but by the Holy Ghost." (I. Cor. XII, 3.)

The apostle of our Devotion in the present generation is the great Cardinal Archbishop of Westminster. What he says in his letter to Doctor O'Connell, "the Apostolic preaching shows that we are under the dispensation of the Spirit. The presence and office of the Holy Ghost pervade all the Apostles wrote. The writings of the Fathers are full of the Holy Ghost. They wrote as in the light of the Day of Pentecost"— can verbatim be repeated of his own writings, breathing as they do indeed the Spirit and the unction of Pentecost. Yet it is the same Cardinal who also gave us his admirable book on "The Glories of the Sacred Heart" which is perhaps the most sublime exposition extant of the Devotion. In this happy manner he dwells on the paramount importance of knowing, adoring, and studying the heart of our Divine Savior:

"Jesus is the Book of Life, and in Him 'are hid all the treasures of wisdom and knowledge,' of Him alone all the mysteries of the Kingdom of God may be learnt: not only because He is the Divine Teacher, but because they are all contained in the knowledge of Himself. When He said, 'I am the Way, the Truth, and the Life; no man cometh unto the Father but by Me,' He declared that all truth was contained in Himself; and when the Apostle said that he judged himself to 'know nothing save Jesus Christ and Him crucified,' he meant the same thing, namely, that he knows Jesus Christ aright, knows the whole Revelation of God. As the radiance which flows from the sun is inseparable from the sun, so is the Revelation of God the radiance which flows from the Person of Jesus Christ. I have said that the Sacred Heart is the key or interpretation of the Incarnation of the Eternal Word. Any one who desires to know the mystery of the Incarnation—and in that mystery of the Incarnation to know, I will say, the whole Science of God—may learn it by reading the Sacred Heart of our Divine Redeemer."

The conclusion, then, "a posteriori," covers the one "a priori" perfectly, that the more a man loves the Sacred Heart of Christ, the more he will be imbued with the glow and ardor of Christ's Spirit, and the more a man is "filled with the Holy Ghost," the more he will concentrate his adoration and love in the Heart of God Incarnate.

So it must be, for it cannot be otherwise. From the Heart of Christ beam forth those rays of a supernatural fire and in this Heart the irradiation of Pentecost finds its source and focus. " *Cor meum et anima mea.*" Therefore, I claim that the union of these two devotions, the one to the "Cor meum" of our Saviour and the other to the Spirit the "anima mea" is vivifying both to the Church as a whole and the individual soul of each one of her children.

Viewed in His relations within the Most Holy Trinity, the Holy Ghost proceedeth from the Father and Son and is Their mutual breathing of infinite love, one God with Them in essence, majesty and perfection.

Viewed in His office in the plan of salvation He is altogether the Promise, the Gift, the Continuator of Christ's mission on earth. As the Son did not seek His own honor, but that of the Father, so the Spirit will glorify the Son.

Viewed in His operations described in the inspired word of the Scripture, this most intimate and reciprocal relation between Son and Spirit shows itself in a still more striking light which is well worth our contemplation.

Sacred Writ frequently and in the clearest terms refers to the Holy Spirit without, however, expressing His name.

Before the advent of the Spirit, which took place on Pentecost, the Apostles were not able to grasp fully this mutual relation between their Master and the Paraclete, hence, we find in His divine preaching the name of the Holy Spirit merely implied at times and in connections that would seem to call for its plain expression. Later on, however, when the Apostles had received the Spirit of Whom the Lord said: "The world cannot receive Him, because it seeth Him not, nor knoweth Him; but you shall know Him; because He shall abide with you, and shall be in you" (S. John XIV, 17), they understood in its full truth this mutual relation and why their Master had so often omitted the name of the Holy Spirit. So, too, must we, animated and enlightened by the same Spirit, be able to read between lines.

It may for instance seem strange, that when our Lord says, "I confess to Thee, O Father, Lord of heaven and earth, because Thou hast hidden these things from the wise and prudent, and hast revealed them to the little ones. Yea, Father, for so it had seemeth good in Thy sight, and no one knoweth who the Son is, but the Father, and who the Father is, but the Son, and to whom the Son will reveal Him,"—(Luke X, 22) it may, I say, seem strange that here no express mention is made of the Spirit. And still the Spirit is understood. When the Lord thus spoke, He was, according to St. Luke, "rejoicing in the Holy Ghost." The mutual revelation of Father and Son is given to men in the Spirit Himself. It may again seem strange, that the Holy Spirit is not expressly mentioned, when after St. Peter's confession of His Divinity our Lord said: " Blessed art thou, Simon, Bar-Jona : because flesh and blood hath not revealed it to thee, but My Father who is in• heaven " (Matth VI, 17). And still the Spirit is here understood, because it is in the illumination of the Spirit that the Father performs the act revealing the Son. Hence, St. Jerome's allusion to the meaning of the Hebrew Word *Bar-Jona*, which is the Son of the Dove. The revelation which according to the analogy of scripture is constantly opposed to the revelation of "flesh and blood," is always the revelation of the Spirit; for, " to us God has revealed by His Spirit " (I. Cor. II, 10). And, when concluding His most solemn farewell on the eve of His passion, the Lord said to His

Father, "I have made known Thy Name to them and will make It known; that the love wherewith Thou hast loved Me, may be in them and I in them" (S. John XVII, 26). He does not here use the word "Spirit" and still most emphatically alludes to Him when He speaks of the substantial love of the Father and Son, that should be in them. We know from Rom. V, 5, that "the charity of God is poured forth into our hearts by the Holy Ghost, who is given to us." This mutual and mystical inhabitation of the Father and Son in our souls is brought about by the Holy Ghost. The Lord therefore in the last verse of His sacerdotal oration implores the Father, to bestow the effusion of the Spirit as the principal fruit of His impending sacrifice, the crowning effect and complement of redemption.

I do not deem that I have been too profuse especially since the nature of the subject seemed to call for it, in enlarging upon this most striking mutual relation between Son and Spirit. What I wished to make clear and inculcate is, as you already perceive, that besides His evident and manifest co-operation in the great work of redemption, the Holy Spirit is very often alluded to in Sacred Writ without actual expression of His Sacred Name.

All that I have said is, it seems to me, abundantly sufficient to show that the unique relation between our Lord and His Spirit bespeaks a most singular relationship between the devotion to the Sacred Heart of Jesus and the devotion to the Holy Spirit. The devotion to the Sacred Heart is nothing else than one of those manifestations of the church's indwelling Spirit which show themselves in various forms and shades according to the necessity of the times. Its aim which is singularly adapted to the needs of the present age is, to make that Heart, full to overflowing with divine love for us, more known, loved and adored. But to have Christ dwell in our hearts by faith . . to be able to comprehend what is the breadth, and length, and height, and depth; to know also the charity of Christ, which surpasseth all knowledge" (Ephes. III, 19) we must first be "*strengthened by His Spirit with might unto the inward man*" (Ephes. III, 16). Hence, the Spirit only will give us the grace of a true devotion to the most Sacred Heart. He with his larger effusion will again irradiate this most adorable furnace of divine love, and be our reward exceeding great.

Nor is there any difficulty in uniting both devotions in their practical exercises. We have never for a moment imagined that the exercises of the devotion to God the Holy Ghost should, as some seem to suspect and fear, supersede, or even in the slightest degree interfere with the practical exercises of the devotion to the Sacred Heart. The more we realize theoretically by the nature of both devotions, the better will we unite them in practice, and thus contribute to their promotion and increase. We doubt not that for immediate and especially popular practice, meditation, and daily exercises, the devotion to the Sacred Heart is by far the more commendable and suitable. Christ, God Incarnate, His most Sacred Heart, the centre of His Humanity will always be the mirror, in which Divine perfection has deposited in human forms, the inexhaustible treasure of our meditations. However, the devotion to God the Holy Ghost will take, a secondary, but to my mind, very important part in enabling us to profit by this devotion to the Sacred Heart, in strengthening us in the Spirit unto the inward man and in drawing us nearer and nearer to the Sacred Heart.

True, it is not so rich in practical exercises and meditations, for, the Spirit takes from and reveals the Son. True, it imposes no obligations and has for its aim but the awakening in us of a lively consciousness of our necessity of the Spirit's indwelling in our souls and of constant prayer to obtain a large share of His divine effusion. Nevertheless, has not every other special devotion its birth and life and crown from the Holy Ghost, and should He only have no special devotion? Should He only be lost sight of in our devotions? I grant that were devotion to God the Holy Ghost to always have the place which it should occupy in connection with other devotions, the necessity of a special devotion to the Holy Spirit would to a great extent disappear.

Were we to precede our other devotions by either saying or singing the "Veni Creator," were we to accustom ourselves to supplicate the Holy Ghost before administering or receiving the Sacraments, in fine, were we priests always alive to the necessity of imploring light from the Holy Spirit before entering upon our daily pastoral duties and sacerdotal functions, and ever careful to reserve for our own greater private devotion and for the public devotion of the people the sacred time immediately preceding and following Pentecost, it would be more difficult to establish claims for a special devotion to arouse zeal for the honor of the

Holy Spirit. But since the contrary seems to be the prevailing custom, the necessity of this devotion and its claims for a place among the very first are at once established. This was evidently the opinion of Rt. Rev. Bishop Keane of Richmond, when in his pastoral, speaking of devotions in general and this in particular, he said: "It is indeed far from advisable to have too many devotions, but the spirit of piety cannot but impel us to have *some;* we should choose the best, and no one certainly can fail to recognize that this devotion to the Holy Ghost must be among the very best. It is equally unadvisable to undertake too many pious practices; for experience shows that the effort to say too many prayers and crowd too many exercises into the time that can be daily given to them is ordinarily the destruction of attention and fervor in all the prayers that are said, but the devotion to the Holy Ghost is not liable to this objection. As it is already stated on the certificate of membership (of the confraternity of which we shall speak in the following part), the only obligation is to be enrolled with a sincere desire and resolution to love and honor the Holy Ghost, to think of Him more frequently, and to correspond to His grace more faithfully." It is also advisable that this devotion should occasionally manifest itself in prayers, but ever be it known that no obligation whatever is attached to any of the exercises of the devotion, and therefore, neither dread nor scruples should have place in those who embrace its practice. Let no one, however, fall into the error too common regarding a devotion, which in its practices, unlike other devotions, implies no obligation of measuring its value and the profit to be desired from it by the lightness of its obligation. As I have already tried to make clear, the chief aim of this devotion is to awaken in the mind a consciousness, having for its foundation faith and for its actuation prayer, that we are under the ministration of the Holy Ghost. All other benefits that may accrue from this Devotion will be considered secondary and accidental, and might as well have been attained by any other devotion.

The motto then of what we say and do to promote this devotion must be; "It is the Spirit that quickeneth; the flesh profiteth nothing; the words that I have spoken to you, are spirit and life." (John VI, 64.)

With this explanation of the relation of our devotion to the devotion of the Sacred Heart, we feel that we have also indicated its relation to all other devotions whatever may be their name, their nature, or purpose. After God Incarnate the one that enjoys the most clear, most intimate, most mystical union with the Holy Ghost, is His Spouse, the ever Blessed Virgin. In her Immaculate Conception she appears in the full radiancy and splendor of His light and grace, "all fair without spot or wrinkle."

In the Incarnation overshadowed by the Holy Ghost, she received the Eternal Word. On Pentecost, in the midst of the Apostles, she again as mystical Mother of the Church received the Holy Ghost: that was by virtue of the Holy Ghost framed and formed and vivified around her from whose virginal flesh, the Son of God assumed the spotless garment of His most Sacred Humanity.

In God's numerous Saints, the seven gifts of the Holy Ghost infused in holy baptism, are constantly expanded and enriched in their souls by His frequent inspirations. Those now triumphant and stationed before God's throne in His eternal kingdom of glory, are but the ripe and perfect fruit gathered from the mystical vine and matured under the influence of the Spirit as by the rays of a supernatural Sun. So that far from obscuring or interfering with the devotions in honor of the mysteries of Faith, the Blessed Virgin or the Saints, the devotion to God the Holy Ghost will serve to give them additional life and light. Thus, this devotion will prove a most efficacious means to enrich and quicken the growth of the supernatural seed and hasten to their full development and perfection, the fruit and flowers of the Church, the garden of God. Thus, it will cultivate and fertilize the mystical garden of our souls, so that these various devotions will each in its own time and place increase, improve, confirm, and glorify whatever is good and holy, and thus verify in fact the beautiful, sublime, grand sentiments which led by the hand of God's Church, we so often utter in the following prayer: *" Thou shalt send forth Thy Spirit and they shall be created, and Thou shalt renew the face of the earth. May the glory of the Lord endure forever; the Lord shall rejoice in His works. I will sing to the Lord as long as I live; I will sing praise to my God, while I have my being. Let my speech be acceptable to Him; but I will take delight in the Lord"* (Ps. 104, 30-34.)

7.

The Devotion to God the Holy Ghost and the fruits it is expected to bear.

Having compared our devotion to a plant or a tree it is meet that in this chapter we reach the conclusion that should follow from the comparison.

If then, as Scripture tells us, " every good tree bringeth forth good fruit " and " a good tree cannot bring forth evil fruit " (Matth. VII, 17, 18) a devotion so divine, so altogether supernatural as ours, must certainly bring forth good, nay, the very best fruit that the most godly could desire. And if, as Scripture informs us, we are made aware of the quality of the tree by its fruit, " By their fruits you shall know them ", a new light, a greater appreciation, a broader field, must undoubtedly be in store for this devotion the more its value are estimated from its fruits and results.

We have already, at least implicitly, spoken of the fruits of this devotion.

The larger effusion of the Holy Ghost which is the recognized aim and end of this devotion is exactly the fruit which we, who cultivate it, hope to acquire. It remains then for us to trace and designate the various ways in which the manifestations, signs, and characteristics of the desired larger effusion afford us certainty that we have been made its recipients. To assign a special fruit as the result of this devotion, may indeed, at first sight, seem difficult, since the Holy Ghost Himself the one great gift which includes all others, as St. Francis of Sales beautifully remarks, has been communicated in the divine economy to our souls.

"The glorious St. Paul says: 'The fruit of the Spirit is charity, joy, peace, patience, benignity, goodness, longanimity, mildness, faith, modesty, continence and chastity' (Gal. v. 22, 23). But see, Theotime, how this Divine Apostle, counting these twelve fruits of the Holy Ghost, puts them down as a single fruit; for he does not say, 'The fruits of the Spirit are charity, joy,' etc., but only 'the *Fruit* of the Spirit.' Now here is the mystery of this manner of speaking: 'The charity of God is poured forth in our hearts by the Holy Ghost, who is given to us' (Rom. v. 5). Yes, charity is the one fruit of the Holy Ghost, but because this fruit has an infinite number of excellent properties, the Apostle, who wishes to exhibit some of them by way of sample, speaks of this single fruit as if it were many, on account of the multitude of properties, which it contains in its unity. On the other hand, he speaks of all these various fruits as one fruit because of the unity in which this variety is comprised. So, too, one who would say that the fruit of the wine is the grape, wine, brandy, and the drink 'that cheers the heart of man' (Ps. CIII. 15), would not mean that these were the fruits of different kinds, but merely that though it is only one fruit, it has, nevertheless, many different qualities, according to the various ways in which it is employed." (Love of God, book XI. ch. 19.)

Under the sun's burning rays, in an arid, parching mid-summer, the thirsting earth, the fading flowers, and the withering foliage, betoken a want to which the earth itself cannot minister.

An immediate reaction must come; the dying life of the vegetable world must be called back; the yawning, thirsting earth must get what it craves, else universal barrenness ere long will ensue.

At length, the heavens in seeming pity

for the throes of earth, little by little, gather a dense, black, frowning cloud, the thunder peals, the lightning flashes and the firmanent yields to the earth a refreshing rain. The departing life of vegetating nature returns, the fields, the foliage, the flowers, the crops renew their healthy hues and new life seems to have been infused into all nature. All the energies of nature have been quickened. But who will tell us what particular energy has been benefited most by this benediction of the skies.

Again the physical condition of a man has lost its normal healthfulness, is undermined, exhausted by sickness, or worn out by manual or mental labor; his case seems desperate. Something must be done to stay the fast speeding life and restore him to his health. Medical skill is employed, a salubrious climate is sought, tender care is constant and soon the shattered frame gains strength, the pulse gets back its normal pace, the blood goes its rounds in healthful order, the muscles assume their wonted agility and the man is himself again. Who can tell the organ or part of that man's frame that has been benefited most by the influence of science and nature when the whole man seems new. So it is exactly with the effusion of the Spirit which we expect as the fruit of this devotion. Internally, invisibly inundating the spiritual man it will diffuse new life into the soul and call forth into full play and christian-like action all her gifts and energies. What our Lord says of His own divine mission on earth: "I have come that they may have life, and may have it more abundantly," (S. John X. 10) must also be said of the Spirit's mission towards our interior and supernatural life.

A new effusion of the Holy Ghost procured through a fervent devotion to Him, will have the happy result of bringing that Divine Guest nearer to our souls, so that we will the better know and feel His illumining, fortifying and consoling presence. It is a truth of divine revelation, that the Holy Ghost dwells personally in the soul of the just, the Apostle emphatically declaring: "Know you not that you are the temple of God, and that the Spirit of God dwelleth in you. The temple of God is holy, which you are" (I. Cor. III, 16).

His indwelling in our souls is precisely the medium through which we will know Him, feel Him, perceive His visitation and form that mystical communication with the Father and Son for which our Divine Saviour on the eve of His passion so solemnly prayed when He said: "that the love, wherewith Thou hast loved Me, may be in them and I in them" (S. John XVII, 23). By degrees this personal presence will become more intimate, more felt and more secure.

Besides, a new effusion of the Holy Spirit procured by a fervent devotion to Him, will have the blessed effect of augmenting in our souls created charity, which though distinct, yet is not separable from the Holy Ghost. Under the richness of its heavenly influence, sanctifying grace the only true life, the only real nobility of the human soul will largely increase. As light and heat are not the sun, but emanations from it, so, too, sanctifying grace and charity, whilst they are not the Holy Ghost, are heaven-given indications of His indwelling in the soul. "The sun in the sky" Cardinal Manning says, dwelling on this subject, "is always the fountain of light and heat. But the light and heat are not always with us, for they may be intercepted by the clouds. Moreover, the light and the heat are the emanations from the the sun; they are not the sun; they do not constitute its being or its existence; they flow from the fulness and the power of light which radiates from the sun. So it is with God the Holy Ghost. He is the center of

light and love: But the light and love are
not the Holy Ghost, they are the action of
the Holy Ghost upon the soul; and therefore there is a distinction to be drawn between the Uncreated Charity of God, Who is
given to us, and the created charity of God,
which is grace infused into the soul. The
Uncreated Charity of God is the Holy Ghost
Himself. The Holy Ghost therefore personally dwells in the heart of those who are in
the state of grace, and unites Himself to
them. But the created charity of God is, as
I have said, like the sun's light and heat.
Wheresoever the sun is, there, by the action
of its light and heat, it gives life and form,
and perfection and fruitfulness, and maturity
and ripeness to all things. These qualities
and perfections are deposited, as it were, on
the face of the earth; they become the possession and the properties of the earth and
of the trees and fruits throughout the world.
So it is when the Holy Ghost is in the soul.
The love of God and of our neighbour is
like the ripeness and the fruitfulness which
the sun bestows upon the works of creation.
These are all infused into the soul, and are
left abiding in the soul as qualities and properties and perfections belonging to it. It
is by that created grace that the soul loves

God with all its strength, and its neighbour as itself."

A new effusion of the Holy Spirit brought about by fervent devotion to Him will arouse, stir up, call into full development and harmonious action all these supernatural habits, infused into the soul as the Spirit's dowry in the moment of our regeneration or justification: The Theological virtues, the gifts of the Holy Ghost, even the moral virtues lie in the depths of our soul like dormant energies and powers, so that the inspirations of the Spirit finding these gifts spread and expanded, like sails spread to catch the wind, will impel our souls onwards on the way to God, and verify in us the Prophet's saying: "They that hope in the Lord, shall renew their strength, they shall take wings as eagles, they shall run and not be weary, they shall walk and not faint." (Isai. XI, 31.)

Moreover, besides, this general revival, which is the main fruit or consequence of a new effusion of the Holy Spirit into our souls, there are some manifestations of the indwelling Spirit, which indicate His presence and influence with a kind of unmistakable certainty. Wherever Holy Writ speaks of a man as "full of the Holy Ghost," the manifestations of the indwelling Spirit become

discernible either in his person, words or
deeds.

These more specific manifestations, which,
with all propriety may be termed *expansions*
of the soul, will, too, prove a result of the
new effusion of the Spirit procured through
a fervent devotion to God the Holy Ghost.
As steam cannot be kept within a tight vessel, but bursts forth and sets in motion the
heaviest machinery, so does the Spirit, when
working in His plentitude, fill the soul, expand its energies, urge them into activity
and insist upon spreading His influence far
and wide. The beginning of such an inward power is a more than ordinarily living
faith. What a vast difference, then, is between faith and faith, between the faith of
the man who, wavering like a wave of the
sea, which is moved and carried about by
the wind, receives nothing of the Lord, (Jas.
I, 7,) and the faith of the man who unwaver-
ingly shall say to the mountain: Take up
and cast thyself into the sea, and it shall be
done," (Matth. XXI, 21.) What a striking
contrast there is between the faith of most
men who, whilst they do not dare deny them,
scarcely accept with implicit obedience the
truths of revelation proposed to us by the
authority of the church—and the faith of the
Saints and holy men who have realized these

truths, and before whose enlightened minds supernatural revelation in all its certainty, sublimity and harmony has stood as the greatest of all realities!

Besides this world of faith all other things are light and fleeting as dust. It is a grand reality full of light and intelligence. It is the brilliant object calling for love and fidelity. This flashing up of the light of faith in a soul, is a manifestation that the Spirit shines upon it, just as the morning sun shedding its effulgent rays upon the surrounding scenery, gives it a lustre and attractiveness which, before it did not have. In a transport of such intense faith, the soul with our Lord "rejoices in the Holy Ghost," (Luk 10–21), with Mary the spirit "rejoices in God the Saviour" (Luk I, 47,) and with St. Francis of Sales, rapt by the beauty of faith, man exclaims, "*Hoc doctus Plato nescivit.*" It is therefore but a simple consequence in virtue of natural evolution that such a living faith should generate love and enthusiasm, and that light thus intensified would be the centre radiating warmth and strength and fire.

Thus we see that the second manifestation of a larger effusion of the Spirit procured by a fervent devotion to Him, is an *habitual peace,* which the world cannot give, a spiritual joy which is a foretaste of bliss only experienced by the godly, and a supernatural serenity, the jewel by excellence of the elect. "The kingdom of God which is not meat and drink; but justice and peace and joy in the Holy Ghost" has then arrived in a soul. (Rom. XIV, 17.)

The prayer of the Apostle for the Romans has then obtained fulfilment in a soul; "Now the God of hope fill you with all joy and peace in believing; that you may abound in hope and in the power of the Holy Ghost," (Rom. XV, 13.) This Joy or spiritual sun-shine may from time to time be obscured by the passing clouds of temptation or adversity, but it is habitual, hence Sacred Writ most strikingly alludes to joy and power whenever mention is made of the Holy Ghost and His divine presence. A power indeed it is, for even this joy of mind and heart transforms itself into a propelling power, an impetuous zeal, which shapes the overflowing sentiments of the heart into words and speech, by means of which it shows itself outwardly and has a blessed influence upon others. This brings us to the third manifestation of a larger effusion of the Holy Spirit attained by a fervent devotion to Him which consists in our souls being filled with holy *zeal* for God's glory, the salvation of souls and the prerogative of faith—a zeal which will so fire our souls that our mouths will perforce give vent to it in words of power and in speech replete with spiritual unction. It was an adage amongst the Rhetoricians of the Quintilian age, that: " *Pectus est, quod dissertos facit,*" and again ; *Qui non ardet non accendit.*" A popular proverb has it: "From the fulness of the heart, the mouth speaketh." The inspired word gives expression to the same truth with reference to the mutual relation between faith and preaching, saying: " Having the the same spirit of faith, as it is written ; I believed, for which cause also I have spoken ; we also believe, for which cause also, we speak also." (II Cor. V, 13.)

The zeal, the power, the unction of speech and predication are collectively a signal manifestation of an effusion of the Spirit, and as such must at once appear highly desirable in the priest, whom the following Apostolic utterance concerns: " Necessity lieth upon me to preach the Gospel ; for woe is unto me, if I preach not the Gospel " (I. Cor. IX, 16).

Hence it was on the great day of Pentecost, so signalized by the solemn effusion of the Holy Ghost, that the ministry of sacred preaching was inaugurated, and the Christian pulpit for the first time received its solemn consecration. Again we are reminded of the same beautiful connection existing between the Holy Ghost and the word of power in the solemn strains of the Veni Creator, the crystallization of all the praises of the Holy Ghost, when we say : " *Sermone dittans guttura.*"

" The fulness of His promised word,
Who hast all speech at thy command."

Word impels to action, and becomes a grand medium within the command of the speaker swayed by zeal, encouraged by success and conscious of victory to breathe and communicate to others the power which swells his own bosom. So that potency of speech evolves into thirst for reformation, indomitable courage, great power of action and finally triumphal success. These then are the last but perhaps not the least fruits for us whom it becomes to be powerful in word,— these evolutions wrought in the soul by a new effusion of the Holy Spirit attained by a fervent Devotion to that Divine Person. " I will give you a mouth and wisdom," said the Lord, " which all your adversaries shall not be able to resist and gainsay" (S. Luke XXI. 15.) Our Lord himself tells us about this Invisible Speaker's using the tongue of his Apostles : " For it is not you that speak, but the Spirit of your Father that speaketh in you" (Matth. X, 20). Filled with the Holy Ghost the Apostles after Pentecost proved as fearless and irresistible as they had been before timid and pusillanimous. They, having heard what the chiefs and ancients had said to them, "with one accord lifted up their voice to God, saying: Lord, Thou art He that did'st make heaven and earth, the sea and all things that are in them, who by the Holy Ghost, by the mouth of our father David, Thy servant, hath said: Why did the Gentiles rage, and the people meditate vain things: The kings of the earth stood up, and the princes assembled together against the Lord, and against His Christ? For of a truth there assembled together in this city against Thy holy child, Jesus, whom Thou hast annointed, Herod and Pontius Pilate, with the Gentiles and people of Israel, to do what Thy hand and their council decreed to be done. And now, Lord, behold their threatenings, and grant unto Thy servants, that with all confidence they may speak the word, by stretching forth Thy hand to cures and signs and wonders, to be done by the name of Thy Holy Son Jesus. And when they had prayed, the place was moved wherein they were assembled; and they were all filled with the

Holy Ghost, and they spoke the word of God with confidence " (Act. IV. 24–32).

I have always considered this passage of the Acts one of the grandest in Scripture. Here we have in quick succession after the first and great Pentecost the evident, unmistakable signs of a new effusion of the Holy Ghost. Here we have in the solemn words of the old dispensation the first grand intonation of the triumphal song of the Church, the mystical Jerusalem of the new covenant, a triumphal song ascending as the battle cry of light against darkness from the midst of the persecution which had broken out upon the Apostles. Again the City of Thorns is the scene of the persecution of Christ in the persons of His confessors, as she was but a short time before the scene of His persecution in His own Divine Person. But in the present as in the past His glory must appear, accordingly the Spirit of power the Glorifier of the Son is hailed from on high with fervent tongues and godly hearts. In quick response He descends with such power and in such plenitude that nature acknowledges the Almighty pressure; the place moves, all are filled and speak with a confidence, courage and power—speak as never men spoke before. Down the ages with maturity of nineteen hundred years upon her brow, ages in fact for her of uninterrupted persecution, the grand old Church of Christ, the grand old Church of the Popes, the grand old Church of Rome has sent up this triumphal song of light against darkness. But the end is not yet and cannot be till, guided by the Almighty Spirit from above she will have finished her divine mission and reached with all the glory of triumph the kingdom for which she so gloriously battles. Then as well as now can she break forth in the inspired words of the Psalmist: "Many a time have they fought against me from my youth, let Israel now say, many a time have they fought against me" (Ps. 128, 1). Her confidence in every trial and contest is as stable as the veracity of her Divine Founder whose infallible words are at stake: "The gates of hell shall not prevail against her" (XVI. 18). Her confidence of victory in every persecution receives fresh impulse and inspiration from her consciousness of the promise of a new effusion of the Holy Spirit. Do you ask proof? Read the Acts of the Apostles, that history of the infant Church, that book by excellence of the Holy Ghost. Read the history of the Church, especially the dark and bloody annals of her persecutions and behold her coming forth with the crown of victory upon her brow,

Read the lives of God's Saints, count the victories in supreme trials which have crowned their lives the world over, because, they have confided in Him who has overcome the world and have been made powerful to do all things in Him who has given them strength. Where the Spirit is, there, too, is victory. For the Soul that is filled with the Holy Ghost there is no such word as fail, be the holy enterprise what it may. Her greatest difficulties under the divine influence of the Spirit are transformed into rounds of the ladder which leads up to victory. In the heat of the divine presence of the Holy Ghost, the shackles forged in narrow-mindedness, formalism, pedantry and false nationalism which bind and restrain the energies, the strength of the individual are melted and "the law of liberty reigns supreme."

Undoubtedly the two great objects of a man's national regard are his kindred and his country. Blasted forever be the false, foully false imputation with which the world rings, that Catholics cannot love their country. Far from being true, it is the doctrine of Catholic Theology, that by the gift of piety a man is bound to love his country. The laudable and justified pride of every man is that, which he has from the advantages, history and glories of his nation. No people, no race, no nation, is without its peculiar advantages and glories: so, too, every people has a providential mission to fulfil. But the nationalism which would, if it could, limit the very power of God and destroy the universality, unity and Catholicity of His Church, was gloriously consumed in the miraculous fire of the great Pentecost.

God's Church is essentially and in the highest sense of the phrase "*Unum ex pluribus.*" And yet, strange to say, false nationalism in some sense lives and has manifested itself down the ages, but always to be conquered and "overcome"; for it is of this world, and Christ has conquered and "overcome the world."

"We are not, indeed," says the Cardinal with special reference to England, and we might repeat it of ourselves, *mutatis mutandis*: "such lovers of our country that if an Apostle came to us from Judea, we should stone him with stones, or stop our ears or harden our hearts against him. We do not believe that every teacher sent from God ought to be an Englishman. We do not believe that all matters of spiritual judgment and doctrine are to be decided within the four seas of England. No, because that would be an impiety—an impiety against God, an impiety against Jesus Christ, an impiety against the Holy Ghost, an impiety against the whole revelation of faith, an impiety against the whole Christian world. We know that when the Apostles were sent out with a divine commission to make disciples of all nations, the nations listened to them, all Jews as they were. They subdued the cultivated Greeks, and the imperial Romans, and our barbarous forefathers into one family. And within the circle of revealed truth, all these national distinctions were abolished. In Jesus Christ there is 'neither Jew nor barbarian, nor bond nor free.'"

In this great country more than in any other does it become people never to forget the foregoing intimation of the scriptures. For it is the secret of America's glory that on this continent all nations under heaven meet as they did in Jerusalem on the day of Pentecost.

People of all nations constantly pour into this new world and are amalgamated, transformed into one national body essentially *unum ex pluribus.* Here a wide field is open to the people of the earth to promote their interests which so long suffered from the deficiencies and mistakes of the social management in the old world. Here the latent energies and abilities of every nationality are challenged, called forth and put in action by the energy, competition and ambition for which our nation is noted. On this great continent the amalgamated masses of every nation with their united talents and united efforts can reach and show to the world a degree of civilization, never known to the people of the ages that are past. To effect this, however, every vestige of the spirit that bespeaks narrow-mindedness and false nationalism must be completely and forever stamped out. Praiseworthy in the highest sense though it be for us, who have made this the land of our adoption to cherish a dear remembrance and love for the land of our birth; ever be it far from us to retard the progress, thwart the onward march to greatness, or aim a death-blow at the life of this nation of our adoption by any effort to transplant and put into its life old and unsuitable characteristics of other nations. Not less are they enemies to the growth, development and prosperity of the nation who, nourishing a spirit of false nativism, would in their delusion exclude all physical and mental resources from abroad and in their hour of prosperity proudly boast of their self-sufficiency. Man left to himself is at best selfish and narrow, and the individual characteristics for better or for worse become those of the nation. Hence, to prevent all short-comings, to establish a new and great nation, all selfishness and narrow-mindedness must be abandoned and a true Catholic, which is a true American, broadmindedness must take their place; but to effect this the Holy Spirit is required —the Dove that ever hovering above, becomes to the nation not a mere figure but a glorious reality.

Our nation without fail will be made the happy recipient of this divine boon by devotion to the Holy Ghost, for the promotion of which it is our great pleasure to contribute this our humble effort. Thus far we have but considered faith, joy, power of zeal, courage, success which may with all propriety be called *expansions* of the soul effected by the influence of the Holy Spirit. Before concluding, however, it would seem to become us, in a cursory way at least, to give our attention to some characteristic *restraints* effected through the influence of the Holy Ghost. Though the expansions which we have considered are true characteristics of the indwelling of the Holy Ghost in our souls, it is nevertheless amazing how well the devil who assumes at times the appearance of an angel of light can counterfeit them in persons totally devoid of God's Holy Spirit. Hence, it is safe to say that the restraints form a more certain criterion from which to judge of the Spirit by which a man is influenced. I will content myself with mentioning three, which to my mind will amply, and unmistakably indicate the Spirit of God, or proclaim His absence.

The first and decidedly the most important is a *loving filial submission* to our Holy Mother the church in all that she teaches, proposes, commands or even advises us to think and believe. The Church is the home here below of the Holy Ghost; she is the mystical body of Christ and the Holy Ghost is her soul, and as the body cannot live without the soul so He the Christ-given Soul can never desert her and thus contrary to Christ's promise allow her to be prevailed. against by the gates of hell. The souls of the just are individually temples of the Holy Ghost and in the divine economy will not be deserted by Him unless driven out by man's abuse of free will in the commission of mortal sin. But His divine operations are too often thwarted by lesser sins and omissions, hence, the correction of these is truly a new effusion of God's Holy Spirit for the individual soul. It evidently follows since the Holy Ghost, the Spirit of truth, is the same in the Church, as He is in the individual soul of a just man, that he in whose soul the Holy Ghost is, will be lovingly submissive to the Holy Ghost in the Church.

God could have dispensed with an external organization such as the Church and through the Divine Spirit have accomplished in the souls of men all that the Church accomplishes. But such was not His divine pleasure. For His own wise reasons He chose to establish the Church, and authorized her to teach the world whatever He had commanded, promising at the same time to be with her till the end of time. Therefore, it is evidently false and absurd to suppose that the Holy Ghost, the soul of the church, the very incorporation of the visible body built by Christ upon the rock, actuating all its living members and speaking through the visible authority of that body, actuating and inspiring the individual soul of the man in grace, should inspire the Church to teach, dictate and command; and inspire the man to find fault with the teaching, quibble at the dictation, or murmur against the command. Wherever such a disagreement is found, there it is certain a spirit other than the Holy Spirit has influence. This cannot be in the Church over which the Holy Spirit reigns supreme, it must therefore be in the soul where the indwelling of the Holy Spirit is at the option of the free will of man. Whilst it is his choice to be under the influence of the Holy Ghost he enjoys the freedom of the children of God; but the moment he concludes to banish the Holy Ghost by the commission of mortal sin, he becomes an abject slave to a spirit entirely and necessarily antagonistic to the Holy Spirit. The harmonious response of a ready obedience to the Church in everything is a sure sign that a soul is under the influence of the Holy Ghost—it is simply the Holy Spirit echoing His own voice, but when the discord of disobedience shows itself, it is quite evident, that another Spirit occupies the place of the Holy Ghost. Full and implicit obedience to the authority of the Church is the characteristic trait of the soul, really and truly the sanctified temple of the Holy Ghost, and it is the true and only safe road to perfection, the road traversed by all the saints. As the operations of the Holy Ghost in the soul can be retarded or frustrated in a greater or less degree without totally depressing Him, so the more prompt, the more universal, the more loving the obedience and attachment to the Church, the greater evi-

dently is the influence of the Holy Ghost.
All who know the Church as she really is,
to be the mystical Body of Christ having
for its Soul and guidance the Holy Ghost
and His hallowed voice and light, conceive her to be the tabernacle of God
among men, the nearest approach to the
Beatific Vision and the union of the
human soul with God.   Our obedience then
must not confine itself to her dogmas, but
must embrace in full harmony the whole
spirit which pervades the discipline, worship, and devotions of the Church, " *Ubi
ecclesia ibi Spiritus*,"—" *Sentire eum ecclesia* "
—The " *Spiritus Ecclesiasticus* " is then the
necessary consequence of such obedience.
Then as becomes true children of the
Church we will lovingly appreciate whatever
the church does or advises us to do.   Then
whims and tastes will give place to strict
fidelity to her ceremonies and liturgical
functions.   Then the words, forms and sentiments of prayers having the impression of
the designation and sanction of the Supreme
Pontiff will have our preference.   Priests
and people will be not only of one body,
but also of one spirit and mind—" the mind
of Christ."

Another sign that the Spirit of God occupies the soul is a *sincere reverence **and***

appreciation for the doctrine of the Saints and theologians of the Church. The Saints have been under the influence of the Holy Spirit to an extraordinary degree. The unanimous belief of the Saints is the unmistaken sense of the Holy Ghost. In the pre-eminence to which their sanctity has raised them, the Saints even here below have seen and comprehended truths which are beyond our reach. So, too, the doctors of the Church, in whom great natural light has been associated with the supernatural gift of the Holy Ghost and has been by them raised eminently above itself, have been numbered amongst the teaching authority of the Church and have been esteemed as men of more than ordinary light.

The third sign that the Spirit of God reigns in the soul is a *wholesome suspicion and fear of all novelty* or socalled originality, and an honest, humble mistrust of ourselves. Tertullian says: "From the order itself it is manifest that what is first in tradition is from the Lord and true, what is afterwards brought is foreign and false." The forms, definitions, and terminology may be new, but the underlying truth is as old as revelation. *"Aliqua scire, et de aliis prudenter dubitare"*—that is to say there are some things which it behooves a man to know of himself and others which he must, to be prudent, doubt and mistrust.

No man who knows himself can constantly confide in his own light. Confidence in one's own light is deemed by those outside of Catholic unity a virtue, but within the pale of unity it is branded as a most dangerous vice. As the Greeks said: "If we cannot sail, we must row;" "if we have no divine guidance by the Spirit of God, breathing through the Church, we must painfully toil onwards by the stretch and reliance of our strength." (Card. Manning, Eccl. sermons V, VII, p. 328.)

How all-important then for us, God's priests set in the ecclesiastical firmament as so many signs and guides of others, are these last three signs of the divine sway of the Holy Spirit in the soul: How earnestly should we impress these truths on the minds of the people lest they yielding to the spirit of independence, subjectivism and false liberty be Catholics only in name, but Protestants in their views; and as St. Paul has it: "tossed to and fro, and carried about with every wind of doctrine by the wickedness of men, by cunning craftiness by which they lie in wait to deceive." (Ephes IV, 14.)

In conclusion then let us say that if such

be the blessed fruits which a true devotion to God the Holy Ghost is calculated to produce, and if from the fruits we must know the tree, what a healthy, what a valuable plant, what a desirable tree in God's vineyard is this devotion and how fragrant and attractive are its flowers, how delicious and refreshing its fruit! We have but plucked sparingly of its abounding, rich and delicious fruit for you, dear reader, but the taste will suffice to tell you of the quality of the tree. The fruits of the Spirit, as enumerated by St. Paul, are many and various.

All the fruits of a fervent devotion to God the Holy Ghost, it is out of the power of man to enumerate or even imagine; for only God knows the number and richness of His own favors to a devoted soul. Whatever can be obtained by prayer, (and what is there, that it is well for us to receive, that cannot be obtained by prayer?) can be procured by means of this devotion. Yea, the Holy Ghost will instruct us how to pray and enlighten us as to the objects of our petitions. We cannot better conclude this our unpretentious exposition than by the words of St. Paul in reference to the Holy Ghost, the source of all benediction, sanctification and salvation, praying in all devoted souls: " *But you have received the Spirit of adoption of sons, whereby we cry: Abba: Father. For the Spirit Himself giveth testimony to our spirit, that we are the sons of God. Likewise also the Spirit helpeth our infirmity: for we know not what we should pray for, as we ought; but the Spirit Himself asketh for us with unspeakable groanings. And He that searcheth the hearts, knoweth what the Spirit desireth: because He asketh for the Saints according to God."* (Rom. VIII, 14, 16, 26, 27.)

PART II.

The Confraternity of the Servants of God the Holy Ghost.

"When you founded the Confraternity of the Servants of the Holy Ghost, I felt a lively sense of thankfulness. It was the embodiment of a devotion to which for more than thirty years I owe all the chief blessings and graces of my life."

Cardinal Manning to Very Rev. Rawes, the founder of the Confraternity, 1879.

1.

Origin of the Confraternity.

Hitherto we have only enlarged upon the
devotion to God the Holy Ghost, without
yet having spoken of the " Confraternity of
the Servants of the Holy Ghost." As with
all propriety we distinguish between religion
and its visible embodiment, the Church, so
with the same propriety we can analogically
distinguish between a doctrine and its corresponding embodiment in a confraternity
or association. A special devotion to God,
to a Divine Person, to Jesus Christ in the
various mysteries of His life, death and
glorification, to the Blessed Virgin, to the
Angels and Saints, to a mystery of our Holy
Religion can exist, be practiced, bring forth
fruit and flourish without necessarily being
embodied into what we call a confraternity
with special approved membership, rules,
obligations, privileges and organization.
Devotion, as well as Religion, is at first
something internal, spiritual, and as such is
the universal source or origin of all external

worship. But, though internal, it cannot long conceal itself; for the nature of the operations of the Soul is such that they speedily make themselves felt for good or for evil outwardly. Hence devotion no sooner takes firm root in a soul than it breaks forth into outward acts of worship, takes shape and form in various ways, and gradually develops into a corresponding external organization in the Church. By a certain law of crystallization working in the Church of God, every internal religious event soon becomes externally perceptible, soon binds together by a spiritual bond of common feelings and views the minds of pious people already impressed and influenced alike by the same internal devotion. Gradually their internal union leads to an external gathering into a society, which, under the fostering care and controlling guidance of the Church, develops into what may aptly be called a minor subordinate organization in the great divine human organization—the Church of God. Thus by the co-operating agency of the Holy Spirit in individual souls first inspiring them with the idea of such a devotion and in the Church as a whole, approving and controling such a movement, a Confraternity is created.

Devotion and Confraternity stand to each other in similar mutual relation as matter and form, soul and body, the letter and the quickening Spirit. Devotion without an embodiment in a Confraternity can exist, but it will not fully develop, it will not wield a universal and permanent influence, or spread or attract or produce the practical, lasting result which mark and follow a devotion shaped into the organic form of a religious or pious association.

A Confraternity without the corresponding internal devotion, is like a plant without life, a letter without the vivifying spirit, a body without the soul—a dead form. Both must be united to attain the special end of the devotion. Man is a social being and words of importance can only be accomplished " *unitis viribus*," that is, by the power of association and organization. Thus the embodiment of a special devotion in a Confraternity gives, as a rule, more growth to the internal devotion of the individual members, because it provides the appropriate means and rules to cultivate, to increase the devotion in general, and secure the end at which it aims. Finally, a Confraternity eventually becomes a corporation enlarging its proportions, exercising a telling influence in its ever widening circles and proving a leaven of spiritual revival not only to the thousands of its individual members, but frequently to the whole Church.

It is generally upon some devout soul that the illumining and warming irradiation of the Holy Spirit first falls, aiming at bringing forth in the mystical garden of God the bud of a fragrant flower. As knowledge is the first and vital condition of all true worship, dogma the source of devotion in general and a clearer and more distinct perception of some truth the cause of some specific devotion, the Holy Ghost, selecting one or some devout souls as fertile ground for the seed of His new plantation, spreads His own mind upon the surface of their minds just as the sun spreads its image upon the surface of the placid lake ; and just as the disk of the sun is reflected perfectly from the lake's surface, the disk of God's divine mind is reflected from their pious minds. Like the magnet, they soon attract other persons with minds and souls of similar cast and ere long a communion of devoted souls is formed. Nothing then remains for the full formation of a Confraternity but the sacred seal of the Church's approval. The society of devoted souls is but a natural outgrowth of the internal life of the Church ; and when she sets her seal of approval upon it, when she bestows upon its rules, obligations and practices, her blessings, indulgences, and privileges, she but enriches the fertility and growth of her own internal life with a celestial and supernatural dew.

This is the history of the Confraternity of the Servants of the Holy Ghost. Without difficulty can we trace the various stages which the development of the Devotion to God the Holy Ghost reached ere it became the grand organization known as the Arch-confraternity which at present is the source of so much glory to the Holy Ghost, so much honor to the Church, and so much good to souls. Though this devotion is as old as the Catholic faith, yet whilst we here trace its gradual formation into a confraternity, we will content ourselves with considering it in that more striking revival, spread, and expression, which have decidedly marked it in our own days. Many a devout mind, indeed, startled by the ever increasing encroachments of sensuality and materialism upon modern society, has again turned towards the Holy Ghost, the source of infallible truth and supernatural grace; but, without doing injustice to anyone, we feel entitled to say that it is under the auspices of his Eminence, Cardinal Manning, Archbishop of Westminster, that this Devotion began to flourish and to spread. It is the great Cardinal himself whom "the kindly light" from above has led from the twilight of faith, outside of the pale of the true Church, to the noonday of the perfect revelation, as given on Pentecost day, and preserved and administered in Christ's one and only true Church. It is he who being "a light that shineth on a dark place, until the day dawn, and the day star" shall arise upon an entire nation, can tell the world: "It gives me opportunity to say, that from the hour I saw the full light of the Catholic faith, no shade of doubt has ever passed over my reason or my conscience. I could as soon believe that a part is equal to the whole, as that Protestantism in any shape, from Lutheranism to Angelicanism, is the revelation of the day of Pentecost." (Letter to the Archbishop of Toronto. Feb'r. 24, 1886.) The books of Cardinal Manning on the Holy Ghost, His Temporal and His Internal Mission, and the same Cardinal's luminous comments on the Adoration of the Divine Paraclete, on the Ministration of the Spirit under which we are, on the Dispensation of Divine truth by the Holy Ghost, on the workings of the Sanctifier in our souls,—on the Day of Pentecost, never setting upon

God's Holy Church on earth—these truly Apostolic writings have beyond doubt done the main part and have been chiefly instrumental in awakening and spreading the Devotion to God the Holy Ghost. It, therefore so happened, that one of his spiritual sons, *the late Very Rev. Father Rawes*, Superior of the Oblates of St. Charles introduced into London by the Cardinal, first conceived the idea to found such a Confraternity. Meeting, of course, with the hearty approval of the Archbishop, the plan quickly matured, and it was concluded that the first Confraternity should be established in the Church of the Oblates of St. Charles, St. Mary of the Angels, Bayswater, Westmoreland Road, London. This was done, and the Church that first enjoyed the honor of having had the present Cardinal as its Rector has ever since been distinguished as the sacred nest of the mystical Dove, the starting point of this Devotion and the center of all the Confraternities of the Servants of the Holy Ghost spread over the globe.

The author of this little volume still remembers with much pleasure, that, while spending in London the winter of 1875–6, he daily said mass in this church long before it became the famous centre of the establishment of the Confraternity of the Servants of the Holy Ghost.   Later on in 1884, when again he visited Europe and St. Mary's Church, he had the pleasure of meeting there the saintly Father Rawes, the immediate founder of the Confraternity.   It was a happy idea of Father Rawes' successor in the rectorship of St. Mary's to call upon all the Servants of the Holy Ghost for material aid to erect in that church a monumental altar in honor of God the Holy Ghost and in memory of His faithful servant, the late Reverend Father Rawes.

In Lent 1877, the first Confraternity of the Servants of the Holy Ghost was established.   God shed many graces upon it, and the members prayed very earnestly for the sanction and blessing of the Vicar of Jesus Christ.   Hence, the Cardinal Archbishop sent the following petition to Rome, which with the corresponding answer may be considered the first official document, concerning the Confraternity:

1. Petition of His Eminence, the Cardinal Archbishop of Westminster:

"The Cardinal-Archbishop of Westminster, prostrate at the feet of your Holiness, humbly recounts that Pope Pius IX., of illustrious and happy memory, graciously granted at the prayer of the said petitioner, in the year 1877, an Indulgence of seven days to all who say the Doxology seven times in honor of the Holy Ghost, the Giver of all gifts and the Guide of the infallible Church, and that henceforth the aforesaid devotion was spread among the faithful, not without fruit.

"The same petitioner now again approaches your Holiness to make known that the Rev. Father Rawes, Oblate of St. Charles, in the Diocese of Westminster, has successfully begun a Society whose end is to increase the adoration of the Holy Ghost, and that he has enrolled in it about twelve members.

"The object of this Society is to spread childlike affection for the Third Person of the Blessed Trinity further and further, to increase it, and so to bring about the growth of a more intense love for Him who is the Fountain of truth and holiness, the author of the supernatural life in us, and in every way the most loving Giver of grace both to the innocent and to penitents.

"In order, therefore, Most Blessed Father, that the beginnings of the aforesaid devotion may be strengthened and unfolded with increased fruit, the Cardinal-Archbishop of Westminster most humbly supplicates your Holiness to vouchsafe to give this Society your Apostolical blessing and indulgences."

"Rescript of His Holiness, Leo XIII., of March 10th, 1878, erecting and indulgencing the Confraternity.

Confraternity of the Servants of the Holy Ghost.

Our Holy Father Leo XIII., by a Rescript dated March 10th, 1878, has approved and indulgenced this Confraternity:

1. He graciously sanctions the name of the society: "*The Confraternity of the Servants of the Holy Ghost.*"

2.　He grants the following indulgences :—

a.　Plenary :

1.　On the day of enrollment.

2.　At the hour of death, on invoking the Holy Ghost.

3.　On Whit Sunday.

4.　On the Feast of the Annunciation of Our Lady.

b.　Partial :

1.　Seven years on every day in the Octave of Pentecost.

2.　One hundred days to all the members who say the Angelic Salutation devoutly three times every day, and seek for the patronage of the Mother of God.

3.　One hundred days to all the members who attend the monthly meetings.

The only obligation is to be enrolled.

A glance at the Holy Father's Rescript will show at once how correctly we have spoken in the foregoing part, regarding the light and few obligations which this Confraternity imposes upon its members.　They are actually only two : *first :* to have an earnest purpose to promote, according to our ability and the intention of Holy Church, a greater worship and glory of the Holy Ghost among men ; *secondly :* to be enrolled or to have their names recorded in the Register of the Confraternity by an authorized priest.　From all that we have so much insisted upon it becomes evident, that this Devotion by no means can interfere with or lessen the practical exercises of other devotions.　It will by immediate application to the Holy Spirit only direct the salutary waters of this Fountain of life to all the various flowers in God's garden, to the various devotions of Holy Church and thus vivify, increase and make them more fruitful. Thus it will rather prove to be the means of making all its members so many organs of the Holy Ghost for the furtherance of other devotions, verifying the inspired text: "He that believeth in me, as the scripture saith, out of his belly shall flow rivers of living water. Now this he said of the Spirit which they should receive who believed Him: for as yet the Spirit was not given, because Jesus was not yet glorified." (S. John VII, 39). As a matter of course, many other practices and pious exercises are advisable to attain more certainly and eminently the end of the Confraternity. Those who have time and feel inspired with devotional feeling to do more towards an end so divine and rich in blessings are earnestly exhorted to be generous in their devotion. Nevertheless, let us never forget that only the two forementioned obligations are essential and that all else is but secondary, commendable, and in no way obligatory. To awaken in us and in "others the consciousness of the presence and indwelling of the Holy Ghost, not only in the Church as a whole, but in each one of us," is to use the words of Cardinal Manning, the first and last object of our endeavor and aspirations be, the way or practice of attaining it what it may. To bring about this consciousness and to further and spread it we believe in one essential and general means, namely, prayer, fervent prayer, constant prayer, daily prayer, prayer in common, prayer directly addressed to the Third Person of the Most Holy Trinity, —God the Holy Ghost. The startling contrast between the children of iniquity in our days, and the Servants of the Holy Ghost cannot be more drastically described than in the words of St. Jude the Apostle: "These are they, who separate themselves, sensual men, *having not the Spirit*. But you, my beloved, building yourselves upon your most holy faith, *praying in the Holy Ghost*, keep ourselves in the love of God, waiting for the mercy of our Lord Jesus Christ unto life everlasting." (S. Jude I. 20, 21.)

It is this "praying in the Holy Ghost" which the Cardinal recommends so forcibly in his already quoted oration, saying: "I will only give you further three intentions for which to pray. The first is for your own sanctification. Be not content to linger in your own faults or your temptations. If you are generous to God He will be more generous to you. Pray that you may be sanctified in body, soul, and spirit. Pray that all the faculties of your intellect, all the affections of your heart, all the acts of your will, all the habits of your life may be guided, governed, and sanctified by the Holy Ghost. The second intention is to pray to Him for the conversion of sinners. Single out some one who has fallen from the truth or from the grace of baptism, or some one who has never known the truth or has never had the great grace of perfect faith, to penance, and to God. Lastly, pray for the Conversion of England. There is visibly a breathing of the Holy Spirit over the face of England. Now, for fifty years a change has been passing upon it, which is not from the nature nor from the man. England has lost much, but it has retained many things, Englishmen believe that Christianity is the revelation of God, and that the Holy Scriptures are the inspired Words of God. They are impatient of human teachers, and refuse to be told by man what to believe. But if they could find a Divine teacher they would gladly listen and believe. They are not mockers nor scoffers, as some men are. Many are yearning for unity with the Church throughout the world, and for the presence of Jesus upon the altar. Pray to the Holy Ghost that the

Spirit from the four winds may breathe upon England and revive its faith.   The seed
which is sown is being needed scantly, and
the furrows are few, but God can multiply
every grain a hundred-fold. The day may not
be far off when the fields shall be white for the
harvest, and the Lord of the harvest shall.
send forth the reapers to gather abundantly
from the face of England the sheaves that
are ripe for His garner."

With a special reference to the chosen and
approved title, "Servants of the Holy Ghost,"
Father Rawes then selected a few passages of
the inspired word to emphazise and magnify
this title.   As they may arouse in us the
sentiments of a salutary pride and spiritual
joy, we give them as follows :

The Servants of the Holy Ghost :

1. " I will not now call you *servants;*   for he
knoweth not what his lord doeth. But I have
called you friends ; because all things whatsoever
I have heard of My Father, I have made known to
you " (St. John XV. 15.)

2. " As free, and not as making liberty a cloak
for malice, but as the *servants* of God " (I. St. Peter
II. 16.)

3. " So you also, when you shall have done all
the things that are commanded you, say: We are
unprofitable *servants ;* we have done that which we
ought to do " (St. Luke XVII. 10.)

4. I. " Paul and Timothy, the *servants* of Jesus
Christ " (Phil. I. 1.)

II. " Paul, a *servant* of God " (St. Tit. I. 1.)

III. " James, the *servant* of God, and our Lord Jesus Christ " (St. James I. 1.)

5. " Hurt not the earth, nor the sea, nor the trees, till we sign the *servants* of our God in their foreheads " (Apoc. VII. 3.)

6. " Singing the canticle of Moses, the *servant* of God, and the canticle of the Lamb" (Apoc. XV. 3.)

7. " There shall be no curse any more; but the throne of God and the Lamb shall be in it : *and His servants shall serve Him;* and they shall see His face ; and His name shall be on their foreheads " (Apoc. XXI1. 3, 4.)

Thus the first step was taken towards embodying and securing and spreading this most salutary devotion of our time and age. The " *Lumen in coelis* " had shone graciously upon the pious undertaking. With feelings of spiritual joy and truly Apostolic zeal, the first Rector of the Confraternity then could address the first members of the Confraternity as follows:

" The higher anything is the more the devil seeks to lower it, and the brighter it is the more he seeks to darken it, and the purer it is the more he seeks to defile it. He will not let our Confraternity alone. His filthy fingers will be on it some day, sooner or later. But he cannot pluck up plants which our Heavenly Father has planted. He cannot curse him whom God hath not cursed. If the Lord our God be with us, then with us is the sound of the victory of the King.

But it depends on our faithfulness to Jesus and our faithfulness to the Holy Ghost. I do, therefore, earnestly, as if they were my last words, beseech the Servants of the Holy Ghost, by the mercies of God, never to seek after new lights nor to walk in new ways, but to be guided by the ancient lights and to walk in the ancient ways. "A path and a way shall be there, and it shall be the holy way This shall be unto you a straight way, so that fools shall not err therein " (Is. XXXV. 8.) Three things will keep you safe. They are love for the Heart of Jesus in the Blessed Sacrament; love for the Mother of God and trust in her; and uttermost loyalty to the Vicar of Jesus Christ and the Apostolic See. Seek always, therefore, to grow in the love of God, as the Saints have grown in that love from the beginning and seek, like them, as St. Paul says (2. Cor. III. 18), "to be changed to the same image from glory to glory, as by the Spirit of the Lord."

2.

Object, Rules and Obligations of the Confraternity of the Servants of the Holy Ghost.

The object of the Confraternity, as approved by the Holy Father, is " to spread more widely and to increase more and more filial affection and burning love for the Third Person of the Most Holy Trinity, the Fountain of Truth and Holiness, and the Author of our supernatural life, who is also in every way the giver of grace both to the innocent and to penitents." This very same object of our devotion, as here defined in the words of Father Rawes, may again be explained, perhaps somewhat more minutely, in the following words: " The object of this Confraternity is, to arouse the Catholic clergy and laity to greater devotion in the practice of that faith, which the Church professes concerning the Third Person of the Godhead, in these words of the Nicene Creed:

"And in the Holy Ghost, the Lord and
Giver of life, who proceedeth from the Father
and the Son ; who, together with the Father
and the Son, is adored and glorified ; who
spoke by the prophets."

This devotion will bring down upon us
more fully the Spirit of God, the Giver of
life, and light, and strength, never so much
needed as in these days of pride and unbelief. The Holy Spirit, who is the Gift of
God, enlightens the understanding, strengthens the will to do good and strive against
sin ; He tempers and orders in us the several
affections and passions, and thus restores, in
a measure, that just balance of the soul's
powers, which the sin of Adam had overthrown. He counsels, He guides, He comforts, He seals in us the image of Jesus
Christ. He is not only a present blessing,
but the pledge and earnest of still higher
and better things, which can never be fulfilled in this life. " In this we know," says
St. John, "that we abide in Him, and He in
us, because He hath given us of His Spirit."

It is to awaken and actuate by means of
holy prayer this consciousness of the indwelling Spirit both in the Church and in us individually that Father Rawes has given the
members of his Confraternity the following

special intentions for their most earnest intercession.

   a. "For yourselves," he says, "let your prayers go up to God ceaselessly

   1. That you may always think with the Church, and so kept from dangerous ways.

   2. That you may always have a great reverence for theologians, and turn even from rash opinions, as from sin.

   3. That you may always grow in love and reverence for the Scripture of God.

   4. That you may never doubt the personal infallibility of the Vicar of Jesus Christ.

   5. That the Holy Sacrifice. of the Mass may be more to you day by day.

   6. That the glory of the Mother of God may be more to you day by day.

   7. That, as true Servants of the Holy Ghost, you may always try His voice in your souls by His voice in the Church.

   b. For *others*, let your prayers go up ceaselessly to God

   1. That in all hearts there may be a more childlike love for the Eternal Father.

   2. That in all hearts there may be a more burning love for Jesus and Mary.

   3. That sinners may be brought to the Precious Blood.

4. That the holy may become holier day by day.
5. For the souls in Purgatory.
6. For the Vicar of Jesus Christ, his intentions and needs.
7. For the establishments of Confraternities of the Servants of the Holy Ghost, from the rising to the setting of the sun."

It is to actuate further and increase this consciousness of the indwelling Spirit that some secondary rules, not of obligation but of great usefulness, have been recommended to the members of the first Confraternity. We give them as follows, together with the more or less official " Act of Oblation," made by all the members of the Confraternity in London :

I. Secondary Rules to the Members.

1. The Servants of the Holy Ghost will make a special offering of themselves, soul and body, at least once a day, to the Eternal Spirit of God, adoring at the same time Him who dwelleth in us.
2. Trusting to the Holy Ghost, they will do all that they can to correspond with grace; to walk whiterobed with Jesus; and to follow Him " whithersoever He goeth."
3. They will also do all that they can to

spread and increase devotion to the Eternal Spirit. They will do this especially by prayer, and most of all by prayer before the Heart of Jesus in the Tabernacle.

4. In the Sacrifice of the Mass they will adore the Holy Ghost, the Sanctifier of the Soul of Jesus, "who," in the words of St. Paul, "by the Holy Ghost offered Himself without spot to God."

5. They will also adore the Holy Ghost, glorifying the Heart of Jesus in the Blessed Sacrament.

6. They will adore the Holy Ghost as Sanctifier in His seven gifts, and in the seven Sacraments; and as the Spirit of truth guiding the Church and the Holy See.

II. Act of Oblation to God the Holy Ghost.

On my knees, before the great cloud of witnesses, I offer myself, soul and body, to Thee, Eternal Spirit of God. I adore the brightness of Thy purity; the unerring keeness of Thy justice; and the might of Thy love. Thou art the strength and the light of my soul. In Thee I live, and move, and am. I desire never to grieve Thee by unfaithfulness to grace; and I pray with all my heart to be kept from the smallest sin against Thee. Make me faithful in every thought, and grant that I may always listen to Thy voice, and watch for Thy light, and follow Thy gracious inspiration. I cling to Thee, and give myself to Thee, and ask Thee by Thy compassion to watch over me in my weakness. Holding the pierced Feet of Jesus, and looking at His five Wounds, and trusting His Precious Blood, and adoring His opened Side and stricken Heart, I implore Thee, Adorable Spirit, helper of my infirmity, so to keep me in Thy grace that I may never sin against Thee with the sin which Thou can'st not forgive. Give me grace, O Holy Ghost, Spirit of the Father and the Son, to say to Thee, always and everywhere: Speak, Lord, for Thy Servant heareth.

O Holy Ghost, Third Person of the Blessed Trinity, Spirit of truth, love, and holiness, proceeding from the Father and the Son, and equal to them in all things, I adore Thee and love Thee with all my heart. Teach me to know and seek my last end; grant me the holy fear of God; grant me compunction and patience; and suffer me not to fall into sin. Give me an increase of faith, hope, and charity, and bring forth in my soul all the virtues proper to my state of life. Make me a faithful disciple of Jesus, and an obedient child of the Church. Give me an efficacious grace to keep Thy commandments and to receive the Sacraments worthily. Give me the Four Cardinal Virtues, Thy Seven Gifts, Thy Twelve Fruits; raise me to perfection in the state of life to which Thou callest me; and lead me, through a happy death, to everlasting life, through Jesus Christ, our Lord. Amen.

O Spirit of Wisdom, preside over all my thoughts, words and actions, from this hour until the moment of my death.

Spirit of Understanding, enlighten and teach me.

Spirit of Counsel, direct my inexperience.

Spirit of Fortitude, strenghten my weakness.

Spirit of Knowledge, instruct my ignorance.

Spirit of Piety, make me fervent in good works.

Spirit of Fear, restrain me from all evil.

Spirit of Peace, give me Thy peace.

Heavenly Spirit, make me persevere in the service of God, and enable me to act on all occasions, with goodness and benignity, patience, charity and joy, longanimity, mildness, and fidelity. Let the heavenly virtues of modesty, continency and chastity adorn the temple Thou hast chosen for Thy abode. O Spirit of Holiness, by Thy allpowerful

grace, preserve my soul from the misfortune
of sin.   Amen.

Seven "Glorias," in honor of the Holy
Ghost, to obtain His seven gifts, for the dif-
fusion of the Faith and intentions of Our
Holy Father, the Pope.

Many other exercises could of course, be
devised to further and obtain the same end.
The Holy Spirit, dividing to each, as He will-
eth, will, without fail, always inspire His
devout servants with new practices and
pious observances calculated to secure the
sanctification of their own souls and the
souls of others.   Notwithstanding that, however, a few more suggestions may not be out
of place here.   Amongst the most practical
means of securing the end of the Confraternity, we name and recommend :

1. To recite *daily* the hymns, " Veni Creator Spiritus," and " Veni Sancte Spiritus."
(We give the text of these hymns together
with the indulgences to be gained by their
recital in the devotional part of this volume.)

2. To say devoutly, if the members are
Priests, the seven orations to the Holy Spirit,
as given in the end of the Roman Breviary
in preparation for Holy Mass and forming
the conclusion of the so called " Accessus
Sacerdotalis ad Altare."

3. To offer with a special intention to glor-

ify the Holy Ghost, the " *Tierce* " of the Divine Office. It is the Canonical Hour which celebrates the *special time of the day* when the Holy Ghost descended upon the Apostles. Hence, a special mention of the Holy Ghost is made in the respective hymn and during the Octave of Pentecost the solemn invocation "Veni Creator" must be substituted in its place.

4. To invoke the Holy Ghost before making a resolution of importance, before studying, spiritual reading, preparation for preaching, the reception or administration of the holy Sacraments.

5. For *Priests*, to say more *frequently*, perhaps *monthly*, as far as the rubrics and circumstances will allow it, the *Votive Mass of the Holy Ghost.*

6. To observe with more than ordinary devotion the *"great Novena,"* preparing us immediately for Pentecost and beginning Friday after the Feast of the Ascension of our Lord. This is *"the Novena" par excellence* ordered by our divine Saviour, observed by Mary and the Apostles and crowned by the glorious effusion of the Spirit on Pentecost day. (We intend to say more about it in the next volume " Pentecost.")

7. To celebrate with a most special solemnity, joy and devotion, the great Day of

Pentecost and its Octave, the "Metropolis Festorum" as St. John Chrysostom calls it, *The Feast* of the "Servants of the Holy Ghost."

————————

3.

Privileges of the Confraternity of the Servants of the Holy Ghost.

It is scarcely necessary to dwell more profusely on the Privileges of the Confraternity. The greatest privilege that can be hoped for, is without doubt the Effusion of the Holy Ghost in His plenitude, with His seven gifts, His divine fruits, His power and wonders. Other Privileges, as the various indulgences bestowed upon the Confraternity with the Blessing of the Vicar of Jesus Christ on earth, have already been recorded and can be found in the Pontifical Rescript, erecting canonically the Confraternity.

Only one word more on the three Patrons of the Confraternity, as assigned it by His Holiness. In the Brief of Approbation the Holy Father gives the servants of the Holy Ghost as special Patrons: 1. *The Immaculate Virgin Mary ;* 2. *St. Paul, the Apostle of the Gentiles ;* 3. *St. Thomas of Aquinas, the Angelic Doctor.* It will at once appear, how appropriately these Saints have been chosen.

1. *The Immaculate Virgin Mary, conceived without original sin*, is, as we have already stated, the "first fruits and perfect examplar" of the Holy Ghost's operation in individual souls. She, especially, in her Immaculate Conception, is the "woman clothed with the moon beneath her feet and on her head a crown of twelve stars:" (Apocal. XII, 1.) that is to say the virgin fair and unspotted, full of grace and radiant in heavenly beauty by the very irradiation of the Holy Spirit. Besides, this Immaculate Spouse of the Holy Ghost has been chosen to be the special Patroness of the Catholic Church in the United States, which happy coincidence throws a new light on the peculiar relationship of this, our Devotion as already dwelt upon in Part 1st, to our country and nation.

2. *St. Paul, the Apostle of the Gentiles*, is the great Apostolic organ, called not by Christ in the state of His humility on earth, but called most immediately by Christ glorified in heaven, and by the power of the Spirit. His very conversion is described by the inspired pen of St. Luke as "the filling with the Holy Ghost." "According to the wisdom given him" (II. Petr. III. 17) he has left more than all the other Apostles to the

TO THE HOLY GHOST.

Church of God in the treasure of his inspired writings, and has dwelt more profusely than any of the inspired writers upon the Holy Ghost's transcendant operation in the plan of salvation. (For information on this consult especially his letter to the Romans and the two which he addressed to the Corinthians.)

In his personal character he shows more than any other Apostle the features of the American character sanctified by the power of divine grace; the broad mind of Christianity before which melt away all the national differences between Greek and Jew and Barbarian, and in which all are one in Christ; the universal spirit of the Catholic Church embracing all the world in one supernatural unity; the energy and pushing ahead in the great task before him; the consciousness of his civil rights and the noble pride of being a citizen of the great world-wide Roman empire, yet more than that, of being a servant of Jesus Christ; the inspired enthusiasm securing him a success and victory unequaled by any one of his successors.

3. *St. Thomas of Aquinas, the Angelic Doctor*, is the representative of the holy Doctors of the Church, and the Holy Spirit's illumination in these select organs of Divine revelation. The holy Doctors of the Church are men

whom the Spirit of wisdom, of understanding and of intelligence has filled in a more than ordinary degree and who, uniting eminent sanctity with excellent learning, now "shine as the brightness of the firmament" and "as stars to all eternity" (Daniel XII. 3.) Amongst those "stars," however, St. Thomas of Aquinas shines like the sun, and in his sublimely enlightened mind the rays of divine wisdom, shining forth from others before and after him, concentrate as in a focus. "He is," says Leo XIII. in his Encyclical, "likened to the sun, for he warmeth the whole earth with the fire of his holiness, and filleth the whole earth with the splendor of his teaching."—"His doctrine," says Innocent VI., quoted in the same Encyclical: "above all other doctrines, with the one exception of the Holy Scriptures, has such a propriety of words, such a method of explanation, such a truth of opinions, that no one, who holds it, will ever be found to have strayed from the path of truth; whereas any one who has attacked it, has always been suspected as to the truth." How fittingly then this matchless Doctor of God's holy Church completes the Trio of the Patrons given to the Servants of the Holy Ghost! Mary Immaculate is the representation of the Holy Ghost's sanctifying power. St. Paul represents the Apostolic zeal and success, given by the Spirit on Pentecost day. St. Thomas is the representation of this divine wisdom which the Spirit, indwelling in the Church, diffuses over all the mystical body of Christ, but most especially bestows upon the select organs for the better instruction and greater illumination of all others.

4.

The Archconfraternity of the Servants of the Holy Ghost.

The last development of the Confraternity, its canonical erection into an Archconfraternity, almost immediately followed its first establishment. So great was the number of applicants for enrollment, so numerous were the places in which the Devotion thus organized seemed to meet with unexampled welcome and success, that it was thought expedient, to petition Rome without delay for the erection of the Archconfraternity. Both Documents, the Petition and the Pontifical Rescript, follow here:

1. Petition for the erection of the Archconfraternity:

"Most Holy Father—Cardinal Manning, Archbishop of Westminster, prostrate at the feet of your Holiness, humbly makes known that the Confraternity of the Servants of the Holy Ghost, already blessed by your Holiness, has been spreading much in England, and also in Philadelphia, in the United States of America. Therefore the petitioner supplicates your Holiness to deign to raise this Confraternity now established into an Archconfraternity, in order that it may have the power to aggregate to this Archconfraternity the Confraternities in other places."

1. Pontifical Rescript erecting the Archconfraternity.

"Our Most Holy Lord, Leo XIII , by Divine Providence Pope, informed by me the undersigned, Secretary of the Sacred Congregation de Propaganda Fide, graciously deigned to grant the request made, *pro gratia, juxta petita.*

"Given at Rome from the house of the said Sacred Congregation de Propaganda Fide, the above year and day, *gratis quocumque titulo.*

[L. S.]   J. B. AGNOZZI,
                                Secretary."

Thus the prayers of many fervent Servants of the Holy Ghost were heard and the Holy Ghost, the Sanctifier, was glorified. The above given decrees were solemnly published in the Central seat of the Archconfraternity, now established, in the Church of St. Mary of the Angels, Bayswater, London, on June the 5th, 1879, by His Eminence Henry Edward Cardinal Manning, Archbishop of Westminster. On this occasion His Eminence, the august Protector and intellectual Author of our Devotion, delivered his sermon, quotations of which are so frequently occurring in this little volume. Now the root was laid deep in the ground and it could spread far and wide.

On the following Pentecost day 3000 names were received in London from the Archbishop of Philadelphia. About 5000 from England and Ireland were received in quick succession. Wherever this Devout Confraternity became known, it was generally and enthusiastically welcomed. From Rome the late Cardinal *Franzelin,* the eminent Theologian, wrote to Father Rawes: "It only remains for me to beg the Holy Spirit to pour forth abundantly His graces by means of this Devotion for the greater Sanctification of the holy, and for the justification of sinners."

From the same sermon of Cardinal Manning, quoted above, we also learn, that the petition for raising the Confraternity to an Archconfraternity, properly speaking, originated in *America.* He says: "The Archbishop of Philadelphia (Most Rev. Wood, D. D.) then sent a petition to the Holy See, praying that the Confraternity in his Church should be elevated to an Archconfraternity." As a Confraternity it could only associate members and not incorporate Confraternities. This petition was presented to the Holy See: our Holy Father on the 6th of April last

granted the petition, and elevated our Confraternity to an Archconfraternity, to be the
centre and head of Confraternities throughout
the world. We have since heard of aggre-
gations made to the Archconfraternity from
France, Italy, Germany, Switzerland. The new
world, however, and in this the leading
country, the name of which seems almost
synonimous with America, the *United States*,
soon saw these Confraternities spring up like
mayflowers.

We have already spoken of its establishment in *Philadelphia*. On August, 26th,
1879 it was with the approbation of Cardinal
McCloskey, Archbishop of *New York*, introduced into the Church of St. Ann of that city.
The Rector of that church, the Rt. Rev.
Monsignor Preston, Vicar General of the
Arch-diocese of New York, was the zealous
promoter of the cause of the Holy Spirit in
that city and took occasion to publish a little
volume containing some admirable sermons
on the subject and entitled " The Divine
Paraclete " (New York 1879). More yet than
that has been done for the spread of this
Devotion in this country by the Rt. Rev.
John Joseph Keane, D. D., Bishop of Richmond, and now the appointed Rector of the
new Catholic University of America. In a
special pastoral, which the Reader will find

at the end of this chapter, the Bishop expresses his wish; "that a confraternity of the Servants of the Holy Ghost should be established in every Mission throughout the Diocese, and that every Catholic that has made his first communion should be enrolled in this beautiful devotion." It is, in fine, especially Bishop Keane, to whom we, the Servants of the Holy Ghost, in gratitude owe the warm and solemn commendation, which this Devotion to God the Holy Ghost has met with on the part of the Most Reverend and Right Reverend Fathers of the Third Plenary Council of Baltimore. Through the direction of these Apostolic Fathers the Confraternity has now found its way into those sacred nurseries which above all other places ought to be its home, possessing a soil most rich and congenial for this heavenly plant— into our Seminaries, Colleges and Convents. In 1883 the Confraternity was established in the Provincial Seminary of *St. Francis of Sales*, near Milwaukee, Wis., and also in the Mother-house of the *Sisters of St. Agnes, Fond du Lac, Wis.* In both places, the establishment took place with the direct sanction of of the authority of the Most Rev. Michael Heiss, Archbishop of Milwaukee. The Rev. *Augustinus Schneider*, O. S. B. of the Benedictine-Abbey of St. Vincent's, Beatty, Pa. strenuously and successfully worked for the spread of our Confraternity in the various houses of the order of St. Benedict. He had the Confraternity established in *St. Vincent's Abbey* and had it aggregated to the Archconfraternity in June, 1887. The same year saw the introduction of our Confraternity into the *Abbey of St. Meinrad O. S. B.* in *Indiana*, into the Priory of *Mount Angel O. S. B.*, Marion Co., *Oregon*, and into *St. Mary's Benedictine Abbey at Newark, N. J.* Several of the houses at the *Franciscan Order*, as in *Louisville, Lafayette, Ind.*, etc., also petitioned for an introduction of this devotion.

The most important step, however, towards reaching the goal we are aiming at, was probably made, when the Rt. Reverend Bishops John Ireland of St. Paul and John Keane of Richmond, immediately after the Council of Baltimore, went to Rome. During their stay in the American College, Bishop Keane addressed its student on the subject and the Rt. Reverend Monsignore *Dr. O'Connell* determined upon making this Devotion *the Devotion of the American College.* The letter of Cardinal Manning to the Doctor, which follows in extenso at the end of this chapter points to the importance of this step and is a manifestation of the joy the great Cardinal must have felt in hearing such good news from the eternal

city.   It is to be hoped that the example set
by the American standard seminary will by
degrees be imitated all over the country.
Just before starting the publication of this
volume we heard of the establishment of the
Confraternity in the *Seminary of St. Thomas
of Aquinas, of the Diocese of St. Paul, Minn.*,
and reasonably, we may presume, that in
some other places, which have not come
under our notice, the same idea has taken
shape and the Devotion has been introduced.
To *facilitate* as much as possible the introduction of the Confraternity into any Seminary, College, Religious Community or
Parish, we thought it well to give in this
second part all necessary information.
Hence, a priest desiring to have the Confraternity established and affiliated to the Archconfraternity, must:

1. Ask his *Bishop* for the *canonical erection*
of the Confraternity, by laying before him
for approval the Statutes thereof.   The Bishop's *will* and *order* is sufficient to have the
Confraternity canonically erected.   He also
must appoint the Rector of the Confraternity.

2. A Certificate, of the erection, signed by
the Bishop's hand and having his seal
attached, giving the name of the diocese,
· church, etc., and also the name of the Rector,
must then, together with the letters of peti-

tion for aggregation to the Archconfraternity, be sent to the President thereof, at present the *Very Rev. Robert Butler, D. D., Rector of St. Charles College, St. Charles Square, in London.* A sample of such a Certificate is the following, given in Latin:

DE CONFRATERNITATE SERVORUM SPIRITUS SANCTI ARCHICONFRATERNITATI AGGREGANDA.

Per has praesentes litteras testamur Confraternitatem Servorum Spiritus Sancti in Ecclesia......
.... apud
... . legitima
auctoritate fuisse canonice erectam; ejus Rectorem designatum esse Rev. ....
ejusque finem ac statuta ex corde approbantes, consensum Nostrum praebemus ut Archiconfraternitati illius nominis in Ecclesia S. Mariae de Angelis, apud Bayswater, Londini in Anglia, a Sancta Sede erectae aggregetur.

Datum .... die .... 18...
....

Then he will receive *Letters of Aggregation,* sealed with the seal of the Archconfraternity, making the Confraternity a sharer in all the indulgences and spiritual graces of the Archconfraternity. The text of such a Diploma is the following:

LITTERAE AGGREGATIONIS ET ASSOCIATIONIS

Archiconfraternitati,

SERVORUM SPIRITUS SANCTI,

Juxta Rescriptum Summi Pontificis Leonis XIII,

die 6. Aprilis 1879.

In Ecclesia Patrum Oblatorum S. Caroli, dicta

S. MARIAE DE ANGELIS,

Apud Bayswater, Londini, in Anglia, die 5. Junii
1879.

Canonice erectae.

DILECTIS NOSTRIS IN CHRISTO.

Confraternitas Servorum Spiritus Sancti, in
Ecclesia ... . auctoritate R. P. D. eius Ordinarii, canonice erectae Sodalibus

SALUTEM IN DOMINO SEMPITERNAM.

Quum .... praedictae
Confraternitatis Rector, aggregationem Archiconfraternitati nostrae Servorum Spiritus Sancti et
communicationem indulgentiarum postulaverit,
Nos, Archiconfraternitatis Moderator, ipsamque
totam repraesentantes, virtute Rescripti supraci-
tati, solo Dei amore adducti ac devotione erga
Spiritum Sanctum, Tertiam Personam Sanctissimae
Trinitatis, Doctorem Ecclesiae, Fontem veritatis
infallibilem gratiae omnimodo tum innocentibus
tum poenitentibus Doctorem, Auctorem sanctitatis;
attentis insuper R. P. D. Ordinarii litteris testi-
monialibus, dixi .... quibus
tum de canonica Confraternitatis erectione tum de
consensu Ipsius ad aggregationem certiores facti
sumus ; Confraternitatem eandem per has praesentes nostras, juxta facultatem Apostolicam Nobis
impertitam, associamus et aggregamus eiusque tum
existentibus tum futuris Sodalibus Indulgentias et
spirituales gratias Archiconfraternitati nostrae a
S. Sede nominatim concessas largimur et com-
municamus in Nomine Patris, et Filii, et Spiritus
Sancti.

Datum apud Ecclesiam S. Mariae de Angelis
supradictam hac die ....

Pontificatus SSmi. Dni. Nostri.................
anno..........
....S. P. D.
Archiconfraternitatis Moderator.
....
Archiconfraternitatis Secretarius.

4. Now the connection is established.
Nothing remains, but to open a book for
enrollment, in order to carry out the idea of
the Devotion and to participate in all the
blessings of the Divine Paraclete.

5. One more suggestion may be in place
as to how the Confraternity can be given life
and external importance in a *Community*.
For this purpose I would propose (*a*) to have
no special meetings, when there are *already*
Sodality meetings and so forth. Simply in-
troduce those meetings with the "Veni
Creator," etc., reserving a *Special Conference*
for Pentecost time. (*b*) Every morning at
mass of the *Community* the "Veni Creator"
with the seven orations before mass, should
be sung or recited. (*c*) When possible, the
Votive Mass of the Holy Ghost should be said
monthly. Have it said with some solemnity,
accompanied by singing, etc. (*d*) The *Great
Novena*, after Ascension should be kept with
extraordinary devotion and by the reading of
books, treating on this Devotion. (*e*) *Pentecost
Day and Octave* should be celebrated with
the utmost solemnity and joy both in

church and out. "Let the seminarians in the church, in the house, even at the table feel that it is *their* feast and the Day, of which the Church sings in the Preface: "*Therefore the whole world exults in overflowing joy.*" (Rom. Missal.) (*f*) It would certainly be very good and prove a source of many graces *if the Confraternity for all the Priests of a Diocese would be established in the Cathedral,* so that then on the occasion of a Diocesan or Provincial Synod, which is always opened with the Mass of the Holy Ghost, the Priests in some still higher sense would unite in the Holy Spirit and be "congregati in Spiritu Sancto."

However, far more than all our poor words can do towards furthering our holy cause, will be effected by the powerful language embodied in the two official documents, which shall now give a conclusion to this Part. We have already quoted from them, but deem it commendable to place them in their full extent before the reader. The first is the Letter of Cardinal Manning to Dr. O'Connell, and the second is the Pastoral Letter of Bishop Keane of Richmond.

1. Letter of Cardinal Manning to Rt. Rev. Mgr. O'Connell D. D., Rector of the Amrican College at Rome.

ARCHBISHOP'S HOUSE.

Whit Sunday, 1887.

Rev. and dear Father:—

I had hoped to write you a letter, as you desired, to reach you on this great feast, but I have been obliged to wait and write you on this day. You have done well in making the devotion of the Holy Ghost the devotion of the American College, and the bishops of America have set us all an example in their forwardness to promote this adoration of the Sanctifier. As the Son is the Way to the Father, the Holy Ghost is the Way to the Son ; for it is but by the Holy Ghost that the Father draws all men to the Son. The Apostolic preaching shows that we are under the dispensation of the Spirit. The presence and office of the Holy Ghost pervade all the Apostles wrote. The writings of the Fathers are full of the Holy Ghost. They wrote as in the light of the day of Pentecost; especially St. Thomas, St. Augustine, St. Basil, St. Didymus, St. Gregory of Nazianzum, and St. Athanasius. The Person, the Presence, the Office of the Holy Ghost pervade their writings also in continuity with the writings of the Apostles. In all its supreme acts the Church proceeds as if in the day of Pentecost, by invocation of the Holy Ghost; from the election of the Roman Pontiff to the election of a bishop, from an Oecumenical Council to a provincial and a diocesan synod; from the consecration of a bishop or priest to the confirmation of a child. The feast of Pentecost, the Mass and Office of the Holy Ghost, teach by

the authority of the Church the special adoration
due to the Holy Ghost, in His Mission, Advent and
Office, as Christmas and Easter the special adoration due to the Incarnation and Advent of the
Son.   How, then, is it that this truth, which is like
the luminous ether of the Church, has been so
slightly and seldom practiced by private devotion.
Our   Lord   ordained   and   commissioned   His
Apostles, and yet commanded them to wait till
they should receive the Holy Ghost coming upon
them.   Is not this, then, the devotion for bishops
and priests?   Are not Christians the anointed, and
is it not the devotion for all Christians?   How can
we be spiritually minded or supernatural in the
out it?   Are not men spiritual and supernatural in
the measure in which they have fellowship or
communication with Him?   But I am writing
truisms.   Is not the peril of the day the unspirituality of men and the revival of naturalism in the
world?   And how can this be met by a diametrical and supreme antagonism if not met by preaching the Holy Ghost and making our priests His
disciples?   Lastly, it is this devotion that
illuminates and infuses the light of all dogmas of
the faith.   All things are visible in the light of the
sun, so all truths from the Holy Trinity to Extreme
unction are made manifest by devotion to the Holy
Ghost.   If we were *pleni Spiritu sancto*, we should
understand the divine tradition of the Church and
the *Summa* of St. Thomas by a kindred intuition.
And now, my dear Father, I have obeyed you, and
you in turn must obey me.   Ask your students to
offer a Communion for me.   And may the Holy
Ghost make you all apostles of Jesus Christ in
your great and noble land!
    Believe me, always yours affectionately in Jesus
Christ,

✠ HENRY EDWARD,

Cardinal Archbishop of Westminster.

1. Pastoral Letter of the Rt. Rev. John Keane, D. D., Bishop of Richmond:

JOHN JOSEPH KEANE,

BY THE GRACE OF GOD AND

THE FAVOUR OF THE APOSTOLIC SEE,

BISHOP OF RICHMOND,

TO THE FAITHFUL OF THE DIOCESE, GRACE

AND PEACE IN OUR LORD.

Beloved Brethren,—Having requested all the Pastors throughout the Diocese to establish in their various Missions the Confraternity of the Servants of the Holy Ghost, and desiring that you should heartily respond to the holy invitation thus extended to you, we deem it our duty to make known to you in this manner the nature of this devotion, and our reasons for desiring that it should be embraced by all the faithful of the Diocese.

Devotion to the Holy Ghost is a most natural offspring of Christian faith, because the Holy Ghost is the very life and soul of the Christian dispensation.

The Holy Ghost is the Infinite Love of God, proceeding from the Father and the Son, and perfecting the Being of the adorable Trinity, according to that sublime utterance of St. John, ' Deus charitas est,' ' God is Love.'

It was through love that God created and redeemed us; therefore it is that the Holy Scripture shows us that the works of creation and redemption, wrought by the power of the Father and the wisdom of the Son, are finished and perfected by the action of the Spirit of Love, the Holy Ghost. Hence, when our Divine Redeemer had completed

His work on earth, and was about to return to His Father, He said to His disciples: ' It is expedient for you that I go; for if I go not, the Paraclete will not come to you; but if I go, I will send Him to you ' (John XVI. 7.) According to our Saviour's promise, the Holy Ghost came on Whitsunday, from the bosom of the Father and the Son, to finish and carry on for ever the work of Their mercy. He became the soul of the Christian Church, making it into a living body; and all its life has ever since come from Him and depended on Him, and so shall continue till the end of the world. All the divine truth that has ever been taught by the Church, or has ever illumined the minds of her children, has come from the Holy Ghost, ' the Spirit of Truth ' All the grace that has ever been dispensed in her Sacraments, or has ever wrought the sanctification of souls, is the work of the Holy Ghost, ' the Giver of Life.' Whenever we ask a spiritual favour from Almighty God, through the merits of our Divine Saviour, or through the intercession of the Blessed Virgin and the Saints, whether we think of the Holy Ghost or not, the blessing given is the outpouring of His love, the grace received is His gift. Whenever we strive to advance in the way to heaven, to climb the ladder of holiness, the power by which we advance is the action of the Holy Ghost. Whenever we think a good thought, say a good word, or do a good action, it is by and through ' the Spirit of God dwelling in us ' that we do it, since St Paul teaches us that we cannot even utter the holy Name of Jesus ' but by the Holy Ghost ' (I. Cor. XII. 3.)

How great, therefore, and how constant is our debt of gratitude to the Holy Ghost! How intimately is our whole spiritual life pervaded by His influence! The more we learn of our interior life the more we must learn of the work wrought by the power and the love of the Holy Ghost. Not to think of this would surely indicate strange thoughtlessness about spiritual things; and to think of it, and not turn constantly toward the Holy Ghost in thanksgiving, as well as in supplication, would surely be the height of ingratitude. Yet, alas, how much of such thoughtlessness and such ingratitude has not the Holy Spirit to endure at our hands!

In this age, when the spirit of error is trying to make men believe that their life is only like that of the beasts of the field, the Church, guided ever by the hand of God, turns the attention of her children, perhaps more specially than at any previous time, to the interior and supernatural life of their souls, of which the Holy Ghost is the Author. The devotion to the Holy Ghost, together with the teaching concerning our spiritual life with which that devotion is inseparably connected, is unquestionably the best antidote for the materialistic and degrading tendencies of our times.

This general and providential tendency toward devotion to the Holy Ghost has taken form in the Confraternity of the Servants of the Holy Ghost, established in London under the patronage of Cardinal Manning. It had the warm approval of Pope Pius IX., and our Holy Father Leo XIII. approved it in March 1878, and, on the 6th of April 1879, raised it to the dignity of an Archconfraternity, with power to aggregate Confraternities throughout the world. A devotion so conformable to the present providential tendency of the Church, and which has received so solemn approval from two successive Sovereign Pontiffs, cannot fail to recommend itself strongly to all Christians. And especially do we desire to foster this devotion in the Diocese of Richmond, since, from the moment that Almighty God was pleased to lay the burden of its spiritual care on our weak shoulders, we felt impelled to look to the Holy Ghost as the source of all the wisdom and strength needful for the worthy discharge of so weighty a duty, and to put all our administation under His special protection. It is therefore our earnest desire that a Confraternity of

the Servants of the Holy Ghost should be es-
tabished in every Mission throughout the Diocese,
and that every Catholic that has made his or her
First Communion should be enrolled in this beautiful devotion.

No one need be withheld by the fear of multi-
plying devotions, or of undertaking to many pious
practices. It is, indeed, far from advisable to have
too many devotions; but the spirit of piety cannot
but impel us to have *some;*—we should choose the
best, and no one certainly can fail to recognize that
this devotion to the Holy Ghost must be among the
very best. It is equally unadvisable to undertake
too many pious practices; for experience shows
that the effort to say too many prayers and crowd
too many exercises into the time that can be daily
given to them is ordinarily the destruction of attention and fervour in all the prayers that are said.
But the devotion to the Holy Ghost is not liable to
this objection. As it is clearly stated on the certificate of membership, the only obligation is *to be
enrolled,*—with a sincere desire and resolution to
love and honour the Holy Ghost, to think of Him
more frequently and fervently, and to correspond
to His grace more faithfully. It is indeed *advisable*
that such devotion to the Holy Ghost should
manifest itself in some daily practices such
as saying seven times the *Glory be to the Father*
to ask the seven Gifts of the Holy Ghost, or
the recitation of the *Veni Sancte Spiritus,* or the
Veni Creator Spiritus, or the saying of the *Little Office of the Holy Ghost,* or some portion of it. But
none of these practices are of obligation, and therefore they need not inspire dread or scruple.

It is recommended that the members should
assemble for public exercises once a month.
This, again, is not obligatory; but it is very useful,
and our Holy Father has granted an indulgence of
100 days to the members who will attend the
monthly meetings. In order that these meetings
may be more systematic and profitable, it is our

intention to propose, ere long, a form of Sodality organization for the members, and a *Little Office of the Holy Ghost* which might very usefully be recited at the meetings, or as an act of private devotion.

We therefore most earnestly invite all Catholics who have received their First Communion to respond to this our recommendation, when made known to them by their Pastors, and to give in their names without delay for enrolment. A certificate of membership will be given to each one, which also contains a brief summary of the indulgences to be gained by the Servants of the Holy Ghost and the acts of devotion recommended to them. To these is added a short prayer to the Holy Ghost for the enlightenment and conversion of all the souls in the Diocese of Richmond that are outside of the one fold, which we request all the members to say every day, as an act of fraternal charity toward their poor separated brethren.

May our heart be gladdened by a ready and devout response to this invitation on the part of all our faithful people; and may this devotion draw down incalculable blessings on the Diocese, and give endless glory to the Father, the Son, and the Holy Ghost.

Given at Richmond this 18th day of October, the Festival of St. Luke the Evangelist, in the year of our Lord 1879.

✠ JOHN JOSEPH KEANE,

Bishop of Richmond.

PART III.

The Office of God the Holy Ghost.

"I have long thought that the secret but real cause of the so-called Reformation, was that the office of the Holy Ghost, had been much obscured in popular belief."

Cardinal Manning in " Religio via-toris " page 72.

Office of God the Holy Ghost.

The sentence, which we have placed at the head of this chapter is in its transcendent meaning worthy of the man who spoke it. If, then, "the secret but real cause of the so called Reformation, was that the Office of the Holy Ghost had been much obscured in popular belief," we can do nothing better to gradually effect a true reformation of our views, devotions and lives than to place this Office of the Holy Ghost in its proper light and set it before popular belief in all its evidence and all pervading signification. In this third chapter, therefore, we wish to give in logical and chronological order a short but lucid outline of the Holy Ghost's universal operation in the plan of salvation.

We have already enlarged upon the character and the various relations of our Devotion. We have given full information regarding the embodiment of this Devotion, the Confraternity of the Servants of the Holy Ghost. Before, however, entering upon the devotional part of this volume, we deem it expedient to premise in the following pages by way of immediate preparation for actual devotion. Dogma is the source of devotion. "We adore that we know" (S. John IV. 22) and the more a truth of revelation seizes upon our mind, the deeper will be the devotion of our heart. It is consequently not out of place to call popular attention to the most striking facts and events of the Office of God the Holy Ghost, which pervade Christian Revelation. Of the impossibility to understand the mystical unity of the Church without having a clear idea of this Office of the Holy Ghost Cardinal Manning says: "I had not as yet perceived that the unity of the Church is the external expression of the intrinsic and necessary law of its existence; that it flows from the unity of its head, of its life, of its mind and of its will; or, in other words, from the unity of the Person of the Incarnate Son, who reigns in it, and of the Holy Ghost, who organizes it by His inhabitation, sustains it by His presence and speaks through it by His voice ... All this escaped me, while my eyes were holden in the ray of twilight where I had been born." (Temp. Miss. of of the H. G. p. 30.) The same Cardinal tells us, how the scales fell from his eyes and he perceived the full truth of the Pentecostal revelation, as soon, as he began to realize the Office of the Holy Ghost. "Nothing but a lifelong illusion"—he says—"which clouds the reason by the subtleties of controversy, could have held me so long in such a bondage. But nothing, I believe, would ever have set me free if I had not begun to study the question from a higher point—that is in its fountain—namely the Mission and Office of the Holy Ghost" (page 31.)

From this "higher standpoint" a true understanding of the mystery of the Church of God is alone possible. From this "higher point" alone the doctrine of supernatural grace and satisfaction appears in all its harmony and beauty. From this "higher point" alone we understand the harmony and symmetry contained in the manifold action of divine mercy in the plan of salvation. First however, we must know the Holy Ghost himself.

"The unknown God" must first be made known to us. It cannot be denied that the Holy Ghost's operation, though so manifest in scripture and divine tradition is still much obscured from popular belief. The following headings will exhibit the universal doctrine concerning the Holy Ghost and His Office. It will be our aim to make brevity and lucidity especially characterize these explanations. Priests and Theologians, of course, will find nothing new in what we now have to say, but even on their mind the effect will not be lost which must needs be brought about by the logical meditation on the universal operation of the Spirit of God.

(The following Chapters have been so arranged that they could, in connection with the Aspirations and Intentions for prayer added to each, be used and read during the *Novena* preceding and the *Octave* following *Pentecost Day.*

1.

The Holy Ghost in the Most Holy Trinity.

In equal distinction from Judaism, teaching a barren Monotheism and from pagan religions, admitting a multiplicity of Gods, Christian Revelation has as its fundamental creed, that in One God there are three Divine Persons: The Father, the Son, and the Holy Ghost. Our language is too imperfect to express exactly the nature and attributes of the Divine Being. In God *nature existence*, and *essence* are one, because He Himself is His own essence, existence and eternity. *Persons*, among created intelligences, have a distinct subsistence, and also a distinct and separate entity, which by its own limitation can make but one individual. In God, however, the Divine Persons have only a distinct mode of subsistence, since They possess each, and in common the whole divine essence. Hence, we say that there are three Persons in God, not three individ-

uals; since the term "Individual" signifies
a distinct nature, which is impossible to the
divine hypostases, in whom there is one
essence and nature, and therefore one natural or essential mind, will and operation.
Nothing can be added to the clear words
of the Athanasian creed: Such as the
Father is, such is the Son and such is the
Holy Ghost." The three Persons are uncreated, immense, eternal and almighty. Yet
there is only one eternal, almighty, immense
and uncreated God. "The Father is God, the
Son is God, and the Holy Ghost is God.
Yet there are not three Gods, but one God."
The personality of the Holy Ghost consists in this: that He is not the Father,
nor the Son, although one with them in
essence. "In speaking of the nature of God's
Being we necessarily transcend the powers
of reason, but we in no sense contradict rea
son, which in its finite sphere can predicate
nothing of the Infinite. Whilst, there would
be contradiction in the idea of three human
persons in one human being and it would
most certainly be a manifest contradiction to
say that three are one, and one is three; yet,
there cannot be the slightest in the mystery
of the Trinity, which reveals to us the mode
of God's existence. To attempt to see contradiction here would be to reason from

things made and imperfectly comprehended
to the uncreated and incomprehensible.
Now with special reference to the Divine
Person of the Holy Ghost, Catholic doctrine
holds.

1. *That the Holy Ghost is God.*   This is the
evident doctrine of Scripture.   In at least
twenty-five places the Holy Ghost is numbered with both Father and Son.   Now this could
not be done without blasphemy, were He
not one God with them.   He is again expressly called " God " as for instance, St. Peter addressing Ananias said: " Why has Satan
tempted thy heart that thou shouldst lie to
the Holy Ghost . . .   Thou hast not lied
to men, but to God."   (Act. V. 3, 4.)   He is
the author of exclusively divine works; the
Creation, the Incarnation, the Sanctification
of men and, as God, dwells in us as in His
temple ; Scripture says: " Know you not,
that you are the temple of God, and that the
Spirit of God dwelleth in you " (I Cor. III 16.)
" You know not, that your members are the
temple of the Holy Ghost, who is in you,
whom you have from God .. Glorify and
bear God in your body."   (I Cor. VI, 20.)
To Him is ascribed all the divine attributes
as for instance omniscience.—" But to us
God has revealed by His Spirit: For the
Spirit searched all things, yea the deep

things of God. For what man knoweth the things of a man, but the spirit of man that is in him? So the things also that are of God no man knoweth, but the Spirit of God." (I Cor. II, 11.)

2. *The Holy Ghost is a distinct Person* from Father and Son and a true Divine Person and not only some Divine power or energy. Scripture exhibits Him acting as a truly Divine Person, a witness with Father and Son. As He is numbered with Father and Son, so He is also distinguished from them. In some prominent texts of Holy Writ all the three Divine Persons are clearly exhibited, both in the equality of their majesty and in the distinction of their personality. So we read: "But when the Paraclete cometh, whom I will send you from the Father, the Spirit of truth, who proceedeth from the Father, He shall give testimony of Me." (I. John XV, 26.)

3. *The Holy Ghost proceedeth both from Father and Son as from one principle.* This truth has been defined against the schismatic Greeks and is solemnly professed in the "Filioque" of the Catholic creed. Scripture calls the Holy Ghost sometimes the Spirit of God, and also the Spirit of Christ. "Because you are sons, God has sent the Spirit of His Son into your hearts, crying: Abba,

Father." (Gal. IV, 6.) "But when the Spirit of truth is come, He will teach you all truth; for He shall not speak of Himself; but what things soever He shall hear, He shall speak; He shall glorify Me; because He shall receive of Mine, and shall show it to you. All things whatsoever the Father hath, are Mine. Therefore I say: that He shall receive of Mine, and show it unto you," (S. John XVI, 13–16.)

4. *The Holy Ghost, therefore, is the Third Person of the Holy Trinity.* It is manifest that there can be no first in dignity of nature or plenitude of power. In the unity of the Trinity, however, a marvelous order is expressed as clearly as the poverty of our language will admit and revealed as extensively as our finite intellects are capable of grasping. "The Father is made of none, neither created nor begotten. The Son is from the Father alone, not made, nor created, but begotten. The Holy Ghost is from the Father and the Son, not made, nor created, nor begotten, but proceeding." The Father from all eternity communicates the divine essence to the Son and this communication we call generation, by which there is a true filial relation between the Father and the Son. The Father and the Son eternally communicate the divine essence to the

Holy Ghost by an act which we call procession. The Father is the principle of
the Son in the eternal act of generation. The Father and the Son are the principle of the Holy Ghost in the eternal act of
spiration (Spiratio activa.) We say principle
intrinsic and do not use the word "*cause*,"
because all is within the essence of Deity.
Such is the mystery of the Trinity which
declares the divine personality of God the
Holy Ghost. While there is perfect distinction, in regard to personality there is no
confusion, there is also the intimate existence
of one Person in the other by reason of the
unity of essence.

5. *Whilst according to Catholic Theology
the Son is begotten from the Father by the way of
knowledge, the Spirit proceedeth from both by the
way of love.* The Father, who is of none, and
who, is called "the root and fountain of the
whole Deity," begets the Son by adequately
knowing Himself and what He is to the Son
eternally begotten by Him, "the brightness
of His glory and the figure of His substance,"
let no one but that Son presume to tell.
The Father and the Son, as one principle, by
an act of supreme mutual love, breathe forth
the co-eternal Spirit. The Spirit proceeds
from both, the pledge of their mutual
affection and the expression of infinite

beatitude. This completes, so to speak, the circle of the divine productiveness and the Spirit, being one in substance, and equal in power and glory is in the words of St. Bernard, "the sacred kiss of the Father and the Son, as their imperturbable peace, their firm coherence, their undivided love, their indivisible unity." "The Son proceeds from the Father as the ray from the sun. The Holy Ghost from the Father, and the Son as the heat from the ray and the sun. The Son as the word; the Holy Ghost as the breath; the Son as the river from the fountain; the Holy Ghost as the lightning from the cloud. These expressions are all good, but all defective. The ray wants equality; the breath solidity; the river stability. But here the ray is equal to the sun. The heat is consubstantial with its principle. The word says all and is all that it says. The breath goes forth unceasingly, and never breathes its last. The river flows continuously, and abides ever in its source. The fire of heaven burns always and never burns away." (Nouet. Meditations.) It will be part of the beatitude of the Saints to know something of this generation and spiration and to be filled with some faint impulses of this gladness in God, when they see God as He is, and are born into the sphere of the attractions of His being.   When the apostle is transported at the sight of the ways of God in the works of his hands he cries out in wonder: "O the depth of the riches of the wisdom and of the the knowledge of God!   How incomprehensible are His judgments and how unsearchable His ways!" (Rom. XI, 33.)   The Church in the office and mass of the feast of the Most Holy Trinity repeats the same words as the expression of her awe and adoration in the presence of the yet infinitely more unsearchable ways of God within the Trinity, His divine processions.   In adoring this Life of God we are overwhelmed with awe and but able to exclaim with Holy Church, "O Beata Trinitas," "*O Blessed Trinity.*"

ASPIRATION.

I adore Thee, O Most Holy Trinity and I firmly believe all that the Holy Catholic Church teaches us of Thee.   O infinite God, the Father, the Son and the Holy Ghost.   "Who hast granted to thy servants, to acknowledge in the confession of the true faith the glory of the eternal Trinity, and, in the power of Thy majesty, to adore Thy unity, grant that, by steadfastness in the same faith, we may ever be defended from all adversities." Amen. (*Rom. Missal.*)

INTENTION FOR PRAYER.

Pray that faith in the Most Holy Trinity and all the truths of Divine revelation be increased! "*I believe, Lord; help my unbelief!*" (Mark IX, 23.)

2.

The Holy Ghost and the Creation.

All the works of God without the Trinity, as we have already remarked, are common to the three Divine Persons. By way of appropriation, with a special reference to their mutual relations within the Trinity, we ascribe some of those works to the Father, some to the Son, never, however, excluding the other two Persons from a work appropriated to any one of the three. Notwithstanding the fact that the creation, the first and basal of all works without the Trinity is prominently ascribed to the Father, still Holy Scripture also most emphatically commemorates the Holy Ghost in this fundamental work. We read in the first chapter of the first book of Moses: "In the beginning God created heaven and earth; and the earth was void and empty, and darkness was upon the face of the deep; and the Spirit of God moved over the waters" (Gen. I, 1.) Singing the praises of God the Creator, the Psalmist breaks forth into the words: "By the word of the Lord the heavens were established; and all the power of them by the Spirit of His mouth" (Ps. XXXII, 6.) assigning to the Holy Ghost not only a participation in the work of creation, but also the special mission to bring about the " creatio secunda," the world of harmony, order and perfection, to give complement and life and finish to everything. Scripture again says in the words that in a mystical sense are now so often repeated in the divine office of Pentecost time : " Thou shalt send forth Thy Spirit; and they shall be created; and Thou shalt renew the face of the earth." (Ps. CIII, 30.)

As is evident from the liturgical act of blessing the baptismal fonts on Holy Saturday and the eve of Whit Sunday, not only the Holy Fathers but also the Church herself perceives in the spirit moving above the waters of the first creation, a direct allusion to the Third Person of the Trinity, the Holy Ghost. "The Spirit of God," says Cardinal Manning commenting on the Sacred text, " moved over the face of the waters." He impressed upon the first creation, the law of its perfection : He gave to everything its form and fulness to each after its kind " (Internal Mission, pag. 184.) "Hence, we attribute to the Third Person of the Trinity the special office in creation of establishing order, of harmonizing elements that might come in conflict, of causing life and beauty to bloom where, without His celestial touch, all would be dead and shapeless. He is the uncreated beauty shining in the things He touches; the divine order leading created intelligences up to the living unity, which is God. He is the living spring, the living fire, sweet unction and true love." (Preston, Divine Paraclete, pag. 45.) St. Basil therefore justly remarks: "There is no gift whatever that is bestowed upon a creature without a special co-operation of the Holy Ghost." (De Spir. Sancto XXIV n. 55.)

ASPIRATION.

O Divine Spirit, who didst move over the face of the waters of the first creation and who hast also descended on me in the Sacrament of Regeneration in the water and in the Holy Ghost, vouchsafe to rest on me all the days of my life. Without Thee my soul is "void and empty." Without Thee there is darkness on my mind. And without Thy sanctifying breath, there is no life, no growth, no motion towards my supernatural end. Of what use would it be to me, to be created, if I should fail in obtaining the last end of my life, my sanctification and its consummation in eternal glory. "Imple superna gratia, quae Tu creasti pectora." "And with supernal grace inflame the hearts which Thou Thyself hast made."

INTENTION OF PRAYER:

Pray to make a good use of thy talents and all the gifts which God by nature has bestowed upon thee. "*Every best and every perfect gift, is from above, coming down from the Father of lights, with whom there is no change, nor shadow of alteration.*" (James I, 17.)

3.

The Holy Ghost and the Creation of Man.

What the Sacred Text says of the creation of the universe, is altogether different from that which it says of the creation of man, the crown of the entire work of the visible world. When, on the new earth, created for our use, the race of man was to take its place the Three Persons communed together. " Let *us* make man to *our* image and likeness " (Gen. I, 26.) Then man was made with the royal mark upon him, with an intelligent soul, with memory, will and understanding, in the image of the eternal Three who formed him. Moreover, pointing to the double substance, constituting human nature, the Sacred Text says: "And the Lord God formed man from the slime of the earth ; and breathed into his face the breath of life, and man became a living soul." (Gen. II, 7.) The holy Fathers see in this mystical language great mysteries revealed. Distinguishing between "image" and "likeness," they see the first word exhibiting man's natural similitude with God and the second his greater conformity, his participation in divine nature, his supernatural condition conferred on him together with his natural perfection by the same "Spirit of God." They could not help seeing a wonderful and striking harmony between this breathing of the Lord Creator into the face of Adam and the breathing of the Lord Saviour upon his Apostles after His resurrection, saying: "Receive ye the Holy Ghost." (S. John XX.) St. Athanasius says: "First by the Word of God man was made. And the Lord breathed into him the spirit of life and confirmed him with a participation of His Spirit. The same God now confers His Spirit on His disciples, that we may be renovated in the same Spirit, in whom we first were constituted." (St. Athanas. Ad Antioch. 9, 64.) Hence, natural and supernatural life with their perfection and complement were given to Adam by the Holy Spirit.

He infused into his soul sanctifying grace. He infused the habits of Faith, Hope and Charity. He by this power ruled within him and there was by the preternatural gifts of integrity, of immortality, of infused science,

there were harmony between soul and body
and peace, which is the tranquillity of order.
Then no war was known between the rational
and irrational creatures. No one, however,
could give us a more lucid description of
this double action of the Spirit Creator in the
first man, than our Cardinal saying: "The
general work of the Holy Ghost as the
sanctifier of the soul in man, began before the
Fall in the creation of man; for Adam when
created was constituted in the state of grace.
He was not created in, but constituted in,
the state of original justice. The distinction
between created and constituted is this: Original justice was no part of the nature of man;
it was a superadded gift, a supernatural
perfection over and and above the perfection
or integrity of human nature. It was not
due to man that he should have the gift of
original justice; his perfection consisted in
the body and the soul, the faculties and the
powers—intellectual and moral—which constitute the human nature. But original justice is more than this; namely, the gift of a
supernatural grace and state, by the indwelling of the Holy Ghost in the soul, illuminating it by the infusion of His light in the
form of truth; and sanctifying it by the infusion of His grace in the form of sanctity.
This was original justice, and therefore,

Adam was in two ways the son of God. He was a son of God by nature, because he was created by God; and a son of God by grace, because the Holy Ghost dwelt in him. Further, because he had this original justice, he had also two other gifts. He had *immortality* in the body, because he was without sin; and he had a *perfect harmony* and *integrity*, or order, in the soul, because the soul was under the direction and guidance of the Spirit of God. Therefore in Adam there were three perfections; there was the *perfection of nature*, i. e. of the body and the soul; there was the *supernatural perfection*, or the indwelling of the Holy Ghost and of sanctifying grace; there was the *preternatural perfection* of immortality in the body and of harmony in the soul in and with itself. *Such was the work of the Holy Ghost.* We do not indeed certainly know, but many theologians of the Church teach as probable, that in Adam there was by the light of faith an anticipation of the mysteries of the kingdom of God; so that he knew, at least in outline, the ever-blessed Trinity and the Incarnation of God. This at least is certain, that the fulness of light which was in him excluded *all ignorance*, for ignorance signifies the not knowing that which we ought to know. Now Adam had all knowledge which belonged to his state. There was in Adam a nescience of many things. There was much that he did not know; but he was not bound to know, he had no obligation to know, that which was beyond his state. And as his illumination was more than ours, so in like manner the sanctification of the soul of the first man was the most perfect, the most profuse, save only the highest sanctification in the order of grace, of which we shall speak hereafter; namely, that of the *Second Adam* and of *His Immaculate Mother.* Such was the work of the Holy Spirit before the fall of man. (Intern. Mission, page 4.)

ASPIRATION.

O Spirit Creator, God the Holy Ghost! Thou hast made the first man into a likeness of God, not so much by the perfection of his nature, as by the participation of divine nature in sanctifying grace. This grace lost by Adam I can regain by the merits of Christ. Give it to me. Make it grow in me. Confirm me in it in the hour of my death. This is my only true life and without it I am living dead. O Spirit of God, bring about peace in my troubled soul. Extinguish the fire of concupiscence in me. Infuse the light of thy science into the darkness of my heart. Make me aspire to and obtain again immortality of the flesh by Thy internal dwelling in the members of my body, for "if the Spirit of Him who raised up Jesus Christ from the dead shall dwell in you; He that raised up Jesus from the dead, shall also quicken your mortal bodies, because of His Spirit, that dwelleth in you." (Rom. VIII, 11.)

INTENTION OF PRAYER.

Pray God to enable you to know more and more the last end for which man is created and to direct all the acts of your life towards it. "*For what does it profit a man, if he gain the whole world, and suffer the loss of his soul? Or what exchange shall a man give for his soul.*" (Matth. XVII, 46.)

———————

4.

The Holy Ghost and His universal operation after the fall of man.

By an act of disobedience the first creation was shattered. The presence of the Holy Ghost was forfeited. Although in man's soul and body the substantial integrity of his nature was left, yet human nature experienced the three severe wounds of *ignorance, weakness* and *passion*. Thus the Spirit was extinguished, in the first Adam and the grace infused and destined to be transmitted to his progeny was forfeited. Iniquity was triumphant, but only for a moment—to be again overcome by God's mercy according to the saying "where sin abounded, grace did more abound." (Rom. V, 21.) Man was guilty of rebellion against his sovereign master, but God decreed salvation ; man had lost eternal life, but God promised a Redeemer ; man had destroyed the temple of the Holy Ghost, but because of His infinite mercy called forth by this being the first offense did God not yet act with the rigor afterwards preached by the Apostle of the Gentiles; "but if any man violate the temple of God, him shall God destroy. For the temple of God is holy, which you are." (I Cor. III, 17.)

Had God in his wrath withdrawn his Spirit of life, even natural destruction would have been man's well deserved punishment, for, it is written; "If Thou turnest away Thy face they shall be troubled; Thou shalt take away Thy breath, and they shall fail, and shall return to their dust." (Ps. CIII, 29.) Had not God decreed to send a Redeemer, we would have been the eternally doomed captives of the evil one and our inevitable lot would have been the second and most terrible death. " Yet through the mercies of the Lord we are not consumed; because His tender mercies have not failed." (Lament, III, 22.) Towards man only has God in these peculiar circumstances allowed His mercy to take the place of His justice, and from the moment of man's fall opened the period of salvation, "God," says the Apostle; "will have all men to be saved, and to come to the knowledge of truth." (I Tim. II, 4.) From the moment of Adam's fall it was again possible for him to rise, but for him and his generation only possible to rise in view and in the virtue of " the one mediator of God and men, the man Christ Jesus; who gave himself a redemption for all, a testimony in due time." (I Tim. II, 6.) This justification, however, obtained by Christ's redemption has always been applied to men, both before the coming of Christ in the plenitude of time and after it, by the operation of the Holy Ghost, Scripture giving testimony to it in the words: " But you are washed, you are sanctified, you are justified, in the name of our Lord Jesus Christ, and the Spirit of our God." (I Cor. V, 11.)

Hence, there was and is yet a universal operation of the Holy Ghost, extending to all men of all times and in all places. As the atmosphere surrounds the entire globe, so the saving breath of God's Holy Spirit reaches all and is the very atmosphere in which we live according to St. John III, 8: " The Spirit breathed where He will; and thou hearest His voice, but thou knowest not, whence He cometh or wither he goeth." " Grace over all the earth " is the subject of a most consoling paper, in which our great Cardinal ably shows, how we Catholics are by no means narrow minded, how we judge not rashly of the salvation of any man, and how we feel and pray, as did St. Paul in his epistle to Timothy. He says:

"Since the Fall, the Spirit of God has assisted from the beginning every man that has come into the world born of Adam; so that there never yet was any soul which had not sufficient grace, if it had sufficient fidelity to correspond with it, to escape the eternal death." Keep ever in mind this great truth; for it is the foundation of the whole doctrine of grace. There are men so narrow as to say, that no soul among the heathen can be saved. The perfections of God, the attributes of mercy, love, tenderness, justice, equity—all rise up in array against so dark a theology. The word of God declares, first of all, that the Son of God is " the true Light that enlightened every man that cometh into the world." Every soul created in the likeness of God is illuminated by the light of God even in his creation. There never yet was a soul born into the world that had not the light of reason, and the light of conscience, that is, the light of God, shining in the soul. The whole world is the reflection of the presence and of the perfection of God. The reason and the conscience, rightly exercised, can see and read His existence, His glory, and His Godhead, in the works of His hands. Again, the Psalmist says, speaking of God: " He hath set His tabernacle in the sun;" and again, " He cometh forth out of the ends of heaven, and His circuit goeth to

the end thereof again.   There is no one that
can hide himself from the heat thereof.'
That is, the glory, and the majesty, and the
love of God, fill the whole world, pervade all
things, all men are encompassed by it.   No
man can hide himself from the love and the
glory of God.   Go where he may—if he
walk upon the earth, God is there; if he
ascend into heaven, He is there also; if he
go down into the deep, God is there before
him.   Every living soul, therefore, has an
illumination of God in the order of nature,
by the light of conscience, and by the light
of reason, and by the working of the Spirit
of God in his head and in his heart, leading
him to believe in God, and to obey Him.
Once more Saint Paul says, that "God will
have all men to be saved and to come to the
knowledge of the truth;" that is, without
any exception, Jew or Gentile.   And again,
"We hope in the living God, Who is
the Saviour of all men, and especially of the
faithful," that is of those who believe, therefore of all men without exception.   And
the two Pontiffs have condemned as hersey
the following assertions: That the heathen,
and the Jews, and heretics, receive no influence from Jesus Christ, but that their will is
without help, that is without grace, was condemned as a heresy by Alexander VIII.
Again, that there is no grace given outside

the Church, was also condemned as heresy by Clement XI. The work therefore, of the Holy Ghost, even in the order of nature, so to say, that is, outside of the Church of God and the revealed knowledge of Jesus Christ among the heathen is universal in the soul of every individual human being; and if they who receive the assistance of the Holy Ghost are faithful in corresponding with it, God in His unrevealed mercies will deal with them in ways hidden from us. The infinite merits of the Redeemer of the world are before the mercy-seat of our Heavenly Father for the salvation of those that follow even the little light which in the order of nature they receive."

ASPIRATION:

O Holy Ghost, driven out from Thy human temple by the sin of our first parents, but recalled to it by our Divine Redeemer, assist me most graciously, I beseech Thee, that I may never more grieve Thee, never sin against Thee. O Spirit of sanctification, make all men without distinction, come to the knowledge of truth. Draw all men to Christ, our Saviour, exalted on the cross. Let me and all my fellowmen more and more fully perceive "that this is eternal life; that they may know Thee, the only true God, and Jesus Christ, whom Thou hast sent." (S. John, XVII, 3.)

INTENTION OF PRAYER:

Pray for the salvation of the many millions of heathens, and all that sit in the shadow of death. "*This is good and acceptable in the sight of God our Saviour, who wills all men to be saved and to come to the knowledge of the truth.*" (I Tim. II, 4.)

5.

The Holy Ghost and the People Elect.

Iniquity was revelling on earth, when, to accomplish His unsearchable designs, God called one man to be the father of a nation and later on in a spiritual sense, the father of all the faithful, saying to him; "Go forth, out of thy country, and from thy kindred, and out of thy family's house, and come into the land which I will show thee. And I will make of thee a great nation, and I will bless thee and magnify thy name and thou shalt be blessed" (Gen. XII, 1, 2.) Amongst the nations, that went astray, losing more and more the true knowledge of God and "delivered up to shameful affections and a reprobate sense." (Rom. VIII, 27.) God chose one nation to prepare the advent of His Son in the flesh, and He made it the object of His paternal solicitude and extraordinary providence. The Jewish nation with its law, its liturgy, its hierarchy, its patriarchs and prophets, its striking reverses and triumphs—is a wonder of God's wisdom, reflecting alike His judgment and mercies. God the Father, who "hath mercy on whom He will, and, whom He will, He hardeneth" (Rom. IX, 18,) had chosen this people for His divine purposes; God the Son, to be born, according to the flesh from this stock of Abraham and Isaac and Jacob, was the object of all providential dispositions in the history of this people. God the Holy Ghost, was eminently the executor of these plans of salvation in the course of time.

We read that to construct the first temple, Solomon was filled with the Spirit of wisdom to accomplish his work. Much more then for the construction of this material house, the Spirit of God was needed to move over this elect people and bring about by degrees its divinely planned maturity, evolution and profession. And, although there was not such a close and mystical union between the Synagogue of the old law and the Holy Ghost, as exists between Him and the Church of God, still He was its soul and ruling spirit. In all its various institutions and dispositions, He breathed and worked "dividing to all as He willed." In all the evolution of Jewish history, the Spirit of God reveals Himself, a Spirit; "of understanding, holy, one, manifold, subtile, eloquent, active, undefiled, sure, sweet, loving that which is good, quick, which nothing hindereth, beneficent, gentle, kind, stead-fast, assured, secure, having all power, over-seeing all things, and containing all spirits; intelligible, pure, subtile." (Wisdom. VII, 22–24.) He preserved the faith in one God; He held aloof from practical corruption the pure law of God; He moved over the waters of history lest they might submerge the ark of the covenant; He ripened the whole nation for the plenitude of time, and He especially called forth and inspired His special organs and messengers to this same people.

The Holy Spirit given to *Moses*, the great lawgiver of the old covenant was again pro-pagated by the imposition of his hands on the seventy chosen ones of Israel, Scripture saying; "The Lord came down in a cloud, and spoke to Moses, taking away of the spirit that was in Moses, and giving to the seventy men. And when the Spirit had rested on them, they prophesied, nor did they cease afterwards." (Num. XI, 25.) The Holy Spirit prepared *Josue* for the office to which he was chosen, the Lord addressing **Moses**: "Take Josue the Son of Nun, a man in whom is the Spirit, and put thy hand on him." (Num. XXVII, 18.) "The Holy Spirit was with *Othoniel*," the Judge of Israel and "he judged Israel. And we went out to fight, and the Lord delivered Chusan Ras-athaim King of Syra and he overthrew him." (Judg. III, 10.) "The Holy Spirit came strongly upon *Samson* in his captivity, and as flax is wont to be consumed at the approach of fire, so the bonds, with which he was bound, were broken and loosed." (Judg. XV, 14.) The Spirit of the Lord shall come upon thee," said Samuel to *Saul*, after he had taken the little vial of oil and poured it upon his head and kissed him, "and thou shalt be changed into another man." (I Kings. X, 6.) "The Spirit of the Lord had spoken by me and His word by my tongue;" proclaims the Kingprophet *David*, "the man, to whom it was appointed concerning the Christ of the God of Jacob, the excellent psalmist of Israel." (II Kings. XXIII, 1, 2.) "Nobody" says St. John Chrysostom, "thinks, that another Spirit was given to the holy men before the advent of Christ, and another to His apostles, after He had gone hence." (In interpret. Didym, De Spir. So. p. 495.) It is consequently the same Holy Ghost who thus prepared the work of Salvation as He was afterwards sent to complete it.

ASPIRATION.

O God, the Holy Ghost, who hast dwelt in the souls of the just ones before Christ, who hast called

Moses and the great men in Israel, who hast spoken
through human tongues and revealed to mankind the plan of salvation, make me a partaker of
Thy sanctification. O Spirit of the living God, give
me strength, wisdom, understanding. unction, that
I may prove an organ of Thy power towards glorifying Thee and saving others. Come upon me, as
Thou camest on Saul and change me into another
man. I beseech Thee, O Spirit of God most merciful, that Thou mayest never depart from me, as
Thou didst from Saul, when the evil Spirit troubled
him. "Deliver me from my enemies, O Lord, to
Thee have I fled; teach me to do Thy will, for Thou
art my God. Thy good Spirit shall lead me into
the right land." (Ps. 142, 11.)

INTENTION OF PRAYER:

Pray for the conversion of Jews and the whole people
elect. "*To the Israelites belongeth the adoption as of children.
and the glory, and the treatment, and the giving of the law, and
the service of God, and the promises; whose are the fathers, and
of whom is Christ according to the flesh, who is over all things
God blessed for ever. Amen.*" (Rom. IX, 4-6.)

6.

The Holy Ghost and the "Promise of the Father" by the mouth of the Prophets.

In the Nicene Creed we ascribe to the Holy Ghost most emphatically the inspiration of the Prophets, saying: "Who spake by the prophets." Saint Peter, speaking of the prophecy in general, says most decidedly: "Understanding this first, that no prophecy of Scripture is made by private interpretation. For prophecy came not by the will of man at any time; but the holy men of God spoke, inspired by the Holy Ghost." (II Petr. I, 21.) The grand exhortation, given by the first Vicar of Christ on earth, St. Peter, to the faithful of his time, gives full evidence of the double fact, that it is the Holy Ghost, to whom the revelation of God must be ascribed and that it is the same Holy Ghost who spoke both in the prophets of the old and through the Apostles of the new law. "Of this salvation" he says, "the prophets have inquired and diligently searched, who prophesied of the grace to come in you; searching what or what manner of time the Spirit of Christ in them did signify; when it foretold those sufferings that are in Christ, and the glories that should follow; to whom it was revealed, that not to themselves, but to you they ministered those things, which are now declared to you by them that have preached the Gospel to you, the Holy Ghost being sent down from heaven, on whom the Angels desire to look." (I Pet. II, 12.) In the Spirit the prophets saw the coming Messiah and all the circumstances of His advent, person, life, death, glory and kingdom. In the Spirit these holy men in an uninterrupted succession announced the approaching salvation and following judgment. In the Spirit the prophets also announced the crowning event of Christ's salvation, the mission of the Holy Ghost on Pentecost day, the consecration of a new people elect, the Church of God.

To these prophecies of the coming of the Holy Ghost we do here only refer. The Holy Ghost is called, "rite promissum patris" and Christ our Lord Himself commanded His Apostles; "not to depart from Jerusalem, but to wait for promise of the Father." (Act. I, 4.) Which are the prominent " promises of the Father," given us by the Prophets? Let us see: Of the effusion of the Holy Ghost the prophet Joel says: " And you, O children of Sion, rejoice, and be joyful in the Lord your God, because He had given you a teacher of justice . . and you shall know that I am in the midst of Israel; and I am the Lord your God, and there is none besides; and My people shall not be confounded for ever. And it shall come to pass after this, that I will pour out My Spirit upon all flesh; and your sons and your daughters shall prophecy; your old men shall dream dreams and your young men shall see visions. Moreover upon My servants and handmaids in those days I will pour forth My spirit." (Joel. I, 27–29.) St. Peter on Pentecost day solemnly declared that in the effusion of the Spirit, this prophecy of Joel was fulfilled; "this is that which was spoken of by the prophet Joel." (Act. II, 16.) " Being exalted therefore to the right hand of God, and having received of the Father the promise of the Holy Ghost, He hath poured forth this which you see and hear." (Act. II, 33.)

Of the effusion of the Holy Ghost *Aggeus* says: " The word that I covenanted with you when you came out of the land of Egypt; and My Spirit shall be in the midst of you : fear not.   For thus, said the Lord of hosts ; yet one little while, and I will move the heaven, and the earth, and the sea, and the dry land.   And I will move all nations ; and the desired of all nations shall come ; and I will fill this house with glory, said the Lord of hosts." (Agg. II, I.)

Of the effusion of the Holy Ghost the prophet *Zacharias*, says :   "And I will pour out upon the house of David, and upon the inhabitants of Jerusalem, the Spirit of grace and of prayers; and they shall look upon Me, whom they have pierced; and they shall mourn for Him as one mourneth for one only son, and they shall grieve over Him, as the manner is to grieve for the death of the first born." (Zach. XIII, 10.)

Of the effusion of the Holy Spirit the prophet *Isaias* says :   " And there shall come forth a rod out of the root of Jesse and a flower shall rise up out of his root.   And the Spirit of the Lord shall rest upon Him : the Spirit of wisdom and of understanding, the Spirit of counsel and of fortitude, the Spirit of knowledge and of godliness, and He shall be filled with the Spirit of the fear of the Lord   . In that day shall be the root of Jesse, who standeth for an ensign of people, Him the gentiles shall beseech and His sepulchre shall be glorious " (Isai. XI.,1, 2, 3, 10.)

Of the effusion of the Holy Ghost the prophet *Ezechiel* says: "And I will pour upon you clean water and you shall be cleansed from all your filthiness, and I will cleanse you from all your idols. And I will give you a new heart and put a new spirit within you; and I will take away the stony heart out of your flesh, and will give you a heart of flesh. And I will put My Spirit in the midst of you: and I will cause you to walk in My commandments, and to keep My judgments and do them. And you shall dwell in the land which I gave to your fathers: and you shall be My people and I will be your God." (Ezech. 36; 25-29.)

ASPIRATION:

O God, the Holy Ghost, Inspirer of the Prophets, Interpreter of Holy Writ, Teacher of the holy men that spoke to us the words of salvation, pour upon me the Spirit of understanding, intelligence and wisdom. Make me realize the great truths of salvation. Make me appreciate the grace which the prophets foretold would come upon us. Give me a share in "those things which are now declared to us by them that preached the Gospel, the Holy Ghost being sent down from heaven." Let us never forget, that "the glories of Christ followed His sufferings" and let us at the end of this life see Him "on whom the Angels desire to look!"

INTENTION OF PRAYER:

Beg of God to multiply vocations to the sacred ministry and to bestow His most precious gifts on the elect ones of the Lord. "The harvest indeed is great, but the laborers are few. Pray ye therefore the Lord of the harvest, that He send laborers into His harvest. Luk. X, 2.

7

The Holy Ghost and the Mother of God.

As centuries rolled on, the Holy Ghost gradually prepared and finally introduced the period of salvation, sanctifying in an extraordinary degree both the parents of St. John the Baptist and the parents of her from whom the Saviour should spring forth as the flowers budding forth from the root of Jesse. But when the fulness of "time was come, God sent His Son made of a woman, made under the law." (Gal. IV, 4.) It is only required to have a correct idea of the Incarnation of the eternal word, to perceive at once, that "this woman" whom the Holy Ghost was to overshadow in order to bring forth from her the Son of God according to the flesh, had first to be overshadowed, sanctified and favored with all possible grace, to render her worthy of the unique and exalted position, which in the eternal counsels of God she was destined to fill. "Protestants," says Cardinal Newman, "have seldom a real perception of the doctrine of God and man in one person. The world allows that God is man: the admission costs it little, for God is everywhere; but it shrinks from confessing that God is the Son of Mary." (Discourses to mixed Congreg. p. 346.) Hence they cannot perceive the unique greatness and singular plenitude of grace we ascribe to this "woman clothed with the sun," and the central position which her exalted mission demands; and which we most gladly attribute to her because of the sanctifying operation of the Spirit. The Church calls Mary the "Spouse of the Holy Spirit." There is a mystical and reciprocal relation between the Son of God and Mary, between Mary and the Church, and between the Son of God and the Church.

The angelic words, "that the Holy Ghost shall come upon thee, and the power of the Most High shall overshadow thee" (Luke I, 35), can be applied to Mary in *three* succeeding grades of an ever increasing sanctification.

As the spouse of the Holy Spirit, she was *first* overshadowed in the very first moment of her existence, her Immaculate Conception. "It was fitting," says Cardinal Newman, "that she who was to be the instrument of God's bodily presence, should first be a miracle of His Grace; it was fitting that she should triumph where Eve had failed, and should 'bruise the serpent's head' by the spotlessness of her sanctity. Hence the season of grace and prodigy now to be inaugurated, should be exhibited in a special manner in the person of Christ's mother. The course of ages was to be reversed; the tradition of evil was to be broken; a gate of light was to be opened amid the darkness for the coming of the Just. As grace was infused first into Adam from the first moment of his creation, so grace was given to Mary from the first, but in an ampler measure. She began where others end, whether in knowledge or in love. She was from the first clothed in sanctity, sealed for perseverance, luminous and glorious in God's sight. Her's was emphatically "the path of the just, which as the shining light goeth forward and increaseth even to the perfect day." (Card. Newman, Discourses to mixed Congreg. p. 351.) Of her Immaculate Conception, the extraordinary effect of the irradiation of the Spirit on her soul, Cardinal Manning yet more beautifully speaks in the following lines;

" And as in the beginning God first created the light and then both night and day— for the day is light measured by the sun; so before the new creation of God arose, there was a day-spring, a dawn of twilight, a prelude of the brightness of the coming moon. The morning light was the Immaculate Conception of the Mother of God—the first-fruits of the full and perfect sanctifying grace of the Holy Ghost. She was the first and the last in the natural lineage of the children of Adam, in whom sin had no place. The Mother of the Incarnate Son was sheltered and preserved from the inheritance of original sin, so that never for a moment was so much as a shadow cast by sin upon her spotless soul. In her was no privation of grace. From the first moment of her existence she was full of the Holy Ghost. The most perfect work of sanctification that the world has ever seen, purchased by the Precious Blood of the Son of God Himself, and given out of free and sovereign grace is the Immaculate Conception of the Mother of God. Such was the aurora before the sun."

Of her Immaculate Conception, as the necessary requisite for her to be the worthy ark of the new Covenant, the great Doctor of the universal Church, St. Francis of Sales, speaks with his usual charm and unction as follows:

"Thus, God destined first for His most holy mother a favor worthy of the love of a

Son, who, being all wise, all mighty, and all good, wished to prepare a mother to His liking; and therefore He willed His redemption to be applied to her after the manner of a preserving remedy, that the sin which was spreading from generation to generation should not reach her. She, then, was so excellently redeemed, that though, when the time came, the torrent of original iniquity rushed to pour its unhappy waves over her conception as over that of the other daughters of Adam, yet it reached her not, but stopped, as did anciently the Jordan in the time of Josue: for this river held its stream in reverence for the passage of the Ark of Alliance; original sin drew back its waters, reserving and dreading the presence of the true Tabernacle of the eternal alliance."

As the Spouse of the Spirit, Mary was overshadowed the second time in the moment the Eternal Word took flesh from her. In the Incarnation her virginity was not violated by her motherhood, but it received a new consecration and her sanctity and holiness were augmented. Here we quote the marvelous passage of Cardinal Newman:

" Mary was no mere instrument in God's dispensation; the word of God did not merely come to her and go from her; He did not merely pass through her, as He may pass through us in Holy Communion; it was no heavenly body which the Eternal Son assumed, fashioned by the Angels, and brought down to this lower world; no: He imbibed, He sucked up her blood and her substance into His Divine Person; He became man of Her; and received her lineaments and her features, as the appearance and character under which He should manifest Himself to the world. He was known, doubtless, by His likeness to her, to be her Son. Thus His Mother is the first of Prophets, for to her came the Word bodily; she is the sole oracle of truth, for the Way, the Truth, and the Life vouchsafed to be her Son; she is the one mould of Divine Wisdom, and in that mould it was indelibly cast. Surely then, if the 'first fruit be holy, the mass also is holy; and if the root is holy, so are the branches.' It was natural, it was fitting, then so it should be; it was congruous that, whatever the Omnipotent could work in the person of the finite, should be wrought in her. I say, if the Prophets must be holy, 'to whom the word of God comes,' what must we say of her, who was so especially favored, that the true and substantial Word, and not His shadow or His voice, was not merely made in her, but born of her? who was not merely the organ of God's message,

but the origin of His human existence, the
living fountain from which He drew His
most precious blood, and the material of His
most holy flesh ? "

As the Spouse of the Holy Spirit, Mary was
again and for the third time overshadowed
by the power from on high on the great day
of Pentecost. Scripture emphatically states,
that " they were persevering with one mind
in prayer with the women and Mary the
Mother of Jesus." (Act. I, 34.)   Tradition and
art always represent Mary in the midst of the
Apostles receiving the tongues of fire and
being filled with the Holy Ghost. This favor
came upon her not so much for her own sanctification which was already sealed, as to consecrate her, who was already the Mother of
His human body, the Mother of His mystical body. Around her, from whom God had
taken to Himself a human body, the infant
Church, His mystical body should take
shape and form.   Filled with the Pentecostal
Spirit, Mary was now the Mother of the
faithful, not only by appointment such as
afterwards took place as she stood by the
cross of her Son, but by consecration in her
sublime office as Queen of Apostles and
Evangelists and as the organ of the Christian dispensation of truth and grace in a
most singular sense.

ASPIRATION.

O Spirit of God, who hast overshadowed with the power of the Most High Mary, Thy beloved Spouse, in her Immaculate Conception, in the Incarnation and on Pentecost Day, pour upon me tender love, an unbounded veneration, a childlike devotion to my beloved Mother, Mary Immaculate. She is Thy only beloved one! She is given us as our Mother by Christ our Lord. How could we separate her honour from His? Make me, O Spirit of the living God, believe of Mary what the Church believes of her, and love her as the Church loves her. Give me, by the Gift of Piety, a singular Devotion for Mary, so characteristic of all the Saints and Elect. Make her for me "the Morning Star," the "Tower of David," and finally "the Gate of Heaven." Amen.

INTENTION OF PRAYER:

Pray for the signal grace of a tender devotion to Mary the Mother of God. "*He that shall find Me shall find life, and shall have salvation from the Lord, but he that shall sin against Me, shall hurt his own soul. All that hate me love death.*" (Prov. VIII, 34-36.)

8.

The Holy Ghost and the Word Incarnate.

Mary was sanctified to be the worthy tabernacle of God Incarnate. By the overshadowing of the Holy Ghost and the power of the Most High, she in the plenitude of time conceived and a virgin brought forth God Incarnate, as we profess in the Creed; "Who was conceived of the Holy Ghost and born of the Virgin Mary." The execution of the decree of the Incarnation was always principally appropriated to the Holy Ghost, the angel saying to Joseph: "That what is conceived in her, is of the Holy Ghost." (Matth. I, 20.) This, however, is a truism. We do not intend to dwell here on the most incomprehensible and most intimate union in which the Holy Ghost stands to the Eternal Word Incarnate, or upon the singular unction, by which the Holy Ghost poured the entire plenitude of grace created into the human soul of the God-man, the second Adam of the new generation, the great

High Priest of eternal atonement. I wish only to refer to the word of holy Scripture exhibiting to us the most continuous and solemn union with the Holy Ghost, in which God Incarnate on earth was standing and working all the days of His Messianic mission.

"The Holy Spirit had filled Zacharias, the father of the Forerunner, so that he foreknew the day of Redemption:" And Zacharias, his father, was filled with the Holy Ghost and he prophesied, saying: "Blessed be the Lord, the God of Israel, because He hath visited and wrought the redemption of His people." (St. Luke, I, 67.) When the Mother of God entered the house of Elizabeth, Elizabeth was filled with the Holy Spirit, and saluting the virgin, she cried out, with a loud voice, and said: "Blessed are thou among women, and blessed is the fruit of thy womb. And why is this, that the mother of my Lord should come to me! For behold, as soon as the voice of thy salutation sounded in my ears, the infant in my womb leaped for joy." (St. Luke., I, 42.) The Holy Spirit was in *Simeon*, and, having received an answer from the Holy Ghost, that he should not see death before he had seen the Christ of the Lord," he came by the Spirit into the temple" (St. Luke. I, 26), "took the child Jesus in his arms and recognized in Him, the Light of the revelation of the Gentiles, the Glory of the people of Israel, the Sign which shall be contradicted, the piercing of the soul of Mary." (S. Luke. I, 26-34.) "The Holy Spirit," to inaugurate Christ in His public mission, in the solemn *baptism* of the Jordan " descended in a bodily shape as a dove upon Him; and a voice came from Heaven : "Thou art My beloved Son, in Thee I am well pleased." (S. Luke. III, 22.) "The Holy Spirit now led Jesus, filled with the Holy Ghost and returning from the Jordan into the desert," (S. Luke. IV, 1,) until "in the power of the Spirit, He returned into Galilee, and the fame of Him went out through the whole country." (Luke. IV, 14.) "The Holy Spirit" resting upon Him was to Christ the evidence of His Messianic mission, as He solemnly stated, when "teaching in the Synagogue, magnified by all, unfolding and reading Isaias, the Prophet, He found the place, where it was written : 'the Spirit of the Lord is upon Me ; wherefore He hath anointed Me, to preach the Gospel to the poor He hath sent Me to heal the contrite of heart'. . And when He had folded the book, He restored it to the minister and sat down. And the eyes of all in the Synagogue were fixed upon Him. And He began to say to them : This day is fulfilled this scripture in your ears." (St. Luke. IV, 16–21.) The Holy Spirit in the midst of Christ's earthly career again gave testimony, when on the mountain of *Tabor*, the Lord was transfigured, and " a bright cloud overshadowed Him, and a voice coming out from the cloud said : This is my beloved Son, in whom I am well pleased, hear ye Him " (S. Matth. XVII, 5.) The Holy Spirit accompanied the Messiah, wherever He went, as the Apostle says: " evidently great is the mystery of godliness which was manifested in the flesh and justified in the Spirit " (I Tim. III, 16,) until this same " Holy Spirit " prompted our Saviour to " offer Himself unspotted to God, to cleanse by His blood our conscience from dead works to serve the living God." (Hebr. IX, 14.) Even the resurrection of Christ is ascribed to the Holy Spirit. He is declared to be the Son of God " by the Spirit of sanctification which raised Him from the dead." (Rom. I, 4.)

ASPIRATION.

O God, the Holy Ghost, who rested upon our Divine Saviour in all the plenitude of Thy gifts, give me a share in these gifts and make me a partaker of the grace that is in Christ. Let me know more and more, that Christ is the Way, the Truth, the Life, the Resurrection. Make me realize the revelation of St. Peter, that there is no name in which we must be saved, but Christ's. Make me also by Thy sanctifying power a "beloved son of God" who will ever "hear the voice" of Christ in His Church, and offer himself unspotted to God," and cleanse me O Divine Spirit in the blood of my Redeemer "for the service of the living God." Amen.

INTENTION OF PRAYER:

Beg of the Holy Spirit to give you a true devotion to the Most Sacred Heart of Jesus. *"And I will pour out . . . the spirit of grace and of prayers and they shall look upon Me whom they have pierced."* Zach. XII, 10.

9.

The Holy Ghost and the "Promise of the Son."

Before leaving this earth, our Saviour counselled His disciples; "that they should not depart from Jerusalem, but should wait for the promise of the Father which you have heard" (saith he) "through My mouth." (Act. I, 4.) This is proof enough, that the "promise of the Father" given by the prophets, was repeated by the Son and has thus also become the *promise of the Son.*" The operations of the Divine Persons without the Trinity always correspond to their mutual relations within the Trinity: and so it comes, that the Holy Ghost, proceeding eternally from Father and Son, is promised by both in succession, sent from both in time, and only then sent on earth, when the Son had returned to His Father.

This "promise of the Son" begins simultaneously with His Messianic work. When St. John the Baptist saw Jesus coming to him, he said: "Behold the Lamb of God, behold

Him who taketh away the sins of the world
.   And I knew Him not, but that He may
be made manifest in Israel, therefore am I
come baptizing with water." And John
gave testimony, saying: "I saw the Spirit
come down as a dove from heaven,
and He remained on Him. And I knew
Him not; but He who sent me to baptize
with water, said to me: He upon whom
thou shalt see the Spirit descending and
resting on Him, He it is, that baptized with
the Holy Ghost." (St. John I, 29–33.) St. Matthew, in the narrative of Christ's baptism in
the Jordan points still more clearly to this
future baptism in the Holy Ghost on Pentecost day, adding: "He shall baptize you in
the Holy Ghost and fire." (St. Matt. III, 11.)
Repeatedly during His Messianic mission
our Lord alludes to this coming and crowning event of Redemption, as for instance,
when He, on the last and great day of the
festivity, cried, saying: "If any man thirst,
let him come to Me and drink. He that believeth in Me, as the Scripture saith, out of
his belly shall flow rivers of living water."
Now this He said of the Spirit which they
should receive, who believe in Him; "for
as yet the Spirit was not given, because
Jesus was not yet glorified." (St. John,
VII, 37.) The more near, however,

the end of His life approaches, the more distinct, the more frequent, the more emphatic becomes His promise. The nearer the approach of the stormy night of His passion and the eternal day of His glorification at the Father's right hand, the more explicitly the Second Person, Incarnate of the Holy Trinity, refers His disciples to the person, the office, the mission and the impending advent of the Third Person in the same Deity. It is the beloved disciple, who resting on the bosom of our Lord on the last memorable evening before His passion, and imbibing from the Sacred Heart all the secret thoughts and sentiments of Christ, has given us the full and detailed account of this promise of the Son, uttered by Him in His last words to His disciples.

Now the three Divine Persons are repeatedly mentioned together in one sentence. "I will ask the Father and He shall give you another Paraclete, that He may abide with you forever, the Spirit of truth, whom the world cannot receive, because it seeth Him not nor knoweth Him; but you shall know Him; because He shall abide with you, and shall be in you." (S. John, XIV, 17.) Now He tells His apostles plainly, that, although He would go hence, His work would be continued by the ministration of the Spirit

in them, saying: "The Paraclete, the Holy Ghost, whom My Father will send in My name, He will teach you all things and bring all things to your mind, whatsoever I shall have said to you." (V. 26.) Now He lays stress on the truth, that His disciples should not give way to sadness, for, He continues, "I, tell you the truth: it is expedient to you that I go: for if I do not, the Paraclete will not come to you; but if I go, I will send Him to you. And when He is come, He will convince the world of sin, and of justice, and of judgment.   .
When He, the Spirit of truth is come, He will teach you all truth; for He shall not speak of Himself: but what things soever He shall hear, He shall speak; and the things that are to come He shall show you. He shall glorify Me: because He shall receive of Mine and shall show it to you." (S. John, XVI. 7–15.) So our departing Saviour spoke and finally concluding His sacerdotal oration He once more asks the Father for the all comprehending reward of His passion, the main object of His pontifical prayer, the fruit of redemption—the effusion of the Spirit, saying: "And I have made known Thy name to them and will make it known; that *the love, wherewith Thou hast loved Me, may be in them and I in them.*" (St.

John, XVII, 26.) He suffered, died, rose again, but He would not ascend to His seat of glory without having once more repeated His promise: "And I send the promise of My Father upon you; but stay you in the city, till you will be endued with power from on high." (St. Luke. XXIV, 49.) "The promise of the Father which you have heard, He saith, through My mouth" (Act. 1, 4) will now be accomplished. "For John indeed baptized with water, but you shall be baptized with the Holy Ghost *not many days hence*." (Act. I, 5.) Now even the time is appointed. The promise of the Son is finished. Nothing remaineth but to see it fulfilled.

• ASPIRATION.

O God, the Holy Ghost, whom my Divine Redeemer has promised to His disciples, be also my paraclete, my assistance, my consolation in this life! Bring home to my mind the truths of salvation which our Saviour taught us. Give me the peace which the world cannot give. Enable me to shun sin, do justice and escape the judgment of of this world. Confirm me, O Giver of all grace, in a living faith and an immaculate life that I may give testimony to my Lord and Saviour. Amen.

INTENTION OF PRAYER.

Pray for strength to give testimony of Christ and religion fearlessly and courageously, both by word and deed. "*Every one, therefore that shall confess Me before men, I will also confess him before My Father who is in heaven.*" (Matth. X, 322.)

10.

The Holy Ghost and His Advent on Pentecost Day.

"The not many days hence," mentioned by our Lord, passed. "When the days of Pentecost were accomplished" (Act. II, 1) the plenitude of time had reached its culmination and the Son was glorified in the descending Spirit. There is no chapter in the inspired books so luminous, so glorious, so attractive for devout Servants of the Holy Ghost, than this second chapter of the Acts or the authentic narrative of the solemn Advent of God the Holy Ghost on Pentecost day. We do not enter upon a detailed meditation of this chapter, reserving for a future volume to treat of Pentecost. We shall now only point to the difference, that characterizes this advent of the Holy Ghost and distinguishes it from His previous actions, operations, and effusions. The better we realize this difference, the brighter and more luminous must appear to us the feast of the Servants of the Holy

Ghost *par excellence*—Whitsunday or Pentecost: These characteristic differences are the following three:

1. *First: the Holy Ghost had previously come into this world by His universal operations in all mankind, but on Pentecost Day He came through the Incarnate Son;* to continue and to accomplish as the Third Divine Person the work commenced and established by the Second; to be the main fruit and reward of Christ's vicarious passion and death; to be His glorification and to glorify Him in this world. This character of the Holy Ghost's coming on Pentecost alone accounts for the exuberance of gifts and graces, the miraculous manifestations, the power and fulness of His coming, as recorded in the Acts.

2. *The second characteristic difference is, that on Pentecost the Holy Ghost came to create and vivify the mystical body of Christ.* Therefore, the day on which we celebrate the advent of the Holy Ghost is also the solemn anniversary of the divine consecration of God's Church. "Until Pentecost day the mystical body was not complete. There could be no complete body till there was a Head. There was no Head until the Son was incarnate; and even, when incarnate, the completion of the body was deferred until the Head was glorified; that is, until the incarnate Son had ful-

filled His whole redeeming office in life, death, resurrection and ascension, returning to enthrone humanity with which His Eternal Person was invested, at the right hand of the Father. Then, when the Head was exalted in His supreme majesty over angels and men, the creation and organization of the body was completed." (Card. Manning, Temp. Miss., p, 38.) "Christ had found this mystical body as God had found the body of Adam. Christ gave it its divinely ordained structure, organization, institution. As man, however, became a living soul only by the vivifying spirit breathed into him, so the body of the Church become only the mystical body, the living body, the divine-human organization by the effusion of the Spirit on Pentecost day. Then the Church took life and growth. Then the Apostolic Hierarchy as a compact body appeared with Peter as its head. Then the waters of salvation begin to flow into the remission of sin. Then the power of apostolic preaching was first triumphant. Then the Church of the new law began to move, and grow, and extend in the very capital of the old law. St. Gregory the Great, summing up the doctrine of St. Augustine, writes as follows: 'The holy universal Church is one body, constituted under Christ Jesus, its Head. There-

fore, Christ, with His whole Church, both
that which is still on earth and that which
now reigns with Him in heaven, is one Person; and as the soul is one which quickens
the various members of the body, so the one
Holy Spirit quickens and illuminates the
whole Church. For as Christ, is the Head of
the Church, which is His body, the Church is
filled by the same Spirit that it may have
life, is confirmed by His power that it may
subsist in the bond of one faith and charity.
Therefore, the Apostle says, 'from whom
the whole body being compacted and fitly
joined together maketh increase of the
body.' This is that body out of which the
Spirit quickeneth not; wherefore the blessed
Augustine says: 'If thou wouldst live of
the Spirit of Christ, be in the Body of
Christ.' Of this Spirit the heretic does not
live, nor the schismatic, nor the excommuni-
cated, for they are not of the body; but the
Church hath a Spirit that giveth life, because it inheres inseparably to Christ its
Head: for it is written: 'He that adhereth
to the Lord is one spirit with Him.'" (Card.
Manning, Temp. Miss., p. 47.)

*The third characteristic difference is constituted
by the indissoluble absolute union between the
Holy Ghost and the mystical body of Christ, the
Church.* This union is independent of all

finite will and dependent only upon the Divine will, therefore it will be eternally indissoluble. It is constituted by the union of the Holy Ghost with the Head of the Church, not only as God, but as man, and in both these relations this union is indissoluble. There will never come a time when that body will cease to be, therefore, there never can come a time in which its union with the Holy Ghost will cease. The mystical body will exist for all eternity in the perfect number of the blessed. These Divine unions, first of the head with the members; next of the members with each other; and lastly of the Holy Ghost with the body, will likewise be eternal. But that which shall be eternal is also indissoluble in time:—the union, that is, of the Spirit with the body as a whole. Individuals may fall from it as multitudes have fallen. Provinces, nations, particular churches may fall from it; but the body still remains, its unity undivided, its life indefectible, for "all are built together into an habitation of God in the Spirit" (Ephes. II, 22.) This union of the Spirit with the body is a divine act, analogous to the hypostatic union, whereby the two natures of God and man are eternally united in one Person. (According to Cardinal Manning in Temp. Miss. of the Holy Ghost, pages 45–77.)

Hence, the coming of the Holy Ghost on Pentecost day was a solemn, public official coming of the Spirit of truth in His plenitude, through the merits of the Incarnate Son glorified, to create and vivify the mystical body of Christ, His Church, and to dwell, to operate, to live in this Church for all time and in eternity. It is of this personal presence, abiding visitation and never ceasing operation of the Holy Ghost, that St. Augustin writes: "Therefore the Holy Ghost on this day descended into the temple of His Apostles, which He had prepared for Himself, as a shower of sanctification. He came no more as a transient visitor, but as a perpetual comforter and as an eternal inhabitant. He came therefore, on this day to His disciples, no longer by the grace of visitation and operation, but by the very Presence of His majesty; and into those vessels, no longer the odor of the balsam, but the very substance of the sacred unction flowed down, from whose fragrance the breath of the whole world was to be filled, and all who came to their doctrine to make partakers of God." (S. Aug. Serm. in die Pentec. I Tom. V, App.)

ASPIRATION:

O God, the Holy Ghost, who on the glorious day of Pentecost hast actually verified the saying of the

Psalmist: "The Spirit of the Lord hath filled the whole earth and that which contained all things hath knowledge of the voice" (Wisd. 1,) grant, we beseech Thee, that this day may be a lasting day for me. Never, we humbly pray Thee withdraw Thy beatifying Presence. Make us feel the plenitude of Thy indwelling. Be to us not a transient benefactor, but a perpetual comforter. Pour upon us the sacred Unction of Thy consolation and supernatural strength. "O God, who on this day didst instruct the hearts of the faithful by the light of Thy Holy Spirit; grant us in the same Spirit to relish what is right, and ever to rejoice in His consolation. Amen." (Oration of the Church on Pentecost day.)

INTENTION OF PRAYDR:

Pray for the exaltation and propagation upon earth of our Holy Mother the Church. "*Not by an army nor by might, but my Spirit, says the Lord of hosts.*" Zach. V, 6.

11.

The Holy Ghost and the Mystical Body of Christ.

This entire explanation of the mutual relation between the Holy Ghost and the Church would be defective, were we not to say one word more on the mystical Body of Christ. Already in showing the characteristic differences between the Holy Ghost's operation, both before and after Pentecost, we have laid stress on the expression "Body;" and the idea of the Church as "the mystical body of Christ" is truly, what we call, a classic and transcendant notion, both of Scripture and of tradition. It seems to us, that in our days this truth must be more clearly than ever borne in mind, that the Church of God is not merely a society, a congregation of many, a corporation in the large sense of the term, but actually and truly a *body*, a perfect organism, a divine-human, and consequently a mystical organization, vivified by an internal and divine principle of life—the Holy Ghost.

The multitude and fellowship of the just, who from Abel to the Incarnation had lived and died in faith and union with God, constituted the soul of a body which was to be afterwards divinely framed. They did not constitute the Church, which signifies not only the *election* but the *aggregation* of the servants of God; not only the calling *out*, but the calling *together* into one all those who are united with Him. Scripture is abundant in texts exhibiting to us the Church as "Christ's body." St. Paul writes in his epistle to the Ephesians: "One body and one Spirit: as you are called in one hope of your calling. One Lord, one faith, one baptism. One God and Father of all, who is above all and through all and in us all. But to every one of us is given grace according to the measure of the giving of Christ; but doing truth in charity, we may in all things grow up in Him who is the Head, even Christ: from whom the whole body, being compacted and fitly joined together, by what every joint supplieth, according to the operation in the measure of every part, maketh increase of the body unto edifying of itself in charity." (Ephes. IV, 4–16.) The same Apostle writes to the Corinthians: "All these things one and the same Spirit worketh, dividing to every one

according as He will. For as the body is
one and hath many members: and all the
members of the body, whereas they are
many yet are one body; so also is Christ.
For in one Spirit we are all baptized into one
body, whether Jews or Gentiles, whether bond
or free; and in one Spirit we have all been
made to drink. For the body also is not one
member, but many   Now you are the
body of Christ and members of member."
(I Cor. XII, 12–27.) Again he says, writing
to the Ephesians: "He had subjected all
things under His feet, (Christ) and had
made Him head over all the Church, which
is His body, and the fulness of Him, who is
filled all in all." (Ephes. I, 22–23.)

Tradition or the Fathers seem to dwell
upon this most comprehensive comparison
with a certain predilection and to draw from it
the most vital deductions. St. Augustin
remarks on the relation in which the
article of the Church stands to the doctrine
of the Holy Trinity: "In the like manner
we ought to believe in the Holy Ghost, that
the Trinity, which is God, may have its fulness. Then the Holy Church is mentioned;
.... the right order of the confession
remains that to the Trinity should be sub-
joined the Church, as the dwelling to the in-

habitant, and as His temple to the Lord, and the city to its builder."

The same doctor dwells yet more profusely on the Apostolic words "one body, one Spirit," saying: "Listen, members of that body. The body is made up of many members, and one spirit quickens them all. Behold, by the spirit of a man, by which I myself, am a man, I hold together all the members; I command them to move; I direct the eyes to see, the ears to hear, the tongue to speak, the hands to work, the feet to walk. The offices of the members are divided severally, but one spirit holds all in one. Many are commanded, and many things are done; there is one only who commands, and one who is obeyed. What our spirit—that is, our soul—is to our members, that the Holy Ghost is to the members of Christ, to the body of Christ, which is the Church; therefore, the Apostle, when he had spoken of the one body, says: "There is one body." I ask, is this body alive? It is alive. Whence? From the one Spirit. "There is one Spirit."

The following words of S. Gregory of Nazianzen teach expressly the same doctrine: "But now the *Holy Ghost*, is given more perfectly, for He is no longer present by His *operation* as of old, but is present with us, so to speak, and converses with us in *a substan-*

tial manner. For it is fitting that, as the Son
had conversed with us in a body, the Spirit
also should come among us in *a bodily manner ;* and when Christ had returned to His
own place, He should descend to us."

This idea of "the mystical body of Christ"
is the keynote to the understanding of the
entire doctrine of the Church. If the Church
is the "mystical body of Christ," we will at
once perceive, that the Church must be
visible, an organization of various organs and
members with unequal offices and graces, a
variety in a most sublime unity, a human
structure and society with an internal and
divine principle of life and growth and development. We were redeemed by our Divine
Saviour in a human body which He received
from the Virgin Mary by the overshadowing
of the Holy Ghost. The same Lord has also
willed to apply the merits of redemption in
the ordinary way by the instrumentality of
a human body, the Church, created by the
overshadowing Spirit on Pentecost day.
Hence, it is manifest, that in and through
the Church the souls of men must be saved.
The Holy Spirit would not have come in
flaming glory to dwell in this Church, unless
it were to be the sacrament of union with
Him, and the sphere of His sanctifying energies. The Spirit fills the universe with His

immensity, but He dwells with the gift of a substantial union only in the body which is His temple.   Vainly, therefore, shall man seek any other salvation or hope to draw nigh to the eternal Trinity, without the atonement of the Son and the indwelling of the Holy Ghost.   They who seek salvation must come to the earthly home of the Spirit and to the temple where alone the Paraclete "takes of the things of Christ and shows them to His chosen."

ASPIRATION:

O God the Holy Ghost in whom I have also been baptized into the unity of that body of which Christ is the Head, make me, I beseech Thee a partaker of all those gifts that from our Divine Head flow upon all members of His body. Preserve me in the unity of this body in the bond of peace.   United unto one body let us also be one with Christ " in whom dwelleth the fulness of the Godhead corporally and that we are filled in Him, who is the Head of all principality and power." (Col. II, 9-12.)   We thank Thee, O God the Holy Ghost, for the signal grace of having been born in the pale of the true Church.   We beg of Thee, O Spirit of Life, to make this our union with Holy Church ever more close, more intimate, more prolific in grace and sanctification.   Make us not only be *one body*, but also have *one mind* with Holy Church and thus have "*the mind of Christ.*"   Amen.

INTENTION OF PRAYER:

Pray for the grace of a filial attachment to Holy Church and all that belongs to her.   "*Christ loved the Church, and delivered Himself up for it, that He might sanctify it . . . and that He might present it to Himself a glorious Church, not having spot or wrinkle. or any such thing, but that it should be holy and without blemish.*" (Ephes. V, 27.)

12.

The Holy Ghost and the properties, endowments and notes of the true Church.

As Christ's Divinity manifested itself in His humanity, so too must the internal life of the Church, the indwelling Spirit be manifest in this mystical body of which He is the soul. It would be useless to treat of the *properties* and *notes* of the Church before having first established and sufficiently expounded this most essential truth and basis of all others; that the Church as the mystical body of Christ is vivified by the indwelling Holy Ghost. United by the Holy Spirit with Christ the Head, the Church not only appears, but truly is a mystical personality, of which St. Augustin says: "The head and the body are one man, Christ and the Church are one man, a perfect man; He the bridegroom, she the bride, and they shall be two, he says, in one flesh." (St. Aug. in Ps. XVIII, tom. IV–p. 85.)   All the properties and notes of the Church, flow from this principle as naturally as the rivulets flow from the stream's source.   Now these characteristic qualities of the Church so often dwelt upon, are no mere appearances, but real qualities which she possesses always and everywhere in virtue of her principle of life, and therefore, necessarily.   As in the Incarnation there is a communication of the Divine perfection to the Humanity, so in the Church, the perfections of the Holy Spirit become the endowments of the body.

Because the Spirit dwells in the Church, as the Soul dwells in the body, the Church is necessarily *visible*.   The race of men is a visible race, and must be treated as such in all the operations of God.   Our bodies are an integral part of our nature, material and visible.   The human race fell in Adam, its father, and was visibly exiled from Eden, and in its corporate life passed into the shadow of death, away from God.   To redeem us our Lord took a visible body in all things like unto ours, sin only excepted.   Thus is He, the second Adam as visible as the first and hence by necessary consequence, the bodies of the just are quickened with

His life. Through his Humanity He shows Himself to us and by His Humanity He touches us. The action of redemption upon *man* consequently requires the sacraments of a visible Church. Such a visible Church our Lord evidently founded when on earth. He framed it into a visible body, giving it a visible head, Peter, visible superiors, the Apostles, visible worship, sacrifice and sacraments, a visible constitution. All our Lord's comparisons of the Church with a "sheepfold," a "vineyard," a "vine," a "city on the mountain top," a "body," point to this visibility of His Church. Upon this visible Church, then in a visible sign, the invisible Spirit descended on Pentecost day to rest upon it forever. "The external miracles which glorified this day"—writes Msgr. Preston—"in the flames of fire, the rushing, mighty wind, and the gift of tongues, were the signs of a divine power which the world had not known before. The church was formed by our Lord in all its essential framework, and stood ready to receive the supernal guest who was to quicken it and make it the dwelling of God. In this manner the Holy Spirit had never been in the world until this day. He had been one in the operations of the Father and Son. He had blessed the different ages and dispensations with His influence. He had been the unseen author of every good thought and work. All, the race of man had known of sanctity, came from the effusion of His gifts. Now He comes, by a special and personal presence, to complete the work of the Incarnate Son. It was necessary for the Son in our nature to atone for our transgressions, and in that nature to ascend to the throne on high, before the Holy Ghost could thus personally dwell on earth."

Because the Holy Ghost dwells in the Church as in a body, this Church is necessarily and intrinsically one, numerically *one*. Unity here is the intrinsic association of intelligence, will and organization, generated necessarily from within by the personal unity and operation of the Holy Ghost. The property of unity is not extrinsic, but intrinsic and essential. We call a plant, an animal body, an organism, one, not because all its single parts form as independent parts a whole, but because these parts have grown out of one principle, root, embrio, organism, and therefore are essentially one, quickened as they are by the same life-giving principle.

Without the indwelling Spirit the Church would be like any other organization of mere men, liable to constant change. She is, indeed, an organization of men, but not of *mere* men. Her members are bound to each other and to God by the presence and the power of the Almighty Spirit. Hence she must be one. Unity is life and disunion is death. Where the Spirit of life binds the whole structure together, there is of necessity the unity which flows from the fountain of all *oneness*. In this intrinsic and invisible unity the sacrificial prayer of our Lord is principally fulfilled: " That they may be one, as Thou, Father, in Me and I in Thee; that they may also be one in Us." (St. John XVIII, 21.) Of this essential unity to which we can trace as to their common source almost all other properties of the Church, Cardinal Manning again says in one of his lucid explanations:

" This extrinsic unity springs from the intrinsic—that is, from the presence and operations of the Holy Ghost, by whom the body is inhabited, animated, and organized. One principle of life cannot animate two bodies, or energies in two organizations. One mind and one will fuses and holds in the perfect unity the whole multitude of the faithful throughout all the world. The unity of Faith, Hope, and Charity—the unity of the one common Teacher—renders all discrepancies of belief and worship, and renders unity of communion, not a constitutional law or an external rule of discipline, but an intrinsic necessity and an inseparable property and expression of the internal and supernatural unity of the mystical body under one Head and animated by one Spirit. It is manifest, therefore, that division is impossible. The unity of Church refuses to be numbered in plurality. To talk of Roman, Greek, and Anglican Churches, is to deny the Articles: 'I believe in the Holy Ghost, the Holy Catholic Church,' and the Divine relation constituted between them. The relation is a Divine fact, and its enunciation is a Divine truth. St. Bede says, with a wonderful precision and depth : 'If every kingdom divided against itself is brought to desolation, for that reason the kingdom of the Father, Son, and Holy Ghost is not divided.'"

Because the Spirit dwells in the Church of Christ as the soul in the body, His Church is necessarily *indefectible* and *perpetual.* The Church is always the body of Christ and can never, therefore, loose its vital union with the Holy Ghost. This union is indissoluble, and like the union of the two natures in the one Christ, it cannot be sundered. Individual members may perish by separation from the body ; the Church can never decay, grow old or perish. As long as our soul is in the body, we stand erect, we move; no chemical dissolution can sunder the original unity of our system. So, likewise, no essential changes can pass over the Church; no attack of man can prevail against her; for by the life of God in her, she is emancipated from the law of decay. She is imperishable not only because our Lord promised that "the gates of hell would not prevail against her" (Matth. 18), but also by her very nature, since this promise of Christ is founded in the very nature with which He endowed His Church. She may and must suffer, for she is the Church of a Crucified God; she may become the subject of the world's attack; the battle around her may rage with its hell-stamped violence, but the end of time will find her the miracle which she has been since Christ breathed into her a divine soul. Her life is the miracle of the day and the proof that "God is in the midst thereof, and that she shall not be moved though the earth be troubled and the mountains be removed into the heart of the sea." (Gal. 45, 3-6.) And the indefectibility of life which we ascribe to the Church of Christ, and which her continuous existence for nineteen hundred years in the most adverse circumstances amply proves, can be the prerogative of no other than the Roman Catholic Church. To this, her striking evidence of the indwelling Spirit, our Cardinal calls the world's attention, in his last little book, a real gem of apologetical literature, "Religio Viatoris" page 69:

"Where are now the heresies of the East, the Docetæ, the Arians, the Monophysites, the Monothelites, the Eutychians? They either ceased to be or the world has forgotten them. Where are the heresies of the West, the Montanists, the Novatians, the Palagians, the Sacramentarians? In a little while where will be Lutherans, Zwinglians, Calvinists? 'Every plant that my Heavenly Father hath not planted shall be rooted up.' But the mystical Vine abides forever. This one Church founded by our Redeemer, spread into all nations by the Apostles, interpenetrating and uniting all, refusing all nationality, but lifting all nations into a supernatural unity which is indissoluble even when all other bonds of this world are broken and even when the nations are in mutual warfare; this, one universal empire, self-evident as the light, speaking to the eye by its visible presence and to the ear by its living and articulate voice; this is a fact not to be denied, for a city seated on a hill cannot be hid. It is a phenomenon like the

Sun, the Light of the world, an Epiphany, the witness of God manifest in the Flesh."

Because the Spirit of God dwells in the Church as the soul in the body, the Church is intrinsically and absolutely *holy.* The Church lives the life of God, and hence she is holy by this indissoluble union. As the soul informs the body and gives it vitality, so the quickening Spirit vitalizes the Church and fills it with His divine energy. The body animated by the Spirit is "built upon the foundation of apostles and prophets, Jesus Christ Himself being the chief corner-stone, in whom all the building, being framed together, groweth up into a holy temple in the Lord." (Ephes. I, 20–21.) "The Spirit of the Lord rested," according to the Prophet Isaias (XI, 2–3) "upon Christ, even as man, as the second Adam, as the first born of the new generation," and according to St. Peter, "God had anointed Jesus of Nazareth with the Holy Ghost and with power." (Act. X, 38.) From this anointed Head the unction of the Spirit naturally and necessarily flows to the members, and is diffused over the entire body. So the Holy Ghost works unceasingly "for the edifying of the body of Christ, until we all meet in the unity of faith, and of the knowledge of the Son of God, unto a perfect Man, unto the measure of the age of the fulness of Christ." (Ephes. IV, 12–13.).

Because the Holy Ghost dwells in the Church as the soul in the body, she is intrinsically and necessarily and eternally *infallible*. As grace, so flows truth from the Head to the member. As the Church is indefectible, because of her absolute union with the Holy Ghost, for the same reason she is also infallible. Infallibility is only indefectibility with regard to faith and doctrine. What, therefore, is true of the Church of God with reference to her freedom from sin and imperfection, is also true of her with regard to the exclusion of error in teaching and believing. The Church of God cannot err. The body animated by the "Spirit of truth" cannot be liable to delusion and deception. The Church consequently is infallible, not so much because this infallibility is promised to her externally, as because it is promised to her and proclaimed to her, for the reason that she was intended to be the Body of Christ and the voice of His indwelling Spirit. Christ communicated life to His Church to the end that she might carry to completion His work and make known His gospel to succeeding generations. As the incorruptible body of Christ, and the dwelling of the eternal

Spirit, the Church must possess a supernatural knowledge of the truth (infallibilitas passiva) and the power to teach, without the possibility of error. The indwelling Holy Spirit, consequently, imparts to the Church inerrability in receiving divine revelation, infallibility in teaching it, and supernatural unction in imparting it. In these three departments the Church acts as the organ of the Spirit, of whom Christ promised: "When the Paraclete cometh, whom I will send you from the Father, He shall give testimony of Me. When He, the Spirit of truth is come, He will teach you all truth" (St. John XV, 26.) As, then, the Holy Ghost leads the Church into all truth, so does He, likewise, speak through her. There is a mystery in the indwelling of the Holy Ghost in the Church, but there is no mystery in the infallibility of the Church which He vivifies, because, His indwelling supposed, He must be infallible. As, when man speaketh, it is the soul which speaks, though the words are those of a human voice, so it is the Holy Ghost who speaketh by the voice of the Church and her voice is, therefore, that of God, with all the energy and unction of Divinity. Of this possession of divine truth by the Church, as a body, sacred Writ says: "You have the unction from the Holy One, and know all things. You have no need that any man teach you : but as His unction teaches you of all things, and it is truth." (I. S. John II, 20) It is of the utmost importance that we be fully conscious both of this Infallibility of the Church, taken as an organic whole, as the mystical body of Christ, and of the real source of it, the indwelling Spirit of truth. It is because this consciousness was obscured in many christian minds, that so large a number of so-called Catholics was shocked and troubled at the last definitions of the Church in the Council at the Vatican. We have not yet spoken of the different organs of the teaching Church, but whatever we say of them or ascribe to them in authority and Infallibity is reduced to this Infallibility of the Church as a body and the voice of the Holy Ghost.

From this same union of the Church with the Holy Ghost, not only flow the properties, visibility, unity, indefectibility, infallibility, but also the *four Notes* of the Church, as Theologians commonly call them : *Unity, Sanctity, Catholicity* and *Apostolicity.* By these notes the Church is distinguished from all counterfeits, ánd characterized as the true Church, as the " city seated on the mountain, that cannot be hid." (Matth. V, 14.) As notes they strike the eye of the world, because they lie on the surface: as properties they are the ultimate motives for our submission to the Church of God. *Unity*, taken as a note, is the external manifestation of the intrinsic and divine unity, already spoken of; and it involves unity of profession, unity of worship and constitution and above all its creating and sustaining principle—authority. In the present state of Christianity, does not the Unity of the true Church appear the more luminous, the darker the night of dissension and dissolution, outside her pale?

Sanctity as a note is the consequence of the intrinsic Sanctity imparted to the Church by the indwelling Sanctifier. It comprehends the sanctity of doctrine, the sanctity of the means of salvation, the sanctity of the great number of its members, and of the continuous inhabitation of extraordinary graces, gifts, wonders in the Church. Is not the true Church of Christ in our days shining forth in this her sanctity of doctrine, worship and life as the Spouse of Christ described by the Apostle: "Christ loved His Church and delivered Himself up for it, that He might sanctify it, cleansing it by the water in the word of life, that He might present it to Himself a glorious Church, not having spot or wrinkle, or any such thing, but that it should be holy and without blemish." (Ephes. V, 25.)

Catholicity, as a note, is a necessary consequence of the intrinsic oneness of the
Church. Being one and still destined to
save all times and generations, the Church
must essentially be universal as to time,
places and peoples. The Christian Church,
unlike the synagogue, not passing the
bounds of national unity, cannot be bound
by laws of race or nation. By its own vitality it passes from land to land, and there
is no limit to the prolific energy of the Holy
Ghost. It is for all time the City of God,
illumined by the divine presence of the
Holy Ghost. No body or congregation of
men which has not this universality can lay
claim to the participation of the gift of Pentecost. And the fact is wonderful, that no
heretical sect has been able to keep the
name "Catholic," or show the least right to
this title, or wrest it from that Church
which is in name and in fact the Holy
Catholic Church.

So also is *Apostolicity* as a note the mere
and absolute consequence of the intrinsic
unity of the Church. Apostolicity means
conformity to the original Church in doctrine, worship, and especially in the legitimate succession of the true pastors. What
our Lord has instituted in the twelve Apostles, as the patriarchs of the new law, must

continue, for His promises were not made to them as mortal men who could not continue Christ's work " even to the consummation of the world," but to the immortal Apostolate in their legitimate successors. Now there is no succession, in the full sense of the term, outside of the Catholic Church. Where due obedience and submission to the supreme Pastor, in whom the unity of the Apostolate is rooted, has ever been refused, there can be a succession of intruders and hirelings, but not of pastors and Apostolic ministers. This identity, however, of the Church and its perfect conformity with its original can only be brought about and preserved by the identity of the same Divine Spirit, dwelling in the Church, as in the mystical body of Christ.

ASPIRATION.

O God. the Holy Ghost, Thou art the living soul of God's Holy Church and in Thee alone, dwelling in the Church, as in a living tabernacle, the great mystery of the Church of Christ, is intelligible and its wonderful manifestations explicable. In this light, make me always. O Spirit of truth, behold and understand Holy Church. Give me the heavenly revelation of the Father, so that, what flesh and blood do not reveal, I may know and believe of Holy Church, taught by a higher illumination. O Spirit of God, illumining His temple on earth, let the rays of holiness and universality also be reflected on my soul, and make me a faithful and holy member of the One, Holy, Catholic and Apostolic Church!   Amen.

INTENTION OF PRAYER:

Pray for the conversion of the Heretics.   "*A city seated on a mountain top cannot be hid.   Neither do men light a candle and put it under a bushel, but upon a candlestick, that it may shine to all that are in the house.*" (Matth. V, 15.)

13.

The Holy Ghost and the Authority in the Church of God.

The idea of a body also involves the notion of a multiplicity, variety and *inequality* of members. From the doctrine of the gospel, it is evident that our Lord instituted the Church not as a society of equals in authority and ministry, but that he instituted the inequality of superiors and inferiors, of pastor and flock, of teachers and disciples, of supreme, higher, and inferior pastors and ministers. To this inequality and, therefore, variety of ministries, offices and authority, the Apostle alludes whenever he refers to the one divine Authority and its unequal manifestations in the various offices of the Church, as for instance, saying: "God hath tempered the body together, giving to that which wanted, the more abundant honour, that there might be no schism in the body, but the members might be mutually careful one for another. Now you are the body of Christ, and members of member. And God, indeed, hath set some in the Church, first Apostles, secondly Prophets, thirdly Doctors, after that miracles, then the graces of healing, helps, governments, kinds of tongues, interpretations of speeches. Are all Apostles? Are all Prophets? Are all Doctors? "(I Cor. XII, 25–29.)

Now, whatever authority is in the Church and whatever authority the superior organs of the Church enjoy, flows directly to them from the Holy Ghost, the principle of life in the Church of Christ. The words of St. Paul to the clergy of Ephesus: "Take heed to yourselves and to the whole flock, wherein the Holy Ghost has placed you bishops, to rule the Church of God, which he hath purchased with his own blood" (Act. XX, 28), principally refer to the bishops; still they do not exclusively refer to them. They in general assert, that the regime and authority of the superiors of the Church are not of human, but of divine origin—of the Holy Ghost. Opposition, therefore to and rebellion against this authority is a declared sin and crime against the Father and the Son, Scripture stating: "He that despiseth You, despiseth Me, and he that despiseth Me, despiseth Him that sent Me." (S. Luke X, 16.) It is also described a sa direct sin against the Holy Ghost" as when St. Peter reproached Ananias with having "been tempted by Satan to lie to the Holy Ghost." (Act. V, 3.) Now the authority of teaching in the Church is only a part, but chronologically the first, and necessarily the most important part of her Authority in general. First is the preaching and the creation of faith. Then follows the authority to rule and to feed the flock of the faithful. We wish to speak here merely of the authority to teach in the name, with the power, and with the unction of Christ and His Spirit.

That the Church is authorized and even obliged to preach the revelation of Christ, as fully given in the Spirit of Pentecost, is evident both from her mission, to carry on the work of Christ and from His own command: "Going, therefore, teach all nations .. teaching them to observe all things whatsoever I have commanded you: and behold, I am with you all days, even to the consummation of the world." (Matth. XXVII. 20.) That the Church, thus invested with the authority of Christ, to teach all nations, to preserve, explain, proclaim, and defend the deposit of revelation, must be free from the possibility of erring in performing this duty and consequently infallible, is again evident both from the impossibility of carry-

ing out Christ's commission without this
Infallibility and from the promise of the
Spirit of truth, to lead the Apostles into all
truth.   It is beyond all question, that the
Church, teaching mankind is, ever was, and
ever will be infallible, because she is the
voice of the indwelling Holy Ghost.   But
here we only wish to state, when and through
what organs the Church speaks as the voice
of the Holy Ghost.

There is a latent, universal, most mystical
Infallibility in the Church, in virtue of
which whatever has been held and believed
by all, at all times, in all places, must be
true and of Divine revelation.   The inhabitation of the Holy Ghost prevents the
possibility of universal error or intellectual
decay in the mystical body of Christ.   There
is the active Infallibility of the teaching
Church of God, given to the entire Apostolic body of the Episcopacy in union with
its divinely constituted Head.   Whenever
the Episcopate in union with its visible
Head speaks of Divine Revelation, we hear
the voice of the immortal Apostolate; the
Church speaks as Christ's mystical body,
and the promises of Christ given to this
Church take effect.   The Apostolic College
continues in the Episcopate, taken as a whole,
in union with the successor of St. Peter.

The promises of Christ, given to His Church, do not refer to the number, majority or minority of bishops, their learning or worldly position, but to the Apostolic body, which is exclusively to be found where the bishops form one legitimate organization, and consequently are in union with Peter. It is always a manifest sign, that the consciousness of the last source of authority and infallibility of the indwelling Spirit, is obscured in the mind of men, when they attach undue importance to those nearly secondary and human motives that add to the authority of the Church, as for instance, the number of Prelates, their learning and science, their overwhelming majority and so forth.

Finally there is the active Infallibility given to the Head of the Church, in the promise made to St. Peter and his successors, and preserving from error the Vicar of Christ, when he, in his supreme office, using his full authority, teaches the universal Church, what to believe and hold about the deposit of revelation. The inhabitation of the Holy Ghost and the organic Constitution of the Church once admitted, this Infallibility of the Vicar of Christ is a necessary consequence. We can not refrain from giving here the full text of Cardinal Manning's splendid passage on this prerogative of St. Peter and his successors as the Head of the universal Church. He says: "St. Augustine argues as follows of the Head and the body: 'Therefore as the soul animates and quickens our whole body, but perceives in the head by the action of life, by hearing, by smelling, by taste, and by touch, in the other members by touch alone (for all are subject to the head in the operation, the head being placed above them for their guidance, since the head bears the personality of the soul itself, which guides the body, for there all the senses are manifested), so the whole people of the saints, as of one body, the man Christ Jesus, the Mediator between God and man, is Head."

" Now the Pontiffs, as Vicars of Jesus Christ, have a twofold relation, the one to the Divine Head of the Church of whom they are repesentatives on earth, the other to the whole body. And these two relations impart a special prerogative of grace to him that bears them. The endowments of the head, as St. Augustine argues, are in behalf of the body. It is a small thing to say that the endowments of the body are the prerogatives of the head. The Vicar of Jesus Christ would bear no proportion to the body if, while it is infallible, He were not. He would bear also no representative character if He were the fallible witness of an infallible Head. Though the analogy observed by St. Augustine between the head and members cannot strictly apply to the Vicar of Christ and the members upon earth, nevertheless, it invests him with a pre-eminence of guidance and direction over the whole body, which can neither be possessed by any other member of the body, nor by the whole body without him, and yet attaches to him personally and alone as representing to the body the prerogatives of its Divine Head."

Let us conclude this Chapter with a longer quotation from the "Controversies" of St. Francis of Sales. This matchless defender of truth and lately declared Doctor of the universal Church spoke in his days of the Pontifical Infallibility in such unmistakable terms, that, when at the time of the Vatican Council, the true reading of the following passages was discovered in the Archives of palace Chigi at Rome ; these statements of the great Saint led, according to the Bull of Doctorate, many of the Fathers " as by the hand " to subscribe to the definition of Papal Infallibility. We quote from the English translation of the works of the Saint by Rev. B. Mackey, O. S. B. (London 1886.)

The first passage is found in the "Controversies," Part II., Art. VI., Chap. XII., and reads thus : " So when St. Peter was placed as foundation of the Church, and the Church certified that the gates of hell should not prevail against it, was it not enough to say that St. Peter, as foundation-stone of the ecclesiastical government and administration, could not be crushed and broken by infidelity and error, which is the principal gate of hell? For who knows not that if the foundation be overthrown, if that can be sapped, the whole building falls. In the same way, if the supreme acting shepherd can conduct his sheep into venomous pastures, it is clearly visible that the flock is soon to be lost. For if the supreme acting shepherd leads out of the path, who will put him right? If he stray, who will bring him back ? "

" In truth, it is necessary that we should follow him simply, not guide him; otherwise the sheep would be shepherds. And, indeed, the Church cannot always be united in the General Council, and during the first three centuries none were held. In the difficulties then which daily arise, to whom could one better address oneself, from whom could one take a safer law, a surer rule, than from the general head, and from the vicar of Our Lord? Now all this has not only been true of St. Peter, but also of his successors; for the cause remaining, the effect remains likewise. The Church has always need of an infallible confirmer, to whom she can appeal; of a foundation which the gates of hell, and principally error, cannot overthrow; and has always need that her pastor should be unable to lead her children into error. The successors, then, of St. Peter all have these same privileges, which do not follow the person, but the dignity and public charge."

The second passage is found in Chapt. XIV, and reads: "Theologians have said, in a work, that he can err in questions of fact, not in questions of right; that he can err *extra cathedram*, outside the chair of Peter, that is, as a private individual, by writings and bad example.

But he cannot err when he is *in cathedra*, that is, when he intends to make an instruction and decree for the guidance of the whole Church, when he means to confirm his brethren as supreme pastor, and to conduct them into the pastures of faith. For then it is not so much man who determines, resolves, and defines, as it is the Blessed Holy Spirit by man, which Spirit, according, to the promise made by Our Lord to the Apostles, teaches all truth to the Church, and, as the Greek says and the Church seems to understand in a collect of Pentecost, conducts and directs His Church into all truths: *But when that Spirit of truth shall come, He will teach you all truth,* or, *will lead you into all truth.* And how does the Holy Spirit lead the Church except by the ministry and office of preachers and pastors? But if the pastors have pastors, they must follow them, and all must follow him who is the supreme pastor, by whose ministry Our God wills to lead not only the lambs and little sheep, but the sheep and mothers of lambs; that is, not the people only, but also the other pastors; he succeeds St. Peter, who received this charge: *Feed my sheep.* Thus it is, that God leads His Church into the pastures of His Holy Word, and in exposition of this he who seeks the truth, under other leading loses it. The Holy Spirit is the leader of the Churches, He leads it by its pastor; he therefore, who follows not the pastor, follows not the Holy Spirit.

But the great Cardinal of Toledo, remarks most appositely on this place that it is not said *He shall carry the Church into all* truth, but *He shall lead;* to show that though the Holy Spirit enlightens the Church, He wills at the same time that she should use the diligence, which is required for keeping the true way, as the Apostles did, who, having to give an answer to an important question, debated, comparing the Holy Scriptures together; and when they had diligently done this they concluded by the phrase: *It hath seemed good to the Holy Spirit and to us;* that is, the Holy Spirit has enlightened us and we have walked, He has guided us and we have followed Him, up to this truth. The ordinary means must be employed to discover the truth, and yet in this must be acknowledged the drawing and presence of the Holy Spirit. Thus, is the Christian flock led,—by the Holy Spirit but under the charge and guidance of its Pastor, who, however, does not walk at hazard, but according to necessity convokes the other pastors, either partially or universally; carefully regards the track of his predecessors; considers the *Urim* and *Thummim* of the Word of God; enters before his God by his prayers and invocations, and, having thus diligently sought out the true way, boldly puts himself on his voyage and courageously sets sail. Happy the man who follows him and puts himself under the discipline of his crook! Happy the man who embarks in his boat, for he shall feed on truth, and shall arrive at the port of holy doctrine!

Thus he never gives a general command to the whole Church in necessary things except with the assistance of the Holy Spirit, who, as He is not wanting in necessary things even to second causes, because He has established them, will not be more wanting to Christianity in what is necessary for its life and perfection. And how would the Church be one and holy, as the Scriptures and Creeds describe her?—for if she followed a pastor, and the pastor erred, how would she be holy? if she followed him not, how would she be one? And what confusion in Christendom, if one party should consider a law good, and another deem it bad, and if sheep, instead of feeding and fattening in the pasture of Scripture and the Holy Word, occupy themselves in controlling the decision of their superior?

It remains, therefore, that according to Divine Providence we consider as closed that which St. Peter shall close with his keys, and as open that which he shall open, when seated in his chair of doctrine teaching the whole Church.

ASPIRATION.

O God the Holy Ghost, Who hast spoken through the Prophets of old and now, though in a different way, speakest to us in the voice of Holy Church, make me an obedient and faithful child of this Church, ever illumined by Thy light, ever guided by Thy hand, ever preserved from error by

Thy indwelling Presence! Built upon this rock of the Church, I shall myself be firm as a rock. Clinging to the chair of Peter, my faith shall not fail. Sailing in the bark of Peter, I have no reason to fear shipwreck and can confidently hope to reach the harbor of a happy eternity. O Spirit of Truth, keep me always in the spirit of filial love and submission to Holy Church. Amen.

INTENTION OF PRAYER:

Pray for the grace of an unreserved and filial submission to all the teachings and doctrines of Holy Church and especially of the Holy See. " *I have prayed for thee, (Simon) that thy faith should not fail; and thou being once converted, confirm thy brethern.*" (Luke. XXII, 32.)

14.

The Holy Ghost and the Fountains of Revelation.

The Holy Ghost has not been given to the Church to supersede by His teaching and His Assistance, the Revelation given by Jesus Christ and His Apostles, but to continue and complete the work of the Redeemer. The Revelation of the new law was objectively completed by the Holy Ghost coming and resting upon the Apostles, and all the working of the same Holy Spirit in and through the Church is reduced to an ever increasing and ever more perfect introduction into and pronunciation of all truth. The word of God, or Divine Revelation, as given by the Son of God and completed by the Holy Ghost, has partly been written by the inspired writers of both testaments, and has been partly stored up in the "depositum" of faith, as handed down from age to age in the oral Tradition of the Church. *Scripture* and *Tradition* are not so much *two* fountains of truth revealed, as *one*, the waters of which can be distinguished, but actually not separated. From the Day of Pentecost the Holy Spirit has been moving and brooding upon these waters of salvation, always keeping them alive, pure, lucid, by His sanctifying power, as they flow into life everlasting in the souls of the just. Scripture and Tradition form together the "stream of the river that maketh the city of God joyful." (Ps. 45, 5.) The Psalmist continues: "The Most High has sanctified His tabernacle. God is in the midst thereof." (V. 6.) God the Holy Ghost is indeed in the midst thereof, so that Scripture and Tradition are only divine, pure from human ingredients, waters of salvation, when they flow through the City of God, the Channel of all Revealed Truth, the Earthly Home of the Holy Ghost, God's Holy Church.

It is of vital interest to bear this in mind continually, all the more as since the time of the so called Reformation men have tried to bring about an opposition between the word of Scripture and the word of the Church. It is equally important to be fully aware of the truth that the same authority must be ascribed to the written and to the oral word of God, Scripture and Tradition, all the more, as again since the time of the so called Reformation men have been taught to look upon Scripture as the exclusive Divine Revelation, and upon Tradition as a human addition or adulteration of the Word of God. Both are fountains of divine truth; rather they are one stream of revelation, since on the unwritten as well as the written word of God the Spirit of truth equally moves.

Scripture has always been looked upon as God's own handwriting, the inspired text, the word of God par excellence. "Prophesy" says St. Peter, "came not by the will of men at any time: but the holy men of God spoke, inspired by the Holy Ghost." (II Peter I, 21.) St. Paul speaks of "Scripture inspired of God." (II Tim. III, 16.) Our Lord Himself, alluding to Holy Writ of the Old Law, speaks of it as of the word of the Holy Spirit, saying: "How then, doth David in Spirit call him Lord?" (Matth. XXII, 43.) Not only to God, but principally to God the Holy Ghost, the inspiration of Scripture is ascribed and appropriated. He, who has breathed upon the Apostles inspired also their words and writings. Hence the solemn declaration of the Council of the Vatican, summing up all the statements of preceding traditions referring to Scripture: "The books written by the inspiration of the Holy Ghost have God as their author." (Sess. IV, Decr. de Can. Script.)

And still what could Scripture be to us without the voice of the Holy Ghost in the Church? It is the Holy Ghost speaking through the Church, who alone makes us certain about the existence, the integrity, the inspiration of Holy Writ. Hence the saying of St. Augustine that he would not believe the Scripture unless the Church taught him to do so. It is the Holy Ghost speaking in and through the Church, who was speaking to mankind and to the faithful before any written records of the New Testament existed, and who must yet complete the incompleteness of the Scripture. "It was not till faith had been everywhere preached, believed, defined, recorded in the mind of the universal Church, embodied in sacraments, and manifested in its perpetual worship, that the New Testament was formed. By the inspiration and impulse of the same Divine Teacher who had already revealed the whole Truth to the Apostles, it was for the most part put in writing. I may say for the most part, because the written Scripture is not co-extensive with the Revelation of Pentecost, nor with the preaching of the Apostles. The written Scripture presupposes and recognizes in those to whom it is addressed the knowledge of the whole Truth. It is to the Church, guided by the Spirit of God, what the writings and letters of a man are to his personal identity. They would recognize all, but record only a part; imply many things, and express only such things as fall within their scope."

It is the Holy Ghost speaking in and through the Church, who alone furnishes us the true interpretation and genuine sense of Scripture. "Understanding this first," writes St. Peter, "that no prophesy of Scripture is made by private interpretation." (II Petr. I, 20.) "Scripture is Holy Scripture only in the right sense of Holy Scripture. Just as a man's will is man's will no longer, if it be interpreted by those who come after him. If those who survive him, misinterpret the disposition of his property, they defeat his will, they defraud him of his intentions. So it is with the Holy Scriptures, when they are interpreted—God is defrauded of His will and testament, and His people are robbed." (Intern. Miss. p. 238.) "The endless contradictions and steady diminution of truth among those who go by the principle that Scripture apart from the interpretation of Holy Church is self-sufficient, proves abundantly, that this is not God's way of faith. Unless the divine Scripture be read with the light of Pentecost upon its page, there is no divine and unerring interpretation. For, there is no channel through which that light descends to us, but the one only true church of God. "From no other interpreter can we learn the true meaning of Holy Scripture. Through no channel, but the Church alone can we receive the perfect material of faith—that is, the whole revelation of Jesus Christ. A fragmentary Christianity may be put together by texts of Scripture truly understood; but the whole revelation of Pentecost can be known only and through the Church. A correct interpretation of many parts of Holy Scripture may be attained without the guidance of the Church, but a divine certainty that such interpretations are correct, cannot be attained without it. The Church received the interpretation of the Book before the Book was written; for it had the whole revelation in custody before the Scriptures were committed to its charge. It is the sole witness and guardian, both of the meaning and of the Book, and it is itself both the interpreter and the interpretation; present, visible, and perpetual."

And so it is apparent that the living voice of the Holy Ghost in the Church is both antecedent and concomitant completing the word of Scripture. Thus the written word of God is bound up with and mystically united to Divine Tradition. "The New Testament is a living Scripture : it is the Church itself, animated by the Spirit of God, the author and writer of all Divine Truth. He is the *Digitus Paternæ Dexteræ*, the finger of God's right hand, by whom the whole revelation of the New Law is written, not on parchment, but on the living tables of the heart. St. Irenæus, the disciple of Polycarp, who in turn was the disciple of St. John, writing fifty years after the death of the last Apostle, asks: 'What if the Apostles had left us no writings, would it not have been needful to follow the order of that tradition which they delivered to those to whom they committed the churches?' to which many of the barbarous nations who believe in Christ assent, having salvation written without paper and ink, by the Spirit in their hearts, sedulously guarding the old tradition." (Card. Manning, Temp. Miss. p. 179.) The sum of Christian Tradition, therefore, the unanimous belief of the Christian people, the constant doctrine of the great Doctors of Holy Church, the succeeding declarations and definitions of the Church herself,—all these form the treasure of Divine Tradition, preserved pure, interpreted authentically, explained with infallible truth by the voice of the Holy Spirit speaking in and through the Church. And as it is sinful to appeal against the interpretation of Scripture by the Church to human criticism, so is it equally a sin against the Holy Spirit, to appeal from the voice of the teaching Church to antiquity, history, human tradition. "The history of the Church," says Cardinal Manning, "is the Church itself; its world-wide circumference guarded by the universal Episcopate, and its center the fountain of supreme authority; its unbroken succession of Bishops in all nations; its lineal inheritance of the Primacy of the chief of the Apostles; its nineteen Oecumenical Councils: all these things are history, historical documents, testimonies, records and living witnesses. To quote human and uninspired texts against the voice and witness of the universal Church, is no sign of common sense. The scientific historian reads the history of the Catholic Church in one sense, the Catholic Church reads its own history in another. Choose which you will believe."

"To those who do not believe the Church to be a moral "person" endowed with a divine life and light, with a continuous intelligence and an unfailing memory, these words of St. Paul may have no meaning.

To those who believe that the mystical body of Christ has a living and perpetual consciousness of its own divine endowments, of the deposit of the Faith committed to its custody, of its conflicts with error, of its definitions of truth, of the history of its own doctrines,—to such the meaning of these words is that the Church knows itself by an internal and supernatural light. Each man has a consciousness of his personal identity, against which no other man can argue. But his personal identity contains in itself the memory and knowledge on his part in all the fulness of his manifold experience both of internal habits and acts, and of external events and history. And each man alone for himself holds the key of interpretation, and is the sole interpreter. In like manner, no critic or interpreter external to the living consciousness of the Church can prescribe its teaching or revise its judgments."

ASPIRATION.

O God the Holy Ghost, who hast inspired the holy men, spoken to the Prophets and revealed the truths of salvation to the Holy Apostles, infuse into my soul a great love and veneration for the Holy Scriptures. Holy Writ is Thy own hand writing. Holy Scripture is, indeed, the book of books, God's book. "All Scripture inspired of God is profitable to teach, to reprove, to correct, to instruct in justice." (II Tim. III,'16.) Make me obey the Apostle's admonition: "Meditate upon those things, be wholly in these things." (1 Tim. IV, 15.) Give me, in meditating upon Thy inspired word, the unction from above to understand Thy voice and to obey Thy Aspirations. Amen.

INTENTION OF PRAYER.

Pray for the spirit of study and earnest application to all the duties of thy state. Pray moreover, for the love and veneration for Holy Scripture, the book of the Holy Ghost. " *Meditate upon these things, be wholly in these things; that thy profiting may be manifest to all.*" (1 Tim. IV, 15.)

15.

The Holy Ghost and Separation from the Church of Christ.

All that has hitherto been said, has been to show the absolute union, that exists between the visible Church, the mystical body of Christ and the Holy Ghost. "What God has joined together, let no man put asunder," (Matth. XIX. 6) may also be said of this union between the Church and the Holy Ghost. No human power, indeed, will ever divorce this mystical union, formed, and forever absolutely confirmed in the fire of the Pentecostal tongue. Still, man may in self-delusion attempt to destroy the work of God. Man, in rebellion against the authority set by the Holy Ghost to rule the Church of God, has indeed, divorced, not the Church and the Holy Ghost, but himself, his fellow-men, entire nations, particular churches from the one Church, instituted by Christ and sanctified by the indwelling Spirit. Running through ecclesiastical history there are to be found two offenses declared by the Christian law to be capital, or deadly: namely, *heresy* and *schism*, or in other words, the false liberty of opinion, in matters of religious belief, and the wilful separation from the public worship and Sacraments, that is from the external unity of the Church. Why are these offenses punished with excommunication or cutting off from Catholic unity? Why should this twofold use of human liberty be treated as a capital offense and held to be deadly? Why the Apostolic threatenings, even of the meekest of the Apostles, against the authors of schisms and heresies, for even St. John commands us "not to receive a heretic nor to say to him: God speed you." (II. John v. 10.) "No dissent from human teachers can be deadly: no separation from a human organization can by any means be worthy of anathema. Heresy and schism are deadly precisely for this reason: the Teacher from whom heresy dissents is divine; and the unity that schism breaks is also divine. Heresy resists the Divine Witness, the Holy Ghost, the Spirit of truth; and schism resists the Holy Ghost, the Charity of God incorporated in the body of Christ." (Card. Manning in "Religio Viatoris," p. 63.) The authors of any such separation directly sin against the Divine Witness in the Church, the Holy Ghost. Separation of both kinds began under the eyes of the Apostles. St. John writes: "They went out from us because they were not of us." (I. St. John II, 19) and St. Jude: "These be they that separate themselves—not having the Spirit." (St. Jud., v. 19.) The language of the Fathers against separation from the Church is most powerful and all the Fathers exclude from the participation of the Spirit, those who wilfully separate themselves from the Visible Church.

St. Augustine says: "See what ye have to beware of, to watch over and to fear. In the body of a man it may happen, that a member, the hand, the finger, or the foot, may be cut off. Does the soul follow the severed member? While it was in the body it was alive; cut off, its life is lost. So a man is a Christian and Catholic while he is alive in the body; cut off, he becomes a heretic. The Holy Ghost does not follow the amputated limb." (St. Aug. Serm. in die Pentecost. II, Tom. V, p. 1091.)

We have already quoted the saying of St. Gregory the Great: "This is that body out of which the Spirit quickeneth not; wherefore the blessed Augustine says: 'If thou wouldst live of the Spirit of Christ, be in the body of Christ.' Of this Spirit, the heretic does not live, nor the schismatic, nor the ex-communicated, for they are not of the body; but the Church hath a Spirit that giveth life, because it inheres inseparably to Christ its Head; for it is written: 'He that adhereth to the Lord is one spirit with him.'" (St. Gregory in Ps. Paenit. III, p. 511.)

Of course we do not contradict what we have already said about the Holy Spirit's grace over the whole earth. We know that all who are outside of the true and visible Church of God without their own fault can belong to the soul of this Church, and thus be sanctified by the Holy Ghost, whose operation is not limited by the boundaries even of the Universal Church. On one thing, however, we here desire to lay stress; namely, that if the act of separation from the body of Christ is an enormous crime, so also, indeed, is the sad condition of those separated from the union of the Church a great misfortune. We must never lose sight of this truth. We must ever strive to increase in ourselves a horror for heresy and schism. Tolerance and love towards our separated brethren must be accompanied with sentiments of pity, because of the great loss they have sustained and the dangers to which they are exposed. They may have the light of faith, but it is only a twilight showing them a fragmentary Christianity and not the full light of the day of Pentecost. Some of them may possess the grace of the Holy Spirit, but they are bereft of the manifold means to preserve, secure, increase and regain it, when lost by sin. Some of them may have the life of grace in themselves, but they have no participation in the plenitude of truth, life, grace and heavenly gifts, as it is secured in the one house upon which the Pentecost Spirit descended once and remained forever.

The authors of heresies and schisms have always taken some portion of truth from their father's house, when they left it; but like the prodigal of the gospel, they soon squandered it, their only substance. The Christian truth of a fragmentary Christianity, being no longer in conjunction with the whole truth or secured by the living testimony of the Church, soon disappears and dies away before the criticism of human reason. The light which the religious bodies, separated from the Church, seem yet to possess, is not a light of their own, nor comes it from within. It is the light of the illumined house of Pentecost, the true Church, shedding a dim reflex upon those mansions standing around in darkness and in shade. No one, who has not wandered through the desert of infidelity and heresy can fully realize the misfortune of those souls. No one, whose eyes have ever seen the daylight of Pentecost in the true Church, can sufficiently appreciate the blessings of such a condition. Truly, it must be a great difference to live directly under the illumining and warming rays of the Pentecostal sun, and to perceive only a remote, distant, fading glimpse of twilight.

ASPIRATION.

O God the Holy Ghost, author of unity and harmony, keep us always, we humbly beseech Thee, in the unity of the true Church, in the bond of peace. May we never sin against Thee, never commit the sin of those who having not the Spirit, separate themselves. We know " that it must needs be, that scandals come, but woe to that man by whom the scandal cometh." (Matth. XVIII, 6.) Have pity on them, that go astray ! Have mercy, O God of mercy, on those souls, tossed to and fro by every wind of doctrine. Draw to the true sheepfold the sheep of which our Lord said : " And other sheep I have, that are not of this fold ; them also I must bring, and they shall hear My voice and there shall be one fold and one shepherd." (St. John X, 16.) " Almighty and everlasting, God, who savest all and wilt have no man perish, look on the souls that are seduced by all the deceit of the devil; that the hearts of those who err, having laid aside all heretical malice, may repent and return to the unity of Thy truth." Amen. (Oration on good Friday.)

INTENTION OF PRAYER:

Pray for the conversion of all schismatics, especially for the return to the union of the Roman Church of the Orientals and Greeks who persistently deny the Holy Ghost both from Father and Son. "*And other sheep I have that are not of this fold; them also I must bring . . . and there shall be one fold and one shepherd.*" (St. John X, 16.)

16.

The Holy Ghost and the Sanctification of Individuals.

The mission of the Holy Ghost to and the operation of the Holy Ghost in the Church have but one principal end—the *sanctification of individuals.* The mystical relation that exists between the Holy Spirit and the Church of Christ, in an analogous sense also obtains between the Holy Ghost and the individual soul of the Christian. Touching now upon this mystical relation of the Spirit, the Sanctifier to individual souls, we abstain from enlarging here on the more extraordinary ways in which the Author of all Graces is working even outside of the pale of the true Church, and drawing souls from the shadows of death into the kingdom of light. We have already dwelt on this most important truth : "God's grace over all the earth" in the fourth chapter of this part. Divine mercy is above all the works of God, nor can even the boundary lines of God's visible Church on earth

limit or circumscribe the operation of the
Spirit that breathes unto the salvation of all
for whom Christ has died. Not speaking,
therefore, of the extraordinary ways in which
a most merciful Lord deals with those who
without their own fault do not yet see the
"City on the Mountain Top," we can here
only say a few words on the mystical relation of the Holy Ghost to those who, born
again of water and the Holy Ghost by holy
baptism in Christ's true Church, partake in
the fullest sense of the Spirit's sanctifying
power.

"In one Spirit were we all baptized," says
Holy Writ, "into one body; and in one
Spirit have we all been made to drink."
(I. Cor. XII, 11–13.) "The Church of
which Christ is the head, is His body, and
the fulness of Him, who is filled all in all."
(Ephes. I, 22.) "In Him dwelleth all the
fulness of the Godhead corporally: and you
are filled in Him, who is the head of all
principality and power. Buried with Him
in baptism, in whom also you are risen again
by faith of the operation of God." (Ephes. V,
23–30.) These passages of Holy Scripture
confine the gifts of redeeming grace according to the ordinary economy of salvation, to the union with the body of which
Christ is the Head, whence pardon and life

flow.   In this body the Spirit dwells and by His energy the fallen children of Adam are adopted into this body and by regeneration in baptism, put on Christ and joined to His life-giving humanity.   The Holy Ghost is the agent in this work. He is the worker of regeneration; as it is written : " That which is born of the flesh is flesh ; and that which is born of the Spirit is spirit.   Unless a man be born again of water and the Holy Ghost, he cannot enter into the kingdom of God." (St. John III, 5–6.) The operation of the Holy Ghost in the Church is in full accord with the organic life by which the body of Christ is constituted. He is an invisible Spirit, yet by the fact of His inhabitation in an organization of men, to which by His presence He gives supernatural life, He has been pleased to use external signs as the certain means of communicating His graces. As the church itself is the external sign of His presence, or the great sacrament of unity with God, so all the graces by which we are quickened into a new life, are wrought by sacraments, the external signs of the quickening action of the Spirit or living soul of the Church. A brief glance at the sacramental system plainly taught in Holy Scripture will clearly set before us the manner in which the Holy Ghost imparts His life to individuals. We shall only touch the outlines of this argument as it stands in direct connection with our subject. The special relation, therefore, that exists even according to the sacred text, between the Holy Ghost and the Seven Sacraments of the new law, is too conspicuous to be overlooked.

The *Sacrament of Baptism* is the first touch of the Holy Ghost, whereby, with sanctifying grace He takes the fallen child of Adam and admits him into union with the body of Christ, and so with the sacred and life giving humanity of the Saviour, the second Adam. " In one Spirit we are all baptized into one body," and by baptism we are made " the body of Christ and members of member." (I Cor. XII, 13, 27). The Church is the corporate body of the baptized, who make a unity far above all human unities, by reason of the action of the Spirit. This appears still more clearly from the union which baptism gives to the Sacred Humanity of Christ.

"As many as have been baptized in Christ, have put on Christ, and are all one in Him." (Gal. III, 27.) Thus baptism is the new creation, or the new birth, according to the express words of our Lord : " Unless a man be born again of water and the Holy Ghost, he cannot see the Kingdom of God." (St. John, V, 26.) As the old creation presents us the waters of chaos in their darkness, with "the Spirit of God moving upon the face of the deep," so the new creation brings before our faith the waters of baptism filled with the quickening energy of the same Holy Ghost. The fruit of the first action of the Spirit was the material earth, with the race of man in form and soul like unto the eternal Trinity. The fruit of the second and mightier action, in the deeper action of rebel intelligence and disordered wills, is the opening of a "new heaven and a new earth" and the birth of a regenerated manhood, in which appears the face of the Word Incarnate, the Child of Mary, the unfallen Adam, the Lord from heaven." (Preston, Divine Paraclete, p. 137.)

The Sacrament of Confirmation, as well as baptism, imprints an everlasting character on the soul, being, as it were, a touch of the Spirit which can never be effaced. In this sacrament, which completes the new creation the Spirit comes with His sevenfold gifts to strenghten the new creature in his supernatural life, and to illumine his path with "the seven lamps which burn ever before the throne." (Apoc. V, 4.) Thus our supernatural life is fed by the streams which run eternally from the Sacred Humanity, and which are applied by the Holy Ghost, who in the Church is continually " taking the things of Christ " and making them ours. Of this sacrament the Holy Spirit says Himself: " Now He that confirmeth us with you in Christ, and that hath anointed us, is God: Who also hath sealed us, and given the pledge of the Spirit in our hearts." (II. Corinth. I, 22.)

The Sacrament of the Most Holy Eucharist is the central and grandest of all sacramental actions in the Church. Being at the same time sacrament and sacrifice, it holds the central place in the worship of the new law and like the sun among the stars reigns supreme in majesty and holiness. It not only conveys grace, but the Author of grace Himself, and not only unites the children of the fallen Adam to the living Humanity of the Word made flesh, but gives that very Humanity to us to be our food. Here the spiritual life of the Church is nourished by the flesh and blood of its Head. It is the merciful plan of God to feed the new born with this living bread, of which the manna from heaven was only a type. The Lord whose words are " spirit and life " (St. John VI. 64) has plainly told us that the new life imparted to the soul in the sacrament of regeneration must be nourished and fed by the sacrament of His flesh and blood: "Except you eat the flesh and drink the blood of the Son of man, you shall not have life in you. He that eateth My flesh and drinketh My blood hath everlasting life. As the living Father hath sent Me, and I live by the Father, so he that eateth Me, the same also shall live by Me." (St. John VI. 48–58.)   Here is the sacrament in which the supreme power of the Holy Ghost is shown, where the creating words of the God-Man, spoken by His priests in the power of the Spirit, change the bread and wine into the body and the blood of Jesus Christ.   Over this great sacrifice and sacrament the Holy Ghost presides, even as by his energy the sacred Humanity was first conceived in the womb of the Virgin.   When the priest implores His coming down upon the mystical oblation, in the words: "Come, O Almighty and Eternal God, the Sanctifier, and bless this sacrifice prepared for Thy Holy name," the outstretched wings of the Dove are above the altar, even as they were above Christ at the baptism of the Jordan.

The Sacrament of Penance is instituted to restore grace to those who after baptism have forfeited it. Thus life lost or weakened is restored from the same source and in the same sacramental way by which it first was imparted. This power of remission in the Church is the Holy Ghost's, for the word breathed on His Apostles saying: "Receive ye the Holy Ghost; whose sins you shall forgive, they are forgiven them." (St. John XI, 22.) The Holy Ghost must first bring about due disposition in the penitent by enlightening his mind to see the number and grievousness of his transgressions, by moving his heart to detest them, by drawing his soul near to God whom the sinner has deserted, and by helping him to receive this sacrament of mercy in order to obtain forgiveness and the kiss of peace. The Holy Ghost is the direct author of this internal supernatural and sin-destroying sorrow of heart which, an outgrowth of love, divine in its perfection, brings about reconciliation between God and man, even before His minister on earth has pronounced the words of absolution. It is, therefore, the fire of the Holy Ghost that melts the fetters of sin and prevents the eternal doom of misery whenever it meets proper dispositions. These dispositions are also the effects of the Holy Ghost's internal working in the soul of man; and the words of absolution, are the exercise of a power and faculty, bestowed upon Christ's ministers by the same Holy Ghost.

The Sacrament of Extreme Unction shows forth its close and most special relation to the Holy Ghost by its very rite and name: "unction." The Holy Ghost is "*Spiritalis unctio,*" or "unction from above." Whenever a sacred anointing is performed, it is always to signify and confer a special grace of the Holy Ghost. His consoling, strengthening, healing, enlightening and consecrating power is symbolized in the holy oil and sacred anointment. In this sacrament the sacred unction is applied to the departing Christian as the final and supernatural medicine. "When the battle of life approaches its end and the child of the new creation comes to the supreme moment, when he must answer for all the graces and gifts of the Holy Ghost to him in life, then the same loving hand, which 'sealed him for the day of redemption,' (Rom. VIII, 11) will meet him with power once more. Upon the chill waters of death the living Spirit moves and the marks of grace are renewed upon all the senses, that they may awake in the world of realities and 'the believing are signed with the Holy Spirit of promise.'" (Ephes. I, 13.)

The Sacrament of Holy Orders is emphatically the Sacrament of the Holy Ghost, in which He makes perpetual the ministerial priesthood of Christ on earth. In this sacrament Christ breaths the Holy Spirit upon His ministers, as He breathed It upon the Apostles. Hence the essential rite of Ordination, "laying on of hands," which signifies and effects the overshadowing of the Holy Ghost, and the solemn words: Receive the Holy Ghost, and the sacred unction of priest and bishop—all these prominent parts of this sacrament directly point to this relation of Holy Orders to the Spirit of God.

Lastly the Sacrament of Matrimony is the sacrament by which the Sanctifier heals the disorder of our fallen race and sanctifies domestic life, by raising it to a supernatural state: "This is a great sacrament but I speak in Christ and the Church." (Ephes. V, 32.) Its very greatness consists in the wonderful and mystical analogy that exists between Christ and His Church on one side, and the Christian husband and wife on the other. As the first relation was brought about and is preserved by the Holy Ghost, so ought to be the second. "As Christ has loved the Church and delivered Himself up for It, that He might sanctify It, cleansing It by the laver of water in the word of life, that He might present It to Himself a glorious Church, not having spot or wrinkle, or any such thing, but that It should be holy and without blemish, so also ought men to love their wives as their own bodies." (Ephes. V, 25–28.) In one word,—natural love, natural union, the source of natural life, must by the power of the Spirit in this sacrament be sanctified, and consecrated by the supernatural virtue that flows from every sacramental touch of the Holy Ghost.

Thus the sacramental operation of the Spirit reaches all stations and changes of life and social organization. In this view of the work of the Holy Ghost in the individual Christian, we behold the glories of a new creation, the redemption of our race to the life of Jesus Christ. " Our redemption is already wrought; the water and the blood have already flowed, and, with the eternal Spirit, are giving their testimony. They will never cease to speak on earth and their voice ascends before the throne, where it is mingled with the witness of Father, Son and Holy Ghost." (Preston, p. 145.)

ASPIRATION.

O God, the Holy Ghost, who didst not only descend on Pentecost day upon the Church of God, but hast also descended on me in the sacrament of regeneration and filled me with Thy graces and gifts, whenever I received the sacraments of Holy Church; perfect I beseech Thee, the work Thou hast begun in me. " Command Thy strength, O God; confirm, O God, what Thou hast wrought in us." (Ps. 65, 29.) Make me, O Spirit of the living God, appreciate the great, the inestimable happiness of being a child of Holy Church. O Church of the living God, bride of Christ, home of the Holy Ghost, how dear art Thou to me. Thou art the love of Christ's heart; Thou art the reward of His toil; Thou art made white in His blood; Thou art nourished by His flesh. Thou art now putting on Thy raiment clean and white, the sanctification of the saints. Amen.

INTENTION OF PRAYER:

Pray for all the members of Holy Church that they may prove in life what they really are by profession and name: *Christians*, the *anointed ones* of the Lord, the heritage and *people elect* of the Lord. "*The charity of God is poured forth in our hearts by the Holy Ghost who is given to us.*" (Rom. V, 5.)

17.

The Holy Ghost and His Gifts and fruits in the faithful soul.

Sacramental, that is external rites, are the ordinary means by which the sanctification of individuals is effected. Regeneration, justification, growth in holiness and perfection; in short, all transformations of the soul, if thus we may call them, are principally brought about by the application of Christ's grace through the instrumentality of His divinely instituted sacraments. The question now arises in what do regeneration, sanctification, growth in holiness exactly consist, or what are the gifts bestowed upon the christian soul by the Author of all supernatural gifts, God the Holy Ghost. The entire work of sanctification is, as we have said before, not exclusively, but in some sense principally the work of the Third Person of the Most Holy Trinity. If the wonderful works and the harmony of this visible universe call to our mind the omnipotence and wisdom of the Creator, and if the stupendous facts of Christ's redemption on the cross and the preservation and victory of His church in all the trials of this passing world reveal to us the might and mercy of the Saviour; the secret, mystical, yet not less admirable workings of divine grace in human souls bespeak to us the Sanctifier's most inscrutable sway and power in drawing the human soul near to God. Of course we know very little from revelation and experience of these hidden workings of God the Sanctifier. Such knowledge is reserved for the great day of final revelation.

When treating on the various gifts of God the Holy Ghost, books of devotion mention the seven gifts of the Holy Spirit. These seven "dona S. Spiritus" are of course, as their name indicates, the Holy Spirit's most special revelation in the soul of man; but by no means must we confine to them the entire working of the Holy Ghost in the Christian soul. The universal sphere of supernatural grace and sanctification, beginning with the very glimmer of the twilight that dawns upon the infidel soul and makes it turn towards the sun of all justice, and limited only by the fully developed grace, or "the light of glory" in those that by final perseverance have been confirmed in God's love—this boundless

sphere of supernatural grace is the Holy
Spirit's field of action. By substituting the
term "grace" for the action of the Holy
Spirit, we are, it seems to us, prone to forget
the Author of grace and consequently cannot be sufficiently thankful to our great Cardinal that in his admirable book, "The Internal Mission of God the Holy Ghost," he
has treated of supernatural grace in such a
way, as to cause us never to forget, from whom
it flows, whose action it is, to whom it must
be traced. In sketching the supernatural
workings of the Holy Spirit in individual
souls, be it by the instrumentality of sacraments or without them, we follow as a faithful disciple follows the master, the guidance
of our Cardinal. Turning to the life of
our souls, the Divine Guest within us, the
Paraclete in whose consolations we rejoice
we beg of Him to teach us how to speak of
His mighty work. The fruits of the Holy
Ghost in us who are the members of Christ's
Body, are as many and wonderful, as the
attributes of their source can convey to
created intelligences.

1. Analyzing now the various gifts of
Him, who is par excellence, *"Altissimi donum Dei"* we must first name *Himself, His
Divine Presence and Indwelling in the soul of the
just, the uncreated Charity of God.* It is an

article of faith, that the Holy Spirit in a most special way personally dwells in the souls of the just. Sanctifying grace by which we are just can be called both the condition and the consequence of His indwelling Holy Spirit from whose presence it is inseparable. "Grace is, as we have seen, the divine action of a Divine Person dwelling in us, and imparting holiness to us." (Card. Manning: The Holy Ghost, the Sanctifier, p. 57. Little books; IV.) If the Church be the temple of God by reason of the Holy Spirit's dwelling in Her, if it is by the agency of the Spirit that individual men are made members of the one body, then the members of the Church are likewise the tabernacles of the Holy Ghost. Scripture most explicitly teaches this personal indwelling of the Holy Ghost. "In one Spirit we are all baptized into one body, in whom we have all been made to drink." (I Cor. XII, 13.) Again, yet more decisively: "Know you not, that you are the temples of God and that the Spirit of God dwelleth in you? If any man violate the temple of God: him shall God destroy, for the temple of God is holy; which you are." (I Cor. III, 16–17.) "This indwelling of the Holy Ghost in the just is the glory of the new law and the peculiar fruit of the mission of the Paraclete on earth. The formal participation of the divine nature may be understood as an assimilation to God by grace infused, as the effect of the indwelling of the Spirit." (Preston, p. 155.) Thus our Lord declares that He will " send another Paraclete, that He may abide with us forever; the Spirit of truth, whom the world cannot receive, because it seeth Him not, nor knoweth Him. But you shall know Him, because *He shall abide with you and shall be in you."* (St. John, XIV, 16, 17.) This presence of the eternal Spirit is distinct from His gifts, as He is a Divine Person in Himself, and as the author is distinguished from the effects he produces. This abiding of God in us does not simply signify His presence, but a special relation and union of the divine being with our soul. As all the gifts of the natural order are contained in the natural life as their principle, so all the greater glories of the new and supernatural life are contained in the presence and personal action of the Holy Ghost.

2. Next to this personal indwelling of the Holy Ghost, or to charity uncreated, stands *charity created, sanctifying grace infused, the supernatural life.* Theologians, as a rule, speak first of this created grace by which we are made children of God, heirs of heaven,

coheirs of Christ and which is as inseparable
from the personal indwelling of the Holy
Ghost, as this indwelling is from grace
infused. Nevertheless, as our principal
care is to trace all gifts of the supernatural
order to their immediate Author and Source,
God the Holy Ghost, we set first in logical
order the Divine Person whose indwelling
diffuses light and life into the soul. "The
charity, whereby we love God and our neigh-
bors is the created grace, which is distinct
from Him, the uncreated Charity, although
flows from Him: 'The charity of God is
poured forth into our hearts by the Holy
Ghost, who is given to us.' As the sun
sheds abroad light, heat, fruitfulness, and
ripeness upon all things, and these qualities
are distinct from the sun which gives them,
so it is with the created and uncreated charity, which are in us so long as we abide in
Him." (Card. Manning, the Holy Ghost, the
Sanctifier, p. 56.) The justification of man
according to the council of Trent is therefore
far more than a mere remission of sin. It
is a true supernatural sanctification by the
infusion of what we call sanctifying grace.
This is the "communication of the Holy
Ghost" by which "we are illumined, by
which we tasted the heavenly gift, the good
word of God, and the powers of the world to

come, and were made partakers of the Holy
Spirit." (2 Cor. XIII, 13.—Hebr. VI, 4, 5.)
Every created thing in some sense partakes
of the divine being, as He is its exemplary
and efficient cause; and having its origin
from Him by creation, it is to that extent an
adumbration of His perfection. But the
revelation of Christ manifests to us a participation of God above all the dignity and
needs of things created. This participation
is a perfect assimilation to the divine nature
itself by sanctifying grace, which acts upon
the soul and as a supernatural quality transforms it. This is a formal "partaking of the
divine nature" by assimilation to it, and
also an intimate union with God Himself.
Deification, says Dionysius, is assimilation
and union with God as far as possible. A
more distinct declaration is given by St.
Paul when he says that as the face of Moses
was illumined by an uncreated splendor
from his converse with God, so we are transformed by the Holy Spirit into the divine
image. "We all, beholding the glory of the
Lord with open face, are transformed into
the same image, from glory to glory, as by
the Spirit of the Lord." (II Cor. III, 18.)
The faithful, therefore, and the just are partakers in the divine nature, not essentially,
nor personally, but accidentally in part,

and, in fact, substantially. Sanctifying grace is the gift of God infused into the soul, by which proximately, and in the highest degree, we partake of the divine nature. Grace is a thing so noble and sublime that it surpasses the nature of angels and men. This sanctifying grace first expels all mortal sin, just as light banishes darkness. Secondly, it renders a man acceptable to God, making him in the fullest sense of the word, a friend of God. Thirdly, it clothes the soul with sanctity and holiness according to Holy Writ: "Put on the new man, who according to God, is created in justice and holiness of truth." (Ephes. IV, 24.) Fourthly, it makes the just man a son and heir of God. "He has delivered us from the power of darkness, and has translated us into the Kingdom of the Son of His love." (Coloss. 1, 12.) Fifthly, grace is the principle and the cause of good works, making us fruitful trees unto eternal life. Sixthly, grace brings with it all theological and moral virtues and the seven gifts of the Holy Ghost.

3. It would lead us too far to enter now upon a detailed exposition of these further consequences of the indwelling Spirit. We omit what could be said on the *moral virtues* of prudence, justice, fortitude, temperance,

which as habits are infused into the soul together with divine grace. One word only on the supernatural habits of the so called *Theological virtues* and those which, par excellence, are called the Gifts, the Beatitudes and the Fruits of the Holy Spirit. A virtue is a habit. When the power is exercised by uniform and continuous acts, a habit is formed in us by nature. Now the so-called "Theological virtues" are habits and active principles not acquired by, but superadded to nature and infused by the Holy Ghost. These supernatural virtues of Faith, Hope and Charity are necessary to elevate the reason and the will to God as the object of supernatural bliss. *Faith*, then, gives to the intellect a supernatural principle and a supernatural light by which truths exceeding the order of nature, are seen and believed. *Hope* gives to the will a direction towards that supernatural object and to all possible means of attaining it. *Charity* gives a spiritual union by which the intellect and the will are changed and transformed into the likeness of that object of bliss. Faith, Hope and Charity, therefore, are habits which unite the intellect and the will with God, and for that reason they are called *theological*.

4. Now, the *Gifts of the Holy Ghost* though

often called virtues, are something more. It was said of our Redeemer by Isaias the prophet: "The Spirit of the Lord shall rest upon Him: the Spirit of wisdom and understanding, the Spirit of counsel and of fortitude, the Spirit of knowledge and of godliness. And He shall be filled with the Spirit of the fear of the Lord." (Isai. XI, 2. 3.) The parallel between the gifts of the Holy Spirit to the Sacred Humanity and His anointing of the mystical body, is plain and beautiful. Grace flows from the head to the members of the mystical body and the Holy Spirit works unceasingly "for the edifying of the body of Christ, until we all meet in the unity of faith, and of the knowledge of the Son of God, unto a perfect man, unto the measure of the age of the fulness of Christ." (Ephs. IV, 12. 13.) Here, then, we do not speak of those seven Gifts, emphatically called the Gifts of the Holy Spirit, as they are in the Head of the Church, nor as they are in the body of the Church, but as they are in every member of the Church, one by one. They are inseparably united to sanctifying grace and charity. They are seven habits or dispositions, implanted in the soul, permanently abiding in her and giving activity to the will, enabling it to elicit or to call forth certain spiritual acts. The seven

Gifts of the Holy Ghost elicit both from the three virtues of Faith, Hope and Charity, and from the three natural powers of reason, heart and will, the acts which unite the soul with God more intimately and therefore make it more perfect. They are powers enabling the soul to exercise with ease her natural or supernatural perfections; and they are Gifts of the Holy Ghost, because it is He who, by His presence in us, acts upon us. "Just as a harp is mute until a skilful player elicits the harmony which lies in the strings, so the soul of man, though containing the whole power of harmony with the will of God, does not manifest it of its own strength without the assistance of the 'Finger of God' which is the Holy Ghost, touching its faculties, powers and affections, both natural and supernatural." (Card. Manning. Internal Mission, p. 175.) We cannot at present treat more extensively of these Seven Gifts of the Spirit, for we feel compelled to reserve a fuller exposition of them for a future volume. St. Thomas of Aquinas, Saint Bonaventure, Dionysius the Carthusian have delivered to us excellent essays on this subject. No book, however, will with greater lucidity, unction and comprehensiveness bring home to our mind, all that can be said of these Seven Gifts and their inseparable union with the Giver, the Holy Spirit, than our Cardinal's admirable book, "The Internal Mission of the Holy Ghost."

5. *The Fruits of the Holy Ghost* are the acts which are produced by virtues and by the gifts of the Holy Ghost. They are called Fruits because they come from the substance and the sap of supernatural sanctity in the soul, and because they have in them a sweetness both for those who bear the fruits and for those who partake of them. St. Paul counts up twelve fruits which have three relations—to God, to our neighbor and to ourselves, saying: "The fruit of the Spirit is charity, joy, peace, patience, benignity, goodness, longanimity, mildness, faith, modesty, continency, chastity." (Gal. V, 22.)

6. *The Beatitudes* are eight perfections in which the virtues, gifts and fruits rise and terminate. They move and elevate the will to a higher and nearer approach to eternal beatitude, and in so doing they obtain a double reward. They give in this life a foretaste of the eternal beatitude and they insure the attainment of its fulness. In all these gifts of the Holy Spirit the justified soul is a new creature. All these gifts of the Spirit are infused into the soul by a di-

vine operation, and there they must abide, grow, develope and increase. The divine action of the Sanctifier is not only in the beginning of our supernatural life. By actual grace the Holy Spirit continues to act with us through every moment of our probation, aiding us, co-operating with us and giving us a constant increase of both habitual and actual grace as we use the grace we already have. The grace of charity may be increased all our life long from the first moment of reason to the last, if we live in charity and are faithful to its inspirations. It may grow from the least gleam of the smoking flax to the fire of the Seraphim, both by acquisition and new infusion. Charity, then, is the beginning of eternal bliss. Our share in the Beatific Vision will be according to our merit, and our merit will be according to the measure of sanctifying grace or charity; for the bliss of heaven is charity made perfect, and according to the measure of charity in this life will be the glory in the life to come. Such are the daily miracles which the Sanctifier works in the souls of men. His operation baffles all understanding and all calculation. His ministrations are hidden like the ministrations of nature, which though hidden to the eye of man ripen our corn and perfect in form and hue the wild flowers.

ASPIRATION.

O God, the Holy Ghost, who art the charity of the Father and Son, Thine "eyes are as a flame of fire and Thy fervor as the sun in its strength." Dilate my heart by the expansion of Thy love in me, that I may now, in this evil world, love Thee with all my strength. O God, the Father of lights, from whom cometh every best and perfect gift, grant that the seven gifts of the Holy Ghost may have this perfect work in my intellect, and in my will. May the fruits of the Holy Ghost grow in me, that to Thee, my neighbor, and myself, I may be fruitful in every good work and never be smitten with barrenness, by Thy most just sentence. Let me never be cut down for cumbering the ground, but, if need be, let the sharp knife of Thy loving care prune and take away all that hinders my sanctification. Amen.

INTENTION OF PRAYER:

Pray especially for the *grace of final preservance*, crowning the Spirit's operations in us during life: "*Be thou faithful until death and I will give thee the crown of life.*" Apoc. II, 10.

18.

The Holy Ghost and the sin against Him.

Man was created free, and free also he remains under the dispensation of divine grace and the ministration of the Spirit. Whilst the union of the Holy Ghost with the mystical body of Christ is indissoluble, the mystical union of the Holy Spirit with the individual soul is liable to be broken as long as man has not yet consummated his pilgrimage on earth. Man in virtue of his free will, even under the dispensation of divine grace, can resist God. He can slight and neglect the inspirations of the Holy Spirit and hereby "grieve the Spirit." He can go farther and by mortal sin he can "extinguish the Spirit," destroy the temple of the Holy Ghost, reduce his soul to the state of darkness and death, from which by regeneration and justification it was redeemed. He can go farther yet and by direct rebellion against the Spirit commit the sin which the Lord emphatically styles "the sin or blasphemy against the Holy Ghost" and which is the consummation of man's infidelity to the merciful condescensions of infinite love.

Our short explanations of the transcendent office of the Holy Spirit in the whole plan of salvation would be incomplete, should we pass over in silence, the "*sin against the Holy Ghost.*" Sin is a great mystery, the "mysterium iniquitatis," and it is only by the illumination of the Spirit that man, viewing the transgressions of the divine law from a supernatural standpoint, can understand something of this great and awful mystery, of the nature and evil consequences of sin, of the hideous character it shows when studied in the light of faith. Our Lord in His farewell discourses explicitly declares that by the Holy Ghost's coming we should learn what sin is, saying: "When He is come, He will convince he world of sin." (St. John, XVI.) Both in the old creation and in the new, both before the incarnation of the Son of God, and after His ascension into heaven, it has been, it is, and it will be to the end of the world, the work and the office of the Holy Ghost, to convince the world of sin; that is to say, to convince the intellect, and to illuminate the reason of man to understand what sin is, and also to convince the consciences of men of their sinfulness and make them conscious that they are guilty before God. As in the beginning, before the fall of man, man in the light of the Holy Ghost, knew God, His perfections and holiness, so after the fall, God in His mercy has by His Spirit taught men to know, in some measure at least, His perfections and their own sinfulness; but it was only like the twilight preceeding the noonday. We are in the noonday and if in the noonday we are blind to the perfections of God and to our own sinfulness, woe to us in the day of judgment.

Now, in a general sense, every sin is a sin against the Holy Spirit, as far as sin involves neglect of and resistance against the Holy Ghost's operation by divine grace. As there exists the most direct and intimate relation between the Holy Spirit and divine grace, so also has sin in all its forms and degrees a direct relation to this divine Spirit. Again, we must say that in our judgment no man has brought this truth to the front, and shown sin and its direct opposition to the Author of grace, God the Sanctifier, more clearly than Cardinal Manning in his book: "Sin and its Consequences." (London. Burns and Oates. 1874.) Viewing sin in its direct reference to the Holy Ghost, we will here mention some classes of sins. We can according to the inspired Text either "grieve the Spirit" (Ephes. IV. 30), or "extinguish the Spirit" (I. Thess. V. 19), or finally sin "by blasphemy of the Holy Ghost." (Matth. XII, 31.) Here the three classes of sin, as an act of opposition to the Holy Ghost, are distinctly given: *venial sin*, *mortal sin* and the *sin against the Holy Ghost*.

1. We can first "grieve the Spirit," and by this we mean to say, we can oppose, slight, neglect in the most various ways and degrees the incessant work of the Holy Ghost for our salvation and perfection. The Apostle writes to the Ephesians: "Grieve not the Holy Spirit of God : whereby you are sealed unto the day of redemption." (Ephes. IV, 30.) The Holy Spirit has been given us, has been "poured into us," is dwelling in us as in a temple, and His presence, indwelling, inhabitation is not passive, but unceasingly active, so much so that just as the sun never ceases to dart forth its rays, He never desists to shed on us His light and grace. We can, however, at will, neglect or oppose His benignant suggestions. They are the clouds of sinfulness and worldliness that obscure His illumination and neutralize His prolific warmth. The various

forms of sin that involve a direct opposition
against the Holy Ghost will best be understood when considered in their opposition to
the attributes of the Holy Ghost Himself.

The Holy Spirit of God is styled a *Spirit
of truth.* (St. John, XIV, 17.) It is therefore very grieving and vexing to Him,
to have a light esteem of divine truth, to be
indifferently affected towards it, to be slow in
striving to understand more fully the doctrine
of Holy Church. Even without directly denying faith, we can be guilty of infidelity. Divine truths are in our days obscured before
the eyes of men, because "there is none that
considereth in the heart." (Jerem. XII, II.)
Faith comes by hearing, but our age which
has an open ear for the news of this busy
world pays but little attention to the glad
tidings of salvation, as preached the year
round in the power of the Spirit. Christians
themselves hear the word of God, but by
not co-operating with the Spirit's power in
them, they only verify by their own life
the Lord's parable of the seed sown " by the
wayside upon stony ground," and "sown
amongst thorns." (Matth. XIII.) " Blessed
are those," says Jesus Christ " who hear the
word of God, and keep it." (Luke XI, 28.)
The most Blessed of all creatures was the
Spouse of the Holy Spirit who "kept all the

words, pondering them in her heart."
(Luke II, 19.) We grieve the Holy
Spirit by our light-mindedness and dis-
tractions, by not allowing the word of God to
take root in our soul, and prove its power
" more piercing than any two-edged sword :
reaching unto division of the soul and the
spirit," (Heb. IV, 12) and by not relishing
those things which the animal man does
not understand and God has revealed to the
little ones.

The Holy Spirit of God is styled a *Spirit of
grace and holiness* (Rom. I, 4.) It is therefore
vexing to this blessed Spirit when that grace,
of which He is the Author, is rejected, when
there are few that express any regard, show
any desire or manifest esteem for the Divine
boon. A cold heart towards God, a heart
that is disaffected to God, that keeps at a
distance from Him, that will not be engaged
in sweet communion with Him, is a vexing
thing to the Holy Spirit. The grace of the
Holy Ghost in us ever increases by any
faithful use we make of it, and nothing
more grieves the Spirit of infinite perfection and holiness than lukewarmness,
tepidity and wordliness on the part of those
who are called unto His special service ;
separated from this world, honored by higher
vocations, singled out from this wicked

world, and consecrated to His ministry.

The Holy Spirit of God is furthermore
called a *Spirit of power and life.* " It is the
Spirit that quickeneth," says our Lord. St.
Paul tells us, that God hath given us the
"Spirit of power." (II. Tim. I, 7.) It is
therefore vexatious to this Spirit, when we
allow ourselves to be ungenerous, lukewarm,
disinterested in things that are of God, when
we burn not with apostolic zeal, nor are
anxious to fulfil our mission to propagate
God's kingdom.

The Holy Spirit of God is especially
a Spirit *of purity, chastity and virginity.* Chastity is one of the fruits of the Spirit. Both
the shape of a dove and the form of a fiery,
luminous tongue, the two emblems under
which the Holy Ghost visibly appeared on
earth, suggest the angelic purity of which
He is the Author and the Lover. Spirit
and flesh have been antagonists from the
day of the first rebellion. When God
saw that man was flesh, then He said:
"My Spirit shall not remain in man forever."
(Gen. VI, 3.) Hence, all who wish to live
according to the Spirit will first have
to endure the struggle with the flesh; for,
no sin grieves the Spirit more keenly and
directly than sensuality, and yielding to
the passions and lusts of the flesh: "The

flesh lusteth against the spirit; and the spirit against the flesh; for these are contrary one to another .. Now the works of the flesh are manifest, which are, fornication, uncleanness, immodesty, luxury . but the fruit of the Spirit is charity, joy, peace . chastity " (Gal. II, 19,) and "for he that soweth in the flesh, of the flesh, also· shall reap corruption : but he that soweth in the spirit, of the spirit shall reap life everlasting." (Gal. VI, 8.) We have almost touched upon transgressions by which we do not only "grieve," but "extinguish " the Spirit. Even the smaller and slighter faults, by which we "grieve " the Spirit cannot be considered small or slight by those who in the Spirit view the things of God, and bind themselves to war against the "mysterium iniquitatis." It is a general rule that no man sees the nature of sin so clearly as those who are freest from sin; just as no intelligence knows sin with such intensity of knowledge as God Himself. On the other hand, no one is so blind to his own sins, as the man who has most sin upon him. No men know so little of the light of God's divine presence as those whose are covered with sin ; and the more sin they have upon them, the less visible it becomes. Sin stupefies the intellect and the heart; it draws a veil and a mist over the brightness of the intelligence, and it darkens the light of the conscience. Sin, like hemlock, deadens the sense, so that the spiritual eye begins to close, and the spiritual ear becomes heavy, and the heart grows drowsy. (According Card. Manning.)

Secondly, we can not only "*grieve*" the ·Spirit by venial sin or slighter resistance to His operation, but we can, alas, by the commission of mortal sin even "*extinguish*" the Spirit, destroy His temple, ruin His work, reduce our souls to the darkness from which they were freed and bring on them that spiritual death which, in fine, begets the second death of everlasting doom. It is an article of faith that there are venial sins and mortal sins, and that by committing the latter we lose sanctifying grace and all the great blessings of which it is the source. "If any man shall see his brother sin a sin which is not unto death, he shall ask, and life shall be given unto him that sinneth not unto death: I do not say for that any man shall ask. All iniquity is sin, and there is a sin unto death." (I, St. John, V, 16–17.) Mortal sin especially is, what we call the "*mysterium iniquitatis.*" Mortal sin, extinguishing the Spirit and utterly destroying His temple, is a mystery as great and incomprehensible here on earth as grace, regeneration and sanctification. It is, however, only by the light of the Holy Ghost that we can somewhat realize the hideous character and evil consequences of this sin, the extinction of the Spirit. It first strikes the soul dead. The grace of God is the life of the soul, as the soul is the life of the body. One mortal sin separates the soul from God. Secondly it destroys all the merits the soul has acquired. One sin unto death, unless afterwards repented of, utterly cancels the merits of a whole life. All the merits are gone as if they had never been. Thirdly it crushes and kills the very power of serving God and of bringing forth works of supernatural merit. Not all that the sinner does in the state of sin is sin, but he is incapable of bringing forth works unto life eternal. "Just as a tree that has life bears living fruit, and a tree that is dead has nothing but fruit that is also withered and dead, so a soul that is planted in God, as we are all in baptism, strikes its root as the tree by the rivers of water, and increases continually in Faith, Hope and Charity, and in the seven gifts of the Holy Ghost, which expand themselves like the leaves upon the branch, and the twelve fruits of the Holy Ghost unfold themselves and ripen. On the other hand, a soul that is separated from

God is like the tree that is cut asunder at the root, and as the severed tree withers from the topmost spray and every fruit upon it dies, so the soul in the state of mortal sin is separated from God and can bear no fruit unto salvation." (Card. Manning, Sin and its consequences, p. 50, ff.) Fourthly it involves a man in a double debt with God —it involves him in the debt of guilt and the debt of pain; and he will have to pay both. The debt of guilt he must answer for on the day of judgment. The debt of pain he must suffer for before he can see God, either here, or after death in the state of purification: or in hell for all eternity. Every substance has its shadow in this world. You cannot separate the shadow from the substance. Where the substance moves the shadow follows, so every sin has its pain; it matters not whether we think of it or no, whether we believe it or no." (Card. Manning, Sin, p. 53.) All these things, however, can only be perceived in the light of the Spirit. Though we are the children of God, and yet it has not appeared what we are; so it has not appeared what those of iniquity are who have extinguished in themselves the Holy Spirit and have wilfully returned to the bondage of the evil one. Hence we must earnestly entreat the

Holy Ghost, that we may never extinguish Him and that the horror of sin may be increased in our souls. The world does not know sin and calls those transgressions of the divine law merely the necessary results of human weakness. Men have gone so far as to speak of an independent morality, that is a law of morals separated from the Lawgiver, a proud philosophical claim to account for right and wrong without reference to God. This is, says our Cardinal, the stupidity as well as the impiety of our days. For morals are not the dead, blind, senseless relations that we have to stocks and stones, but the relations of duty and of obligation we have to the living Lawgiver, our Maker and Redeemer. Yet here we strike the last degree of sinning against the Holy Ghost. When man by trespassing on divine law not only forfeits grace and extinguishes the Spirit, but directly fights against the Spirit, then he commits the "blasphemy against the Holy Ghost" mentioned in Holy Writ. Of those the words of Isaias will be verified in the fullest sense: "They rebelled and vexed His Holy Spirit. Therefore He was turned to be their enemy, and He fought against them." (Isaias, I, XIII, 10.)

3. By sin against the Holy Ghost in the

strict sense of the term, we signify a special class of sins. To this sin, mentioned on the same occasion by three Evangelists refer the classical words of St. Matthew: " Wherefore I say unto you, all manner of sin and blasphemy shall be forgiven unto men. And whosoever speaketh a word against the Son of man, it shall be forgiven him, but whosoever speaketh a word against the Holy Ghost, it shall not be forgiven him, neither in this world, nor in the world to come." (St. Matth. XII, 31, 32.) These are the words that have vexed so many interpreters by the combination of difficulties involved in their exegesis. What is the meaning of this divine utterance? What is this " blasphemy of the Holy Ghost?" What does it mean to say: "Speak a word against the Holy Ghost?" Why does our Lord in seeming contradiction to His promises of a forgiveness of all sins, beyond exception, declare this sin unpardonable, both in this world and in the world to come? We do not here enter upon a detailed exegesis of this famous passage of Scripture. Although interpreters differ in secondary explanations, they more or less all agree as to the nature of this sin and the sense in which it is declared unpardonable.

The *occasion* on which these words of Christ

TO THE HOLY GHOST.

were spoken was the casting out of a devil that was both blind and dumb, so that the people amazed at the great miracle when witnessing the man who had been blind and dumb, see and speak, concluded from this fact that Jesus must necessarily be the Messiah, the Christ, the Son of God. The Pharisees, however, to blind themselves and others, to counteract the evidence of the fact and proof of Christ's Messianic dignity, to prevent the people from becoming the disciples of Christ, gave out maliciously, that though Jesus did cast out devils (a fact, which they had to acknowledge), yet it was not by any divine power, but merely by the power of Beelzebub, the prince of the devils. The casting out of the devils is here emphatically ascribed to the Holy Ghost. St. Matthew, before giving the narrative of this fact, introduces the Lord, saying: " Behold my servant whom I have chosen, my beloved, in whom my soul hath been well pleased. I will put my Spirit upon Him, and He shall show judgment to the Gentiles." (St. Matth. XII, 18.) Our Lord Himself in His reply to the remonstrances of the Pharisees says: " But if I in the Spirit of God cast out devils, then is the kingdom of God come upon you." (Matth. XII, 28.) According to St. Luke, chap. XI., v. 20, the Spirit of God

is called "the finger of God," just as we now
address the Holy Ghost in the beautiful
Hymn of the "Come Spirit Creator" as
"*Digitus paternæ dexteræ.*" There can consequently be no doubt as to the very nature
of this sin or blasphemy against the
Holy Ghost. What our Lord in His words,
burning with divine wrath, objects to in the
inveterate malice of the Pharisees, is their
wilful and malicious blindness, their perversity in ascribing a work evidently divine
to the enemy of God, the evil one, and their
satanic efforts to prevent others from believing in Him and bowing to the evidence
of divine truth revealed. Saint Thomas of
Aquinas (2*a* 2*ae* 9, 14, art. 1), sees therefore
the nature of this blasphemy of the Holy
Ghost in this wilful blindness of mind and
obstinacy of the will, in virtue of which we
directly resist divine truth revealed to us,
and strive to prevent others from receiving it.

Thus is also solved the question as to its
incapacity of being ever forgiven. Because
our Lord has explicitly declared to His
Apostles that they could forgive all sins and
loosen whatsoever is bound. Some, to evade
the difficulty of this saying, take refuge in
the assumption that our Saviour here makes
use of an Hebrew form of speech which is
frequently met with in Scripture, when the

difficulty of a thing coming to pass is expressed ; so that, then, the words have to be
taken not in an absolute, but in a compara-
tive sense with the meaning : all other sins
and blasphemies shall sooner be forgiven,
then this blasphemy of the Holy Ghost.
Nevertheless, the common and surely the
most certain way of explaining it is this,
that, although from God's mercy no sin is
excluded, if the sinner truly repent of it, still
this sin carries in itself such a perversity of
mind and heart which ordinarily excludes
the spirit of repentance; hence precludes forgiveness, and consequently as a rule is final
impenitence anticipated. This kind of sin is
usually accompanied with such obstinacy
and such wilful opposition to the Spirit of
God, the known truth, that men who are
guilty of it are seldom or never converted,
and therefore are never forgiven because
they will not repent. St. Thomas of Aquinas, (2a 2ae 9, 14 a 3), expressly adds that divine omnipotence and mercy can heal
this deadly disease, yet only in an almost miraculous way. By no means, however, was this sin confined to the wicked
Pharisees of old ; on the contrary, it has
been propagated by their very seed, nor
would we exaggerate in saying, that it has
called forth most disastrous results in the

history of the Church, and is the prominent sin of our days of infidelity and apostasy from truth divine.

The sin of the Pharisees was the sin of their nation. St. Stephan calls the stubbornness of the Jews and their disobedience to the admonitions of the prophets a resisting of the Holy Ghost and consequently a sin against Him. Our divine Lord, "the light that shineth in darkness and which the darkness did not comprehend," (St. John I, 5,) upbraids them with this, by calling to their minds the fact, that not in want of light, that not in inculpable ignorance, but that by the sinning in the malice of their heart against light they did not receive Him, saying: "If I had not come and spoken to them, they would not have sinned: but now they have no excuse for their sin. He that hateth Me, hateth My Father also. If I had not done amongst them the works that no other man hath done, they would have no sin: but now they have both seen and hated Me and My Father." (St. John XV, 24.) And in another passage: "This is the judgment, because the light is come into the world, and men loved darkness, rather that light: for their works were evil." (St. John III, 19.) Here is mentioned this blasphemy of the

Holy Ghost in its root; the evil will, its nature; opposition to truth known, and its punishment: "judgment" and "hatred of the Father." This sin against the light of the divine Redeemer and His Holy Ghost, shining forth from His Church on earth, has always had its developement and has it more than ever in our days of apostasy from Church, Christian revelation, nay, even natural religion. Every eve of Pentecost we read in the Roman Breviary, the description of those men who blaspheme whatever things they know not." And whatever things they naturally know, like dumb beasts, in these they are corrupted." (St. Jud. 10.) In the same Epistle of St. Jude. these sinners against the Holy Ghost in all ages are described as: "Separating themselves, sensual men, having not the Spirit." (v. 19.) To resist them, to withstand the temptation, St. Jude thus exhorts the faithful: "But you, my beloved, building yourselves upon your most holy faith, pray in the Holy Ghost." (v. 19.) Separation from God's Holy Church and opposition to her authority is so great a crime, says Cardinal Manning, because it is opposition to the Divine Spirit embodied in her, a sin against the Holy Ghost. Apostates, Heresiarchs, Heretics and leaders of secession have usually trodden the footprints of those Pharisees. They are and have been generally men who could and did know the truth, who wilfully resisted it, who strove with might and main to check the propagation of truth and in doing so did not shrink from caricaturing truth in the most diabolical way.

Did they not say that our Lord was casting out devils in the power of Beelzebub? Did they not accuse the first Christians and their worship of the most atrocious crimes? Is not our Lord's Vicar on earth proclaimed the Antichrist "the son of perdition?" Have they not dared to pronounce and preach that Church "is the great harlot; Babylon the great, the mother of the fornications, and the abominations of the earth?" (Apoc. XVII.) Thus, men revolting against truth have given vent to their hatred. Thus, "the blasphemy of the Holy Ghost," in its fullest meaning has again been repeated in the history of all heresies and secession from the unity of the Church. There are, however, sins not so horrible, but still possessing the very nature of this "blasphemy of the Holy Ghost," and having a tendency towards this great unpardonable sin of which we are speaking. Profane jesting concerning religion, ridiculing sacred things, atheistical views, involving an opposition against natural light,—all these offences participate of the nature and are closely allied to the sin of blasphemy against the Holy Ghost. Blasphemy against the Holy Ghost in some sense, is the consummation of all sins. It is the ripening into full maturity of the " mystery of iniquity." It produces in the soul a blindness which is only the foreshadowing darkness, final and eternal.

ASPIRATION:

O God the Holy Ghost, Whom I so often have grieved in my life by unfaithfulness to grace and divine inspiration, I repent of all this sinful blindness and stubbornness of my obstinate heart. I have grieved Thee; I have even extinguished Thy light in my soul and destroyed the temple of which Thou hast said : if any man shall destroy it, God will destroy him. O merciful God, do not punish me by denying me the Holy Spirit of repentance! O loving Spirit do not turn to be my enemy and fight against me. Never allow that my sins and shortcomings develope into this sin against Thee, which Thou canst not forgive. "Turn away Thy face from my sins ! Cast me not away from Thy face: and take not Thy Holy Spirit from me." (Ps. 50.)

INTENTION OF PRAYER:

Pray for the grace of having always true, supernatural, perfect contrition for the sins of your life and for the conversion of obstinate sinners. " *Create a clean heart in me, O God, and renew a right spirit within my bowels.*" (Ps. 50, 12.)

19.

The Holy Ghost and the Cousumma-
tion of All Things.

Life on earth is but a pilgrimage. As the
streams pursue their course until they empty
into the immensity of the ocean, so earthly
years roll on until they are lost in eternity.
The importance of this passing life,
lies in the truth of Revelation, that
upon the issue of this life depends man's
endless eternity. Good and evil develope
here on earth like wheat and cockle unto
the day of judgment. The just and the sinner grow in justice and in sin until death
confirms and seals their state. As the office
of the Holy Ghost is so intimately bound
up with the universal economy of salvation,
the Holy Ghost must needs also have a special relation to the final consummation of all
things. So it is. As He is somewhat the
seal and complement of the Divinity, He
also completes and seals the work of salvation and sanctification by the light of glory
and the fire of beatifying love. We will

distinguish three relations of the Holy Spirit to the consummation of all things.

1. *The Holy Spirit is the cause of our bodily resurrection and glorification.* Even in this life the body of the redeemed is, according to Scripture and the Fathers, the subject of redemption as well as the soul. It is evident that the economy of grace respects the whole man, who is constituted of body and soul, and would not be redeemed, if the soul alone were the recipient of mercy. But it is manifest, also, that the Holy Ghost comes to dwell in our bodies, by virtue of their regeneration, and that, consequently, they partake of the fruits of His presence. "Know you not that your members are the temple of the Holy Ghost, who is in you, whom you have from God, and you are not your own? Glorify and bear God in your body." (I Cor. III, 16, 17.) "You are the temple of God, and the Spirit of God dwelleth in you. The temple of God is holy, which you are." (I, Cor. VI, 19–20.) "You are the temple of God, as God saith: I will dwell in them and walk among them." (II, Cor. II, 16.) In Baptism the body is in the Sacred Name touched with the regenerating water, and the whole man is born again in the Holy Ghost. It is not simply in the soul that the Spirit dwells. He also abides

in our bodies, that He may quicken and hallow them. This is even a necessity for the completeness of our justification. The soul, in the condition of sin and condemnation, informs a corrupt body which has no part with Christ. Through nature there is no hope of delivery from death, which reigns over all the children born of Adam. When, however, the supernatural life is communicated, and the soul is awakened in the strength of second birth, to put on Christ and bear His likeness, it is quickened to animate a body which shall likewise be delivered from death and filled with the promise of immortality. The resurrection, then, of the just on the last day, is the necessary consequence of the sanctification of the body. As this sanctification is principally the work of the Holy Ghost, so too, is the resurrection; for in the presence of the Spirit there is life. " If the Spirit of Him, that raised up Christ from the dead dwell in you : He that raised up Jesus Christ from the dead, shall quicken also your mortal bodies, because of His Spirit that dwelleth in you." (Rom. VIII, II.) Quickened in this life by the Breath of the Spirit, hallowed as His temple, and made immortal by the humanity of Christ its head, the body when in the grave but sleeps.

When it shall be called by the voice of the Lord, it shall again appear in new vigor, in the gifts of glory, a true body and still a Spiritual body. On that glad morning the Spirit shall illumine His whole temple. Like the angels of God the glorified bodies shall move at the will of the Spirit and above the laws of nature shall, quicker than the lightning flash, obey the motions of the beatified soul. Subtle like a Spirit, the body, then, puts on the endowments of the glorified soul. Thus it is truly a *spiritual* body, not, because it loses the attributes of matter and becomes a spiritual substance, but, as St. Thomas says, because it is subdued to our spiritual nature and made the organ of the soul joined to God.

2. *In the light of the Holy Ghost the holy souls will see the face of God.* If glory is the fruit, grace is the seed. In proportion to the degree of sanctifying grace in us, will be our measure of " the Light of Glory " by which the saints in heaven see the unveiled face of God. As, then, the Holy Ghost is eminently the Author of grace, which is but the irradiation of His indwelling in the soul, so He is and must be the illuminator of the saints in heaven. Let us, to explain this more fully, give the words of our great Cardinal. In his book: " Sin and its Consequences " he

has a passage on this final relation of the Spirit to the soul confirmed in holiness by a saintly death. " We shall, then," says he, "see God. We shall see His uncreated nature; we shall see that which our hearts cannot conceive; we shall see Him, not by the eyes of flesh and blood, nor by the bare intellect of nature; but by the Light of Glory. The Light of Glory is by the Holy Ghost, the illumination of the intellect by the Holy Ghost. The soul filled with charity will be elevated by the Holy Ghost to the vision of God and to the union of all its power and all its affection with the uncreated Truth and the uncreated Love—that is God Himself. We shall see Him not in His infinity—for the finite mind cannot—but we shall see Him fully. Just as when we see a spark of fire, we see all fire, though the fire has no limit that we can understand ; and as when we see a ray of light we see the whole nature of light, though that light be boundless; so we shall see God. When we shall see His sanctity, purity, wisdom, goodness, power, justice, mercy, pity, compassion, and all the perfections of God, we shall see God, as He is, though not His infinity. And we shall see God the Father in His uncreated essence ; we shall see God the Son begotten of the Father; we shall see God the Holy

Ghost proceeding from the Father and the Son; we shall see the essence of the glory and of the eternal mutual knowledge and of the eternal mutual love of the Three Co-equal Persons in One Godhead. These things surpass both our words and thoughts. In the kingdom of resurrection, however, they shall be manifested to all who enter by that door which is Jesus Christ, by whose light all shall be revealed." (Card. Manning. Sin and its Consequences. Pag. 249.)

The light of glory is, according to St. Thomas, a created splendor, in which the soul receives strength to look upon the divine essence, in its threefold personality and undivided unity. In the power of this light it gazes upon that which, without divine aid, no created intellect could see and live. But in this state of glory, it sees the uncreated light, and in the enjoyment thereof finds its boundless happiness through all eternity.

We have reached the supreme beatitude, in which we shall become, as St. John tells us, like God, and, being truly in Him, possess Him forever. This is the end for which the Paraclete has been poured forth into our souls, in our regeneration; the end for which He in His love and mercy has incessantly worked and bestowed His choicest favors: and now that it has been reached through Him in the light of glory, He completes and irrevocably seals it for our everlasting happiness. Then man has returned to Him, who breathed into man His Spirit. Then the Spirit, once brooding over the waters of the first creation, will fill with a superabundance of endless joy His temple sanctified forever. Then the Third Person of the Holy Trinity, the bond of infinite love between Father and Son, will also be the bond of love that unites in eternal beatitude the creature and the Creator, the redeemed souls and the glorified Redeemer, the sons of God by grace and the Author of all grace and sanctification. "The Spirit and the Bride say, Come. And he that heareth, let him say, Come. And he that thirsteth, let him come. And he that will, let him come and take the water of life freely." (Apoc. XXII, 17.)

ASPIRATION.

O God the Holy Ghost, I beseech Thee through the most precious blood of Jesus Christ, to sanctify me wholly, that my whole body and soul may be Thy dwelling place, and all my words and works may be begun, continued and ended in Thee. Let me bear God in my body. Preserve pure, undefiled and holy this mortal body unto the day when Thou wilt clothe it with light and power and immortality. Stir up in my soul, O Spirit of the living God, that blessed hope in which "we groan within ourselves, waiting for the adoption of the sons of God, the redemption of our body." (Rom VIII, 23.)

INTENTION OF PRAYER:

Pray for the gift and virtue of *chastity* by which especially we keep holy the temple of God unto incorruption. "*But if any man violate the temple of God, him shall God destroy. For the temple of God is holy, which you are.*" (I Cor. III, 17.)

Conclusion:

We have now had a glance at the transcendent Office of the Holy Ghost from the very beginning of creation to its consummation in eternal glory. The brief sketch, given on the preceding pages, can only serve to bring home to our minds and consciousness the Office of the Holy Ghost, "so much obscured in the popular belief" not only of those outside of the Catholic Church, but even of Catholics. In proportion to our knowledge and realization of what Christian Revelation teaches us of the Person, the Mission, the Work, the Office, the Gifts of the Holy Ghost, will grow and increase our true devotion to the Third Person of the Holy Trinity. To bring about, with the grace of God, this increase of devotion, is the sole aim of our writing. This third part, consequently, forms the immediate introduction to the fourth and last part, which will furnish the devout servant of the Holy Ghost with some select prayers and pious exercises for cultivating a practical devotion, now theoretically justified. If by prayer we draw the supernatural light upon us, and in this supernatural light we understood, realize and love the things of God, this is twice and thrice true of all that concerns this Devotion to the Divine Paraclete.

In the Holy Spirit and by His illumination we open our eyes to the things and realities of another world. "We have received not the Spirit of this world, but the Spirit that is of God: that we may know the things that are given us from God." (I Cor. II, 12.) In the Holy Spirit we are transformed into "new creatures," or into "spiritual men," who in opposition to flesh and blood understand the things of the Spirit and relish them. "The sensual man perceiveth not these things that are of the Spirit of God: for it is foolishness to him and he cannot understand: because it is spiritually examined." (I Cor. II, 14.) In the Spirit alone, internally teaching us to believe and understand what externally He speaks to us through His organ on earth, the Church, we know all things: for "who hath known the mind of the Lord, that he may instruct him? But we have the mind of Christ." (I Cor. II, 16.) Without the Holy Ghost illumining, sanctifying and inspiring us, we, as individuals, are animal men and have no part in Christ and His redemption. Without faith in the Holy Ghost who is

living and teaching us through the infallible
Church, the body of Christ, a religious society rejects the Pentecostal mission and Evangelical Office of the Holy Ghost, which specially distinguishes the faith of Catholics from
the faith of Judaism. Finally, without a
fervent devotion to the Holy Ghost and a
proportionate effusion of His Grace upon us,
we will even as Catholics and children of the
Church, remain more or less formal, earthly
minded, sensual, slow to understand and
cold in love.

Let us then apprehend the possibility of
succeeding with God in our efforts and strides
to acquire daily more and more of His divine Spirit. The Holy Spirit is a Spirit of
grace to whom we are to go in all supplication. The more we do so, the more we
honor His divine office, and the better we fulfil our duty, and consequently the larger
will be our share in His divine favors. We
are always to consider our case as one of
great promise when we desire and strive to
acquire and retain the Spirit of God. But
we should take alarm, whenever we detect in
ourselves a growing indifference for the
Holy Spirit of God. We feel death creeping
upon us by degrees, and we regret it not;
death drawing near our vitals, and we mind
it not. But if we, feeling a decay and lan-

guishment ,cry with importunity to God ,the case is not hopeless. He has said, that He will give the Spirit to them that ask for it, and that He will pour out His Spirit upon us. Christ represents the Spirit as a gift given to a child, as a boon from the Father; and as a gift is comprehending all things. Nay, the Spirit is to us as bread to a child; for we can no more live without the Spirit, than a child can without bread. And we may the more boldly ask, because we can suppose ourselves to be nearer the days when there shall be a more general outpouring of the Spirit. This will undoubtedly be when devotion to the Holy Ghost has become more universal and fervent.

PART IV.

Daily Devotion to God the Holy Ghost.

"Are not Christians the anointed, and is it not the devotion for all Christians? How can we be spiritually minded or supernatural without it? Are not men spiritual and supernatural in the measure in which they have fellowship and communication with Him?"

Cardinal Manning to the Rector of the American College, 1887.

Daily Devotion to God the Holy Ghost.

In the preceding parts of this little volume we have dwelt on the Devotion to God the Holy Ghost. We have first endeavored to make clear its propriety and the special features which to our mind characterize it as the Devotion calculated to be accompanied with the most blessed results suited to our age, our country, and though last by no means least, to our priestly state. We have, then, in fidelity to our little program, given full information concerning the establishment, the conditions, formalities and privileges of the Confraternity of the Servants of the Holy Ghost. We have, in fine, by the brief sketch of the transcendent office of the Holy Ghost in the plan of salvation, immediately prepared the reader and introduced him to this the last part of our book, which will furnish every devout Servant of the Holy Ghost with a selection of prayer, and pious exercises calculated to impress him with feelings of devotion. Supernatural truth, known and believed, should not only illumine our intelligence, but also and chiefly our hearts. It should, indeed penetrate our whole being. Dogma, as we have always said, must produce devotion, and a devotion not of mere feeling, but one in prayers, good resolutions, and salutary deeds. Now, however, we wish to lay special stress on the title of this part: "Daily Devotion to God the Holy Ghost." Speaking of the "obligations of the Confraternity of the Servants of the Holy Ghost" we have repeatedly declared that the Confraternity does not in any way burden the conscience or impose any obligation whatever under penalty of sin. Nay, in striking contrast with other Confraternities, this can hardly be said to oblige to anything. Hence there is no necessity of reciting official prayers and exercises. Moreover, we all, at certain times and on special occasions, directly implore, invoke and adore the Holy Ghost by special prayers and appropriate services; as for instance, before and after Pentecost, at the inauguration of our scholastic year, and on all occasions that call for His special light and assistance. Ordinarily, however, the life of the true servant of the Holy Ghost should be characterized by some special daily devotion to God the Sanctifier. Concluding in his book on the "Mission of God the Holy Ghost," our Cardinal writes:

" Therefore in order to do this, I would ask you from this day to the end of your lives to offer *every day* some act of reparation and adoration. Make up your mind now that *not a day shall pass* from this day to your last without some act of adoration to the Person of the Holy Ghost, without some act of reparation made to Him for your own sins and for the sins of other men. Say *day by day* the majestic hymn of the Church, the "*Veni Creator Spiritus,*" or that other, equally beautiful, and even more full of human tenderness, " *Veni Sancte Spiritus,*" or say *every day* seven times the " *Gloria Patri*" in honor of the Holy Ghost to obtain His seven gifts; or make some prayer of your own; raise up your hearts to God, and make, each of you, some short act of reparation and adoration out of the fulness of your soul; or say *day by day:* "O God the Holy Ghost, whom I have slighted, grieved, resisted from my childhood unto this day, reveal unto me Thy personality, Thy presence, Thy Power, Thy seven-fold gifts. One thing I have desired of the Lord: that will I seek after: not wealth, rank, power, worldly home, worldly happiness, or any worldly good, but one drop of that holy flame, one drop of that heavenly fire, to kindle me and set me all on fire with the love of my God. Kindle me with zeal, melt me with sorrow, that I may live the life and die the death of a fervent penitent." (p. 485.) We have given in Italics all the expressions referring to *daily* devotion, as it is our desire to make the word " daily " most emphatic.

The word " daily " is of great significance and importance in a religious and devout life. Devotion in its full meaning is a habit, and a habit is formed only by regular and continued acts. *Daily* mortification and *daily* prayer may therefore be called the two hinges upon which turns a life of sound and true devotion. Hence we are about to furnish a selection of prayers to God the Holy Ghost, for the immediate purpose of making this Devotion practical. Time has not permitted us, to add to the foregoing considerations a complete prayer-book, containing all prayers that in a regular book of practical devotion, might be expected. Nor did we think this a part of our task which consists exclusively in presenting prayers and pious exercises to the devout Servants of God the Holy Ghost for this special service of honoring and adoring with a special worship the Third Person of the Most Holy Trinity. In composing, our little book we did not design that it should in any way supersede other regular prayer-books but rather that it should prove a supplement to be used only on certain special occasions, seasons and feasts of the year. We have confined ourselves here to the offering of those specific prayers to God the Holy Ghost, which, found scattered here and there, seemed to us more beautiful than others and in which we thought the ideas, enlarged upon in the preceding pages, were more exactly shaped into words and expressions.

First, we shall give a number of prayers for daily use, including principally the two liturgical hymns to the Holy Ghost. Because of the most special relations of the Holy Ghost to the Sacraments of Penance and Holy Eucharist, we shall also give under a special heading, some prayers to the Holy Ghost with reference to these two Sacraments. In fine we shall indicate some devotions for extraordinary occasions, and reserve for our next volume, " Pentecost," those prayers that immediately and directly refer to the Pentecostal feast and its liturgical season.

I.

Daily Prayers to the Holy Ghost.

1.

Acts of Faith, Hope, Charity and Contrition.

The acts of Faith, Hope and Charity, rank first, amongst all prayers, because they directly and immediately refer to God and unite us with His Infinite Majesty and Love. They are but the actuation of those habits or theological virtues that by the Holy Ghost were infused into our soul in regeneration or justification. Although the theological virtue of charity is lost by mortal sin, the other two habits remain and are not eradicated by mortal sin, which is directly opposed to them. We should know such correct formulas by heart and say these most meritorious acts frequently. For persons in sickness or in danger of death no prayers are more to be commended than the acts of Faith, Hope and Charity. The act of contrition added to them, is more or less contained, at least implicitly, in the act of Charity, though it is not the same *formaliter*. Whilst, by an act of Charity we love God above all things, because of His infinite goodness, loveliness and perfections, by an act of contrition (perfect), we do the same, but with direct reference to our sins which we consequently detest from motives of the love of God Hence, every act of perfect contrition contains an act of Charity, but not so, at least strictly speaking, *vice versa*. Let it be always remembered that should we, may God forbid, fall into mortal sin, and whilst in that state be in danger of death, having no priest from whom to receive absolution, *perfect contrition*, and *only* this, can save us from eternal damnation. Pray, therefore to the Holy Spirit, for the grace of true, supernatural, perfect contrition and even before stating these acts invoke by a short aspiration to the Holy Ghost His assistance for the worthy performance of things so utterly beyond the capacity of mere nature.

1.

FAITH.

O my God, I firmly believe that Thou art one God in three Divine Persons, Father, Son and Holy Ghost; I believe that Thy Divine Son became man and died for our sins, and that He will come to judge the living and the dead. I believe these and all the truths which the Holy Catholic Church teaches; because Thou hast revealed them, who canst neither deceive nor be deceived.

2.

HOPE.

O my God, relying on Thy infinite goodness and promises, I hope to obtain pardon of my sins, the help of Thy grace and life everlasting, through the merits of Jesus Christ, my Lord and Redeemer.

3.

CHARITY.

O my God, I love Thee above all things, with my whole heart and soul, because

Thou art all-good and worthy of all love. I love my neighbor as myself for the love of Thee. I forgive all who have injured me, and ask pardon of all whom I have injured.

4.

CONTRITION.

O my God, I am heartily sorry for having offended Thee, and I detest all my sins; because I dread the loss of heaven and the pains of hell, but most of all because they offend Thee, my God, who art all-good and deserving of all my love. I firmly resolve, with the help of Thy grace, to confess my sins, to do penance and to amend my life.

5.

A PRAYER FOR OBTAINING CONTRITION.

I have now here before me, O Lord, a sad prospect of the manifold offences, by which I have displeased Thy Divine Majesty, and which I am assured will appear in judgment against me, if I repent not, and my soul be not disposed by a hearty sorrow, to receive Thy pardon. But this sorrow, O Lord, this repentance, must be Thy free gift, and if it comes not from the hand of Thy mercy, all my endeavors will be in vain, and I shall be for ever miserable. Have mercy therefore on me, O Father of mercies, and pour forth into my heart Thy grace, whereby I may sincerely repent of all my sins; give me a true contrition, that I may bewail my past misery and ingratitude, and grieve from my heart for having offended Thee so good a God. Permit me not to be deluded with a false sorrow, as I fear I have been too often, through my own weakness and neglect; but let it be now Thy gift descending from Thee, the Father of lights, that so my repentance may be accompanied with amendment and change of life, and I may be fully acquitted from the guilt of all my sins, and once more received into the number of Thy servants. Through Jesus Christ our Lord. Amen.

2.

FIRST PRAYER TO GOD THE HOLY GHOST.

O Holy Spirit of Grace, be Thou my Wisdom, to teach me my faith; my Understanding, in all my doubts; my Strength against all temptations; my Knowledge, in what belongs to the state of life to which I am called; my Godliness, in all my actions; my Fear, all the day long: that Thou mayst be my Comfort at the last, and my Bliss forever. Amen.

SECOND PRAYER TO GOD THE HOLY GHOST.

O Thou Author of Sanctification, Spirit of love and truth, I adore Thee as the Origin of my eternal welfare, I thank Thee as the Sovereign Dispenser of the benefits that I receive from on high; and I invoke Thee as the source of the light and strength which is necessary to me to know good and to practice it. O Spirit of light and strength, enlighten my understanding, strengthen my will, purify my heart, rule all the movements thereof, and make me docile to all Thy inspirations. Pardon me, Spirit of grace and mercy; pardon my continual unfaithfulness, and the wretched blindness with which I have so repulsed the gentlest, and the most powerful impulses of Thy Grace. I desire by the aid of this same Grace to cease from being rebellious against it, and henceforth to follow its movements with such docility, that I may taste the fruits and enjoy the blessings which Thy Sacred Gifts produce in the soul. To Thee, with the Father and the Son, be all glory forever. Amen.

THIRD PRAYER TO GOD THE HOLY GHOST.

Come, then, O Holy Spirit, come; come, O come, Most Merciful Comforter; come,

Thou Blessed Paraclete; come, Thou Celestial Fire; come, Thou Purifier of sins, Thou Healer of wounds; come, Thou Upholder of the falling, Thou Lifter-up of the fallen, come, Thou Teacher of the humble, Thou Destroyer of the proud; come, Thou Friend of the friendless, Hope of the hopeless, Consoler of the sorrowful, Haven of the weary, Physician of the sick; come, Thou glory of the living, Only Salvation of the dying! Come, O Most Holy, Thrice Holy, Holy Ghost, come, and have pity on me; direct me and defend me; strengthen me and comfort me; confirm me, and gladden me; fit me for Thyself; and having made me fit, dwell in me forever; and grant that my littleness may be acceptable to Thy Greatness, my weakness to Thy Strength, according to the multitude of Thy compassion; through Jesus Christ our Saviour, who with the Father liveth and reigneth in Thy Unity forever and ever. Amen.

FOURTH PRAYER TO GOD THE HOLY GHOST.

O Holy Spirit, be Thou present, and from heaven shed down Thy consolations on them that expect Thee; sanctify the temple of our body, and consecrate it a habitation to Thyself. Make the souls that desire Thee joyful with Thy presence. Make the house fit

for Thee, the Inhabitant: adorn Thy cham-
ber and surround the place of Thy rest with
all virtues; strew its floor with jewels;
let Thy mansion shine with the brightness
of carbuncles and precious stones; and let
the odors of all Thy gifts inwardly discover
themselves; let Thy fragrant balsam perfume Thy residence, and expel whatever is
noisome and the spring of corruption; do
Thou make this joy permanent and lasting:
and this renovation of Thy creature do Thou
continue forever in unfading beauty. Amen.
(A prayer of St. Cyprian.)

3.

Short Prayers to God, the Holy Ghost.

1.

Make me a clean heart, O God, and renew
a right spirit within me. Cast me not away
from Thy presence, and take not thy Holy
Spirit from me. O give me the comfort of
Thy help again, and establish me with Thy
free Spirit.

2.

O God the King of glory, who hast exalted Thine only Son Jesus, Christ with great

triumph unto Thy Kingdom in Heaven: we beseech Thee, leave us not comfortless, but send to us Thine Holy Ghost to comfort us, and exalt us unto the same place whither our Saviour Christ is gone before: who liveth and reigneth with Thee and the Holy Ghost, one God, world without end.

3.

Send, we beseech Thee, Almighty God, Thy Holy Spirit into our hearts, that He may rule and direct us according to Thy will, comfort us in all our temptations and afflictions, defend us from all error, and lead us into all Truth; that we, being steadfast in the faith, may increase in love and in all good works, and in the end obtain everlasting life: through Jesus Christ Thy Son our Lord.

4.

Lamb of God, that takest away the sins of the world, Pour on us the Holy Ghost. Lamb of God, that takest away the sins of the world, send forth on us the promised Spirit of the Father. Lamb of God, that takest away the sins of the world, give unto us the Spirit of Peace.

5.

O Blessed Spirit, who guidest and govern-
est the Church of Christ in all truth, illuminating its Doctors, strengthening its Mar-
tyrs and perfecting its Saints: Thou Bond
of the mystical union between Christ one
Head and us His members, and between the
Church above and the Church below, have
mercy upon us, and keep us in the unity of
the faith.   Amen.

4.

The two Hymns to God the Holy Ghost.

The two following Liturgical Hymns to God the
Holy Ghost are actually master pieces of religious
art. As Cardinal Newman calls the Liturgical
Office of Pentecost the *most beautiful* of all Offices
of the Roman Breviary and Missal, these
two Hymns may be called the most precious
jewels in this set of jewelry, the real " *solitaires*,"
as it were, thereof. According to Cardinal
Manning the " Veni Creator Spiritus " is " the
majestic hymn of the Church " whilst the " Veni
Sancte Spiritus " is " equally beautiful and even
more full of human tenderness." They refer to
each other and complete each other, it seems to us,
as do Dogmatic Theology and Moral or Ascetic or
Mystical Theology.
    Much has been said and published with
reference to their origin and their authors.
It seems to be most probable that " Veni

Creator " has for its author the famous and
saintly Archbishop of Mayence, *Rabanus Maurus*
(850) whilst the " Veni Sancti " was composed by
the angelic monk and singer of St. Gall, in
Switzerland, *Notker Balbulus*, (912). In one of our
projected future Volumes we intend to treat more
fully on these two hymns :

1. VENI CREATOR SPIRITUS.

Come, Holy Ghost, Creator, come,
　The souls which are Thine own invade ;
And with supernal grace inflame
　The hearts which Thou Thyself hast made.

O Thou that art the Comforter,
　The gift of God most high,
The living fount of fire and love,
　Celestial unction from above ;

O Thou who art of sevenfold power,
　The finger of the Father's hand,
The fulness of His promised Word,
　Who hast all speech at Thy Command ;

Enkindle light within our minds,
　With love our wayward hearts inflame ;
And with Thine own undying life
　Give vigor to our mortal frame.

Drive far from us the angry foe,
　And Thy true peace impart within,
That, Thou our leader and our guide,
　We may escape the snares of sin.

Through Thee may we the Father know,
　Through Thee approach the eternal Son ;
And Thee, the Spirit of them both,
　Confess while endless ages run.

To God the Father glory be,
　And to the Son from death arisen,

And to the Blessed Paraclete,
Be praise and ceaseless honor given.
Amen.

---

2. VENI SANCTE SPIRITUS.

Holy Spirit! Lord of light!
From Thy clear celestial height
Thy pure beaming radiance give ;

Come, Thou Father of the poor!
Come, with treasures which endure!
Come, Thou Light of all that live!

Thou, of all consolers best,
Visiting the troubled breast,
Dost refreshing peace bestow :

Thou in toil art comfort sweet ;
Pleasant coolness in the heat ;
Solace in the midst of woe.

Light immortal! Light divine!
Visit Thou these hearts of Thine,
And our inmost being fill :

If Thou take Thy grace away,
Nothing pure in man will stay ;
All his good is turned to ill.

Heal our wounds ; our strength renew ;
On our dryness pour Thy dew ;
Wash the stains of guilt away :

Bend the stubborn heart and will ;
Melt the frozen, warm the chill ;
Guide the steps that go astray.

Thou, on those who evermore
Thee confess and Thee adore,
In Thy sevenfold gifts descend :

Give them comfort when they die;
Give them life with Thee on high;
Give them joys which never end. Amen.

The Sovereign Pontiff, Pius VI., by a brief, May 26, 1796, granted to all the faithful who. once or oftener in the day, with at least contrite heart and devotion, shall say the hymn *Veni Creator Spiritus*, or the sequence *Veni Sancte Spiritus*:

A Plenary Indulgence, once a month, on any day on which, being truly penitent, after confession and communion, they shall pray for peace and union among Christian princes, for the extirpation of heresy, and for the triumph of Holy Mother Church.

An Indulgence of Three Hundred Days to all those who, on Whit-Sunday and during its octave, with at least contrite heart and devotion shall say this hymn or the sequence, praying as above directed.

An Indulgence of One Hundred Days, on all other days of the year, every time that, with at least contrite heart and devotion, they shall say this hymn or the sequence, praying as above directed.

II.

The Holy Ghost and the Sacrament of Penance.

In the diploma of the Archconfraternity the Holy Ghost is emphatically styled "*dator gratiae tum innocentibus tum poenitentibus*." Our divine Lord, conferring upon His apostles the power to forgive sins, gave them first and in a way most significative "the Holy Ghost," Scripture stating: "Then He breathed on them; and said to them: Receive ye the Holy Ghost: whose sins you shall forgive, they are forgiven them and whose sins you shall retain, they are retained." (St. John XX, 22.) Since, by infusion of sanctifying grace, sin is destroyed and the indwelling Spirit banishes sin and guilt from the heart of man, the Liturgy of Holy Church says of the Holy Ghost: "*Ipse est remissio omnium peccatorum.*" (Missa in die Pentecostes). Why is this so? How comes it? Simply because the relation of the Holy Ghost to the spirit, the sacrament and the works of true penance is a most manifold one. The power of absolution is from the Holy Ghost. That which constitutes the essence and soul of our reconciliation with God, true supernatural contrition or all the dispositions required for forgiveness of sins is principally the work and gift of the Holy Ghost. To Him we must have recourse in order to know our sins, to repent of them truly, to confess them duly and to receive sacramental grace validly. Penance is both a virtue and a sacrament. Penance means simply

SPECIAL DEVOTION.   379

repentance. From the beginning of the world the grace of penance has been poured upon men. It is an interior disposition of the soul before God ; and from the beginning the Holy Ghost, whose office it is to convince the world of sin, has convinced sinners of their transgressions, has converted them to penance, and from penance has made them saints. The grace of the Holy Spirit poured upon sinners to convert them, has a double effect, working on both mind and heart; on the mind and intellect, in so far as it gives us light to understand and to know ourselves more truly, and thereby to understand, to enumerate, to measure, and to realize our sins and their gravity ; on the heart, in so far as it enables us to be contrite, to detest sin from motives not of nature, but of faith, and to make acts of sorrow. We are often not conscious enough of the exclusively supernatural character of this entire process. In consequence of minute instruction on how to confess rightly, men oftentimes overlook the principal thing, the interior disposition of the heart, which alone is the soul of all. All depends on this interior disposition and consequently our prayers to the Author of the grace of penance and contrition and forgiveness—the Holy Ghost—are of the greatest importance.

Let us entreat Him to fulfil His office in us and "convince us of our sins." Let us implore His mercy that He may give us the contrition of David, the tears of Peter and the heart-stirring sorrow of Mary Magdalen. Love and contrition alone, as the Holy Ghost gives them, destroy sin, and in proportion to the measure of love and contrition is grace and peace restored to the troubled soul of the sinner. "Her sins, which are many, are forgiven her, because she has loved much." (St. Luke VII, 47.) Here is an example of the grace of penance ; and an example not of penance only, but of perfect and full absolution given in a moment; more than this, a complete restoration of purity given to the most fallen.

We have given amongst the "Daily Prayers" both an oration for obtaining a contrition and a formula for making an act of contrition. Not giving here a full instruction or preparation for the Sacrament of Penance, but only calling attention to the main importance of interior disposition and consequently of the grace of the Holy Spirit, we let follow here only some considerations or motives for contrition, quoting from the official prayer-book which, in accordance with the order of the last Council of Baltimore, will soon be published. No human words, however, will ever be able to express the feelings of a truly repenting sinner so perfectly, as do the inspired words of the Holy Ghost in the psalm of repentance, par excellence.

1.

Considerations to Excite Contrition.

1. Place before yourself, as distinctly as you can, the sins which have come to your remembrance, and their circumstances.

2. Consider WHO GOD IS, *against whom you have sinnend, how great, how good, how gracious to you; that He made you, that He gave His Only Son to die for you, that He made you His Child in Baptism, that He has loaded you with blessings and prepared heaven for you. Consider how patient He has been with you—how long-suffering in calling you and moving you to repent: Say,* O most Loving God, O infinite Goodness, I repent of having offended Thee;

behold me at Thy feet. O my Father, my
Creator, my Benefactor, grant me the grace
of a true repentance, and the blessing of a
free pardon, for Thy dear Son's sake.

3. Consider the infinite wickedness of sin : Say,
O my Saviour, I behold Thee on the Cross,
torn and wounded, Thy sacred Body stream-
ing with Blood: this is the work of my sin.
In Thy Wounds, O my Saviour, I read the
greatness of the guilt and malice of my sins.
By the greatness of Thy pains and sorrows,
O my loving Redeemer, I measure the hate-
fulness of my offences.

*4. Consider the consequences of one mortal
sin : how many souls are now tormented in hell-
fire for one single unrepented, deadly sin : how
many have I not committed !* O my God, how
much do I owe Thee for not cutting me off
in the midst of my sins. Before I fell into
sin, heaven was my home, my inheritance,
my country, my blessed resting-place ; by
sin I have given up my title to the glory of
the Blessed. For the sake of sin I have lost
the love of Jesus, the sight of Jesus, the communion with the Blessed Saints and with
the Angles. O my God, would that I. had
never offended Thee, would that I had never
consented to sin. Behold me now in pity at
Thy feet, full of sorrow and contrition. I
hate sin, which I accursed of Thee ; I re-

nounce all which would draw me away from
Thee; I most bitterly repent my sin and
folly, which would have deprived me for
ever of heaven, if Thou hadst not mercifully
brought me to repentance. I grieve that I
have sinned against Thee, O my God, who
art all-good, all-bountiful, all-worthy of love.

2.

The "Miserere."

There are seven of the psalms of David, which
we call the " Psalms of penance," " Psalmi pœni-
tentiales," as given in the Roman Breviary, namely : Ps. 6, " Domine ne in furore ;" Ps. 31, " Beati
quorum ;" Ps. 37, " Domine ne in furore tuo ;"
Ps. 60. " Miserere mei Deus ;" Ps. 142, " Domine exaudi ;" Ps. 129, " De profundis," and Ps. 101,
" Domine exaudi : orationem meam." Space does
not permit us to speak of all. We cannot omit
however, the famous, " Miserere," that first gave
expression to David's sorrow and contrition and
since then has been repeated over and over by
souls that moved by the Holy Spirit have turned
again to God whom they had for a time forgotten
or offended. The " Miserere " contains repeated
and most expressive allusions to the Holy Ghost.

PSALM 50.

Miserere mei, Deus, * secundum magnam mis-ericordiam tuam.

Et secundum multitu-dinem miserationum tu-arum * dele iniquitatem meam.

Have mercy upon me, O God: according to Thy great mercy.

And according to the multitude of Thy tender mercies: blot out my iniquity.

Amplius lava me ab iniquitate mea, * et a peccato meo munda me.

Quoniam iniquitatem meam ego cognosco, * et peccatum meum contra me est semper.

Tibi soli peccavi, et malum coram te feci, * ut justificeris in sermonibus tuis, et vincas cum judicaris.

Ecce enim in iniquitatibus conceptus sum, * et in peccatis concepit me mater mea.

Ecce enim veritatem dilexisti: * incerta et occulta sapientiæ tuæ manifestasti mihi.

Asperges me hyssopo, et mundabor: * lavabis me, et super nivem dealbabor.

Auditui meo dabis gaudium et lætitiam, * et exultabunt ossa humiliata.

Averte faciem tuam a peccatis meis, * et omnes iniquitates meas dele.

Cor mundum crea in me, Deus, * et spiritum rectum innova in visceribus meis.

Ne projicias me a facie tua, * et Spiritum sanc-

Wash me yet more from my iniquity: and cleanse me from my sin.

For I acknowledge my iniquity: and my sin is always before me.

Against Thee only have I sinned, and done evil in Thy sight: that Thou mayest be justified in Thy words, and mayest overcome when Thou art judged.

For behold, I was conceived in iniquities: and in sins did my mother conceive me.

For behold, Thou hast loved truth: the secret and hidden things of Thy wisdom Thou hast made manifest unto me.

Thou shalt sprinkle me with hyssop, and I shall be cleansed: Thou shalt wash me, and I shall be made whiter than snow.

Thou shalt make me hear of joy and gladness: and the bones that were humbled shall rejoice.

Turn away Thy face from my sins: and blot out all my iniquities.

Create in me a clean heart, O God: and renew a right spirit within me.

Cast me not away from Thy face: and take not

tum tuum ne auferas a me.

Redde mihi lætitiam salutaris tui, * et spiritu principali confirma me.

Docebo iniquos vias tuas, * et impii ad te convertentur.

Libera me de sanguinibus, Deus, Deus salutis meæ: * et exultabit lingua mea justitiam tuam.

Domine, labia mea aperies, * et os meum annuntiabit laudem tuam.

Quoniam si voluisses sacrificium, dedissem utique: * holocaustis non delectaberis.

Sacrificium Deo spiritus contribulatus: * cor contritum et humiliatum, Deus, non despicies.

Benigne fac, Domine, in bona voluntate tua Sion, * ut ædificentur muri Jerusalem.

Tunc acceptabis sacrificium justitiæ, obliationes, et holocausta: * tunc imponent super altare tuum vitulos.

Gloria Patri, etc.

Thy Holy Spirit from me.

Restore unto me the joy of Thy salvation: and strenghten me with a perfect spirit.

I will teach the unjust Thy ways: and the wicked shall be converted unto Thee.

Deliver me from sins of blood, O God, Thou God of my salvation: and my tongue shall extol Thy justice.

Thou shalt open my lips, O Lord: and my mouth shall declare Thy praise.

For if Thou hadst desired sacrifice, I would surely have given it: with burnt - offerings Thou wilt not be delighted.

The sacrifice of God is a troubled spirit: a contrite and humble heart, O God, Thou wilt not despise.

Deal favorably, O Lord, in Thy good will with Sion: that the walls of Jerusalem may be built up.

Then shalt Thou accept the sacrifice of justice, oblations, and whole burnt - offerings : then shall they lay calves upon Thine altars.

Glory be to the Father, etc.

III.

The Holy Ghost and the Sacrament of the Most Holy Eucharist.

The relation of the Holy Ghost to the Sacrament of the Holy Eucharist and the unbloody sacrifice of the mass is, if possible, still more mystical and unique than His relation to the Sacrament of Penance. Because it was by the Holy Ghost that the Eternal Word assumed human nature and the mystery of the Incarnation is, in some sense, continued or repeated in the mystery of Transubstantiation, this miraculous operation or the consecration of bread and wine into the flesh and blood of Christ, is, by the universal tradition of the Church, most emphatically ascribed to the Holy Ghost. This relation of the Holy Ghost to the Holy Eucharist is so prominent, that its solemn expression in the various Liturgies of the Oriental Church gave rise to the protracted controversy between Catholics and the schismatic Greeks, whether "Transubstantiation was affected by the pronunciation of the words of Christ by the celebrating priest, or by this solemn invocation of the Holy Ghost, in which, according to some Liturgies, He is invoked to descend upon the oblation and change bread and wine into the body and the blood of Christ." All Oriental Liturgies contain this so-called "ἐπίκλησις" "epiclesis." Tradition sees a type of this

consuming and transforming fire of the Spirit of
God in the mystical fire, which. in the Old Testament at times came down from heaven and
consumed the sacrifices. And although the Church
has solemnly declared that consecration is effected
by the very words of Christ, intentionally proffered
by the priest ; still the Roman Missal also contains
this "*epiclesis*."

When at the Offertory the priest with uplifted
arms prays: "*Veni Sanctificator omnipotens aeterne
Deus et benedic hoc sacrificium tuo sancto nomini
præparatum*," it is the most solemn invocation
of the Divine Spirit upon the oblation. That
" Sanctificator " here directly refers to the Holy
Ghost, is beyond doubt from the term used and
always appropriated to the Third Person of Trinity. Moreover, we find the same invocation in the
Mozarabic Missal, but more explicitly referring to
the Holy Ghost. There we read : "*Veni Sancte
Spiritus Sanctificator, sanctifica hoc sacrificium de
manibus meis tibi præparatum*." Alluding to this
fact in one of our Latin Dissertations, which we
presented to His Eminence, we were honored by
the following remarks, contained in the Cardinal's
autographic answer : " My belief has always
been that the " *Veni Sanctificator* " is directed to
the Holy Ghost, and reflects all your argument.
The controversy of the Greeks as to the Form of
consecration has obscured this point : and indis-
posed our writers towards your subject, which to
me is beautiful and sweet in the highest degree."
(Card. Manning to the Author. Letter of Oct. 19,
1884.)

By the Holy Ghost, the Blessed Virgin conceived,
for " The Holy Ghost shall come upon thee and the
power from on high shall overshadow thee."
(Luke. I, 35.) " *By the Holy Ghost*, Christ offered
Himself unspotted unto God " (Hebr. IX, 14,) on
the altar of Golgatha as a bloody sacrifice " to
cleanse our conscience from dead works and to
make us serve the living God." *By the Holy Ghost*,

the apostles and through them their legitimate successors were made partakers of Christ's priesthocd
and by virtue of this partaking, using His words,
they consecrate and sacrifice. Hence, the Spirit
of God descended upon the same cenacle where
the Blessed Sacrament was first consecrated.
Hence, the custom of old, to keep the consecrated particles in a silver vessel of the shape
of a dove. Hence, the majestic invocations of
the Oriental Liturgies to the Holy Ghost. Not
only is the Divine Spirit called down to change
bread and wine into the body and blood of Christ:
He is, moreover, called, in order to "make our
oblations *to us* the body and blood of Christ," that
is, to make the Sacrament salutary *to us* and
to give *us* a share in the grace contained therein.
It is, in fine, this same Divine Spirit, whom the
Church in her official prayers asks to prepare us for
a worthy celebration and reception of these divine
mysteries, saying : " *Teach me, thy unworthy servant, by Thy Holy Spirit, to approach so great a mystery with that reverence and honor, that devotion and
fear, which is due and fitting. Make me, through Thy
grace, always so to believe and understand, to conceive
and firmly to hold, to think and to speak, of that exceeding mystery, as shall please Thee and be good for
my soul. Let Thy good Spirit enter my heart, and
there be heard without utterance, and without the sound
of words speak all truth.*"
    What words can be more expressive and more
directly expressing our ideas, than these preceding
words, taken from the oration which the Roman
Breviary gives as a preparation for Holy Mass for
Sundays, as the "Oratio S. Ambrosii ?"
    After the Psalms to be recited before cele-
brating, the Church again places *seven* orations
to the Holy Spirit. In the following pages we
confine ourselves to giving : 1, some of these
orations, contained in the Breviary and translated
into English, which directly refer to the Holy
Spirit ; 2, some Latin orations taken from various

sources ; 3, a Mass of the Holy Ghost, as taken
from the little Manual of the Confraternity compiled by Very Rev. Rawes, D. D.

1.

Orations Before Holy Mass.

FIRST ORATION.

O Great High-Priest, the true Priest, Jesus
Christ, who didst offer Thyself to God the
Father a pure and spotless Victim upon the
Altar of the Cross for us miserable sinners,
and didst give us Thy Flesh to eat and Thy
Blood to drink, and *didst ordain this Mystery
in the power of Thy Holy Spirit, saying, Do this
for the commemoration of Me:* I pray Thee,
by the same Thy Blood, the great price of
our salvation ; I pray Thee, by that wonderful and unspeakable love wherewith Thou
deignedst so to love us, miserable and unworthy, as to wash us from our sins in Thine
own Blood : *teach me, Thy unworthy servant, by
Thy Holy Spirit,* to approach so great a Mystery with that reverence and honor, that devotion and fear, which is due and fitting.
Make me, through Thy grace, always so to
believe and understand, to conceive and
firmly to hold, to think and to speak, of that

exceeding Mystery, as shall please Thee and be good for my soul.

Let Thy good Spirit enter my heart, and there be heard without utterance, and without the sound of word speak all truth. For Thy Mysteries are exceeding deep, and covered with a sacred veil. For Thy great mercy's sake, grant me to approach Thy Holy Mysteries with a clean heart and a pure mind. Free my heart from all defiling and unholy, from all vain and hurtful thoughts. Fence me with the holy and faithful guard and mighty protection of Thy blessed Angels, that the enemies of all good may go away ashamed. By the virtue of this mighty Mystery, and by the hand of Thy holy Angel, drive away from me and from all Thy servants the hard spirit of pride and vain-glory, of envy, and blasphemy, of impurity and uncleanness, of doubting and mistrust. Let them be ashamed and put to confusion that seek after my soul. Let them be turned backward and blush for shame that wish me evil.

SECOND ORATION.

O Great High-Priest, the true Priest, Jesus Christ, who hast mercy upon all, and hatest nothing that Thou has made, remember

how frail our nature is, and that Thou art
our Saviour and our God. Be not angry
with us forever, and shut not up Thy tender
mercies in displeasure. For we humbly
present our prayers before Thy face, not trusting in our own righteousness, but in Thy
manifold and great mercies. *Take away
from me, O Lord, my iniquities, especially . . .
and mercifully kindle in me the fire of Thy Holy
Spirit.* Take away from me the heart of stone,
give me a heart of flesh, a heart to love and
adore Thee, a heart to delight in, to follow,
and to enjoy Thee. And I entreat Thy
mercy, O Lord, that Thou wouldst look down
graciously upon Thy family, as it pays its
vows to Thy Most Holy Name; and that the
desire of none may be in vain, nor their petitions unfulfilled, do Thou inspire our prayers, that they may be such as Thou delight-
est to hear and answer.

THIRD ORATION.

O Great High-Priest, the true Priest Jesus
Christ, I pray Thee for the souls of the faith-
ful departed (especially N.), that this great
Sacrament of Thy love my be to them
health and salvation, joy and refreshment.
O Lord, my God, grant them this day a great

and abundant feast of Thee, the living Bread, who camest down from Heaven and givest life unto to the world; even of Thy holy and blessed Flesh, the Lamb without spot, who takest away the sins of the world; even of that Flesh, which was taken of the Blessed Virgin Mary, and conceived by the Holy Ghost; and of that fountain of mercy which, by the soldiers lance, flowed from Thy most sacred Side; that they be thereby enlarged and satisfied, refreshed and comforted, and may rejoice in Thy praise and in Thy glory.

I pray Thy clemency, O Lord, that on the bread and wine to be offered unto Thee may descend the fulness of Thy blessing and the sanctification of Thy Divinity. *May there descend also the invisible and incomprehensible Majesty of Thy Holy Spirit, as it descended of old on the sacrifices of the Fathers,* which may make our oblations Thy Body and Blood; and may our prayers and offering be acceptable unto Thee, through Him who offered Himself a sacrifice to Thee, O Father, even Jesus Christ, Thine only Son our Lord.

2.

Some Orations in Latin for Priests:

1.

GRATIO AD S. SPIRITUM.

Sanctissime et adorande Spiritus, sine tuo numine nihil est in homine; ex te enim omnis sufficientia nostra. Sine te nihil boni facere, nec statu aut vocatione nostra fungi possumus: custodi animam meam, quoniam sanctus sum; fac servum tuum, Deus meus, sperantem in te. Sanctus sum dono fidei et gratiae, quo me in baptismo sanctificasti. Sanctus quoque sum munere sacerdotii, quo me fungi voluisti; id enim sanctum est; ut autem ei digne respondeam, sanctus esse debeo, id est, segregatus a terrenis purus, castus, multis gratiae dotibus et virtutibus conspicuus. Sed quis sanctum et mundum faciet de immundo conceptum semine? Tu utique, o Deus sanctificator, qui es sanctus sanctorum, a quo omnis sanctificatio nostra. Cor ergo mundum in me crea, et spiritum rectum innova in visceribus meis.

(From a Roman Breviary.)

2

ORATIONES AD SPIRITUM SACERDOTII CHRISTI.

1. *Oremus:* Resuscita in nobis Deus, gratiam salutarem, quam per manus impositionem nobis largiri dignatus es, ut, quos tibi ministros consecrasti, fideles dispensatores inveniamur.

2. *Deus*, qui summus sacerdos et hostia tuo corpore et sanguine reficis ministros, quos tibi consecrasti, concede, quaesumus, ut tui sacerdotii consortes digne ambulemus vocatione nostra et plebem tuam pascere studeamus verbo et exemplo.

3. *Deus*, qui facis angelos tuos spiritus et ministros flammam ignis, emitte Spiritum tuum et renova faciem cleri, ut sacerdotes, velut administratorii spiritus, in ministerium missi, de regno tuo tollant omnia scandala et ignem, quem venisti mittere in terram, in omnium cordibus accendant.   Amen.

3.

ORATIO SUPPLEX AD SPIRITUM S.

Veni, Sancte Spiritus, amor Patris et Filii, mundator scelerum, curator vulnerum, fortitudo fragilium, mœrentium consolator, fulgor intellectus, et vindex libertatis.   Veni e patria felicitatis, et cordis mei penetralibus tam potenter illabre, ut vitia omnia et defectus tuo igne consumas, et omnia peccata mea remittas. Emitte in animam meam lucis tuæ radium, quo illuminante intellectum, quæ tibi sunt placita, videam : quo affectum inflammante ad ea prosequenda tota virtute incumbam. Fac me dignum sacris altaribus ministrum, meque torrente tuæ voluptatis inebria, ut cœlesti suavitate in hac divinissima mensa degustata nihil venenatæ mundi dulcedinis libeat amplius degustare. Imbuat me et perficiat septiformis Spiritus tuus, et ad illum scientiæ gradum fac me pertingere, ad quem Apostolus tuus, cum dicebat se nihil scire nisi Christum et hunc crucifixum. Roboretur infirmitas mea fortitudine tua, vincat bonitas tua malitiam meam, et deformitas mea tua pulchritudine decoretur. Sursum erige me per æternorum affectionem, copula tecum per amoris unitatem, conserva per finalem perseverantiam ; ut tuo ductu revolet anima mea ad te, principium et finem suum, a quo nunquam separetur.　Amen.

(From Cardinalis Bona " De Sacrificio Missae.")

4.

ORATIO SERVI S. SPIRITUS.

Veni, Domine, et regna in servo tuo in plenitude virtutis tuæ, in perfectione viarum

tuarum et in sanctitate Spiritus tui et destrue
omnem potestatem inimici per tuam tuique
Spiritus potestatem ad gloriam Patris.
Amen.

3.

A Mass of the Holy Ghost.

· (From the Manual of the Confraternity).

At the Asperges.

'The earth was void and empty, and darkness was upon the face of the deep, and the Spirit of God moved over the waters: and God said, Be light made; and light was made.'

'I will pour out upon the house of David and upon the inhabitants of Jerusalem the Spirit of grace and of prayers; and they shall look on Me, whom they have pierced.'

'Jesus being baptised forthwith came out of the water; and lo, the Heavens were opened to Him, and He saw the Spirit of God descending as a dove, and coming upon Him.'

'He that hath an ear, let him hear what the Spirit saith to the Churches.'

'Not with an army nor by might, but by My Spirit, saith the Lord of Hosts.

'My Spirit shall be in the midst of you: fear not.'

'When He, the Spirit of truth is come, He will teach you all truth. For He shall not speak of Himself; but what things soever He shall hear He shall speak, and the things that are to come He shall show you. He shall glorify Me because He shall receive of Mine, and shall show it to you.'

At the Judica.

Help me, O Holy Ghost, to make myself ready for the judgment of the Son of Man. I am full of darkness and full of sin, but I have a great longing to be better than I am. Through my own faithlessness I am often overcome by temptation. Thou art my strength against the tempter. I fall when I forget Thee, O Thou Helper of my weakness. I am blind and poor and weak in myself; but Thou pourest on me the riches of grace and makest me see what is right, and givest me strength to do it. Without Thee I can do nothing; but with Thy help I can keep from sin, and grow in grace and enter into life. O ever-living Spirit, dear and precious, make me more and more a child of the light, that I may walk in that light and inherit the promises. Keep always before my eyes the judgment to which I must one day come.

Thou who didst come to the disciples at Ephesus, by the hand of St. Paul, come more and more to us, who are Thy Servants, praying for Thy glory; longing to love Thee more; and longing to be more loved by Thee.

At the Confiteor.

By Thee, Spirit of the Father and of the Son, I confess my sins, and by Thee I am sorry for them. When I look back and see the greatness of my sins, the evil that I have done, and the good that I have not done, how thankless I have been and how wilful, how I have hardened my heart to Thy voice and blinded my eyes to Thy light, my soul is overwhelmed with fear, and faints within me, and crieth out in pain. But when I turn to Thee and rest on Thee, amid the sprinkling of the Blood of Jesus, Thou dost give me great comfort and much confidence in God and the fulness of Thy peace. Thy peace is the peace of Jesus, which the world can neither give nor take away. Not as the world giveth dost Thou give that peace to me. Give me grace, O adorable Spirit, to hate sin and to love justice according to Thy will. Save

me from the guilt of mortal sin; and, if I
fall, grant that I may always hasten to the
Sacrament of Penance, the fountain opened
for the washing of the sinner. Take away
all the evil that is in me, and make my
soul bright with the brightness of the kingdom of God. Let Thy light shine in my
soul, for by Thee we are new-born in light.

At the Introit.

O Holy Ghost, I long greatly to enter
into that Home of God, where Thou dwell-
est in Thy strength, in Thy wisdom, and in
Thy love. There Thou art ever adored by
Saints and Angels; and there Thy Servants
serve Thee and see Thy face. Everything
is worthless but the possession of Thee
and the sight of Thy Godhead, as Thou
fillest all in all. Thou art God over all,
blessed forever more. It is always a hidden joy in my soul that Thou art what
Thou art. I praise Thee and bless Thee
for Thy great glory. Bring me, O uncreated Love, to the city on the heavenly
Mount Sion, from which they who enter go
out no more. It was of Thee that Jesus
said, 'I will ask the Father, and he will give
you another Paraclete, who will abide with
you for ever.'

At the Kyrie.

Have mercy upon me, O Blessed Spirit, because of Thy goodness. In Thy kindness and graciousness cleanse me from my sins. Have mercy upon me; for Thou art God, and I am dust and ashes. Have mercy upon me; for Thou art wise and strong, and I am weak and blind, and Thou knowest whereof I am made. Thou knowest it, for Thou didst make me. With all my strength I turn in my sinfulness to Thee, and ask Thee for Thy help. O, bring me, adorable Spirit, to the Heart of my Lord. Thou art the Helper of my infirmities, and, with great gentleness Thou drawest me upward, giving me light, giving me strength, giving me hope. From the desert Thou bringest me to a land flowing with milk and honey. From the cities of the plain Thy Angel leads me to my mountain-refuge and the shining crest of Libanus. From the tents of Kedar Thou dost draw me sweetly to the Tabernacles of the King, making me glad when I go into the house of my Lord. O Holy Ghost, Spirit of love, have mercy, have mercy upon me. Thou dost gather us from all lands, and dost pour upon us clean water, washing us from all our sins and giving us a new spirit.

At the Gloria.

Glory be to Thee in the highest, O Spirit
of the living God. Blessing and praise and
love and worship and honor and power be
to Thee for ever and ever. May Thy might
be made known among men, and Thy wisdom
to the ends of the earth. May all creatures in
Heaven and in Purgatory and on earth
know Thy love more and more, because of
the greatness of Thy work in the Church of
Jesus. Thou art infinite, immense, eternal.
Thou art in every way equal to the Father,
and in every way equal to the Son. With
the Father and the Son Thou art one God
in Thy indivisible substance. Thou art the
Love of the Father and of the Son. By one
spiration Thou dost ever proceed from Them,
as from one principle. Thou art the bond of
the Ever-blessed Trinity, and Thy life doth
not change. Thou art Thine own beauti-
tude, Thine own glory, Thine own life,
Thou art our life and our comforter, the
Paraclete who came from Jesus. Thou art
the living Water which Jesus gives to those
who believe in Him. Thou art light : Thy
light is come, and thou dost enlighten Jerusalem. Thou, the Lord, hast risen upon
us, and Thy glory is seen upon us. The
Gentiles walk in Thy light, and kings in the

brightness of Thy rising.   There cometh to
Thee the strength of the nations, and Thou
dost abound in the multitude of the sea.
That which is first said of the Incarnate
Word, in another way we say of Thee.   Thy
sons came to thee from afar, and Thy
daughters rise up at Thy side.   'Who are
these that fly as clouds, and as doves to
their windows?   They are gathered together; they come to Thee.   The glory of
Libanus is Thine.   We, Thy Servants, love
Thee with all our strength, and bless Thee
and praise Thee and glorify Thee for ever.

At the Collects.

O Spirit of love, give me grace to know
Thee better, and to taste and see how sweet
and how gracious Thou art.   The joy of the
world is nothing; and the pleasure of creatures is nothing; the desire of the eyes is
nothing; but Thou are all in all, and at Thy
right hand there are pleasures for evermore.
With Thee is the joy which fadeth not, and
the love which ceaseth not.   With Thee
is the day of rest that remaineth for the
people of God.   With Thee is the fulness
of bliss.   O Spirit of glory, let the thought
of this be ever with me, and let the hope
of this be the day-star of my soul.   By the

love that Thou hast for Jesus, save me from
the evil and keep me from sin.   O Spirit of
peace, my own Beloved, I trust Thee and
give myself to Thee.   Thou dost teach me;
for Thou art the Holy Spirit, the Paraclete,
whom the Father sent in the name of Jesus.

At the Epistle.

'There is now, therefore, no condemnation to them that are in Christ Jesus, who
walk not according to the flesh; for the law
of the Spirit of Life in Christ Jesus hath delivered me from the law of sin and death.
For what the law could not do, in that it
was weak in the flesh, God, sending His
Son in the likeness of sinful flesh and of
sin, hath condemned sin in the flesh, that
the justification of the law might be fulfilled in us who walk not according to the
flesh, but according to the Spirit.   For they
that are according to the flesh mind the
things that are of the flesh; but they that
are according to the Spirit mind the things
of the Spirit: for the wisdom of the flesh
is death, but the wisdom of the Spirit is
life and peace: because the wisdom of the
flesh is an enemy to God; for it is not subject to the law of God, nor can be; and
they who are in the flesh cannot please

God. But you are not in the flesh, but in the Spirit, if so be that the Spirit of God dwell in you. Now, if any man have not the Spirit of Christ, he is none of His: and if Christ be in you, the body indeed is dead because of sin, but the spirit liveth because of justification; and if the Spirit of Him that raised up Jesus from the dead dwell in you, He that raised up Jesus Christ from the dead shall quicken also your mortal bodies, because of His Spirit that dwelleth in you. Therefore, brethren, we are debtors not to the flesh, to live according to the flesh, for if you live according to the flesh you shall die. But if by the Spirit you mortify the deeds of the flesh you shall live; for whosoever are led by the Spirit of God they are the sons of God. For you have not received the spirit of bondage again in fear, but you have received the spirit of adoption of sons, whereby we cry, Abba, Father: for the Spirit Himself giveth testimony to our spirit that we are the sons of God: and, if sons, heirs also; heirs indeed of God, and joint heirs with Christ, yet so if we suffer with Him, that we may also be glorified with Him.'

Jesus, King and Spouse, Thou dost ever give to us the joy of Thy Spirit.

At the Munda cor meum.

O Holy Ghost, Uncreated Love of the Ever-blessed Trinity, Thou art living Water and living Fire. Drench my heart in the streams of Thy grace, and make it clean before Thee. Drench my heart in the fire of Thy love, and burn up all the dross in it, that it may be bright in Thy eyes. Adorable Spirit, be to me the water of life. Adorable Spirit, be to me also that flame of judgment and of burning by which Sion and Jerusalem are cleansed.

Jesus, let Thy Holy Spirit dwell ever more and more in my heart.

At the Gospel.

'Amen, amen I say to thee, unless a man be born again of water and the Holy Ghost he cannot enter into the kingdom of God. That which is born of the flesh is flesh, and that which is born of the Spirit is spirit. Wonder not that I said to thee, You must be born again. The Spirit breatheth where He will, and thou hearest His voice; but thou knowest not whence He cometh or whither He goeth: so is every one that is born of the Spirit.'

'Jesus said, If thou didst know the gift

of God, and who is He that saith to thee,
Give me to drink, thou perhaps wouldst
have asked of Him, and He would have
given thee living water .... Whosoever
drinketh of this water shall thirst again;
but he that shall drink of the water that
I will give him shall not thirst for ever:
but the water that I will give him shall
become in him a fountain of water springing up to everlasting life.'

'When the Paraclete cometh, whom I
will send you from the Father, the Spirit
of truth who proceedeth from the Father,
He shall give testimony of Me . 　I tell
you the truth: it is expedient for you that
I go, for if I go not the Paraclete will not
come to you; but if I go I will send Him
to you: 　.. and when He is come He will
convince the world of sin and of justice
and of judgment: of sin, because they believed not in Me; and of justice, because
I go to the Father, and ye see Me no more;
and of judgment, because the prince of this
world is already judged.'

'The Paraclete, the Holy Ghost, whom
the Father will send in My name, He will
teach you all things, and bring all things to
your mind, whatsoever I shall have said to
you. Peace I leave with you; My peace I
give unto you; not as the world giveth do I

give to you. Let not your heart be troubled, nor let it be afraid.'

Jesus, Thou dost feed us with the wheat of Heaven, and dost satisfy us with honey from the rock.

At the Credo.

O Spirit of truth, keep my faith bright and strong. Let it never be dimmed— never be shaken. I love Thee and bless Thee for all that Thou hast revealed in the Scriptures of God. I praise Thee for all that Thou hast taught us by Divine traditions, and by the infallible voice of the Vicar of Christ, and by the Councils of the Church. I bless Thee and thank Thee for the writings of theologians, dogmatic and moral and mystical and ascetic. In their pages I see Thy presence and feel the touch of Thy hand. Thou art ever moving over the waters, as at the beginning. Thou dost ever guide us, and dost ever draw us upward to Thyself. With all my heart I trust Thee and believe Thy word. I believe beforehand all that Thou mayest teach by the Apostolic See till the day of doom. Wisely and sweetly Thou dost order all things from one end of the world to the other: wisely and sweetly, at fitting times, Thou dost teach the Church by the

successor of St. Peter, fixing the ancient
landmarks, and defining doctrines according to Thy will.   As it has ever been, so
it is now, and so it will be till the sign of
the Son of Man shall be seen in Heaven,
when He cometh with clouds, and every
eye shall see Him, and we shall look on
Him whom we pierced.   O Spirit of God,
I trust Thee utterly, and seek Thee always,
and find in Thee the fulness of truth.   Thou
commandest the clouds above, and openest
the doors of Heaven, and rainest down
manna on us to eat, and givest us the
Bread of Life.

At the Offertory.

O Holy Ghost, Thou life-giving Spirit,
overshadow this bread and this chalice of
salvation.   The priest is praying, and saying,
'Come, Thou Sanctifier, Almighty. Eternal
God, and bless this sacrifice made ready
for Thy name.'   Give me grace always so
to offer myself to Thee that I may be to
Thee a sacrifice of light.   Thou givest me
food in abundance: let me not bring upon
myself the wrath of God by sin; let me
not turn back and grieve the Holy One of
Israel.

At the Lavabo.

O Spirit of grace, wash me from my wickedness, and cleanse me from my sins. Have mercy on me, O God, according to Thy great goodness. I have done evil before Thee; I have sinned against Thee; I have wasted Thy gifts and have grieved Thee. If Thou wilt sprinkle me, I shall be made clean : if Thou wilt wash me, I shall be whiter than snow. By the merits of Jesus, and His adorable Blood, I ask Thee to turn away Thy face from my sins, and to blot out all my iniquities. I ask Thee by Thy love of the Incarnate Word, to renew in me a right spirit, and to make in me a clean heart. So wilt Thon strengthen me, and give me joy. Thou wilt give me the joy of Thy glory, that I may give thanks for ever to Thee. In Thy love Thou wilt call me, O Spirit of life, to Thy heavenly kingdom.

At the Secret Prayers.

O Holy Ghost, secretly and silently Thou doest Thy work in the heart. With the Father and the Son Thou dost come to us, and dost make Thy abode with us. Help me to love Jesus, that there may be always this abiding of God in my soul. Turn the wilderness of my soul into pools of water, and the dry land of my spirit into springing wells. Thou dost sow the fields, and dost plant the vineyards; bless me, that I may yield fruit pleasing to Thee. Make me wise, that I may keep Thy commandments, and understand Thy mercies. Great above the Heavens is Thy mercy. Strengthen my soul by the Word of the Lord, for Thou art the Spirit of His mouth.

At the Preface.

O Most Merciful Spirit, I love and adore Thee for Thy goodness. O Most Gracious Spirit, I praise Thee and adore Thee for Thy love. O Spirit of might, who dost break the rocks in pieces, I fear Thee and adore Thee for Thy strength. Thou dost understand all my thoughts; Thou dost know all my ways. Thou givest me Thy gifts of grace in Thy love and wisdom. 'By wisdom the house shall be built, and by prudence it shall be strengthened. By instruction the store-rooms shall be filled with all precious and most beautiful wealth.' Give me the wealth of Thy grace, and build up the house of my soul. Rise always in me, and let Thine enemies be scattered: and let Those that hate Thee fly before Thy face. Let me not lose hope through weariness in the day of distress. I can do nothing of myself; but in Thee and with Thee I can overcome and be faithful, and walk even here with Jesus in white.

Our Lady of the Holy Ghost, pray for me.

At the Canon.

'Who among men is he that can know the counsel of God? Or who can think what the will of God is? For the thoughts of mortal men are fearful, and our counsels uncertain. For the corruptible body is a load upon the soul; and the earthly habitation presseth down the mind that museth upon many things: and hardly do we guess aright at things that are upon earth; and with labor do we find the things that are before us. But the things that are in Heaven who shall search out? And who shall know Thy thought, unless Thou give wisdom, and send Thy Holy Spirit from above: and so the ways of them that are on earth may be corrected, and men may learn the things that may please Thee?'

'O, how good and sweet is Thy Spirit, O Lord, in all things: and therefore Thou dost chastise them that err, by little and little; and dost admonish them, and speakest to them, and concerning the things wherein they offend, that, leaving their wickedness, they may believe in Thee, O Lord.'

'So much then as Thou art just, Thou orderest all things justly; thinking it not agreeable to Thy power to condemn him who deserveth not to be punished. For Thy power is the beginning of justice, and because Thou art Lord of all Thou makest Thyself gracious to all. For Thou showest Thy power when men will not believe Thee to be absolute in power; and Thou dost convince the boldness of men that know Thee not. But Thou being master of power judgest with tranquillity, and with great reverence disposest of us; for Thy power is at hand when Thou wilt.'

Great is Thy strength, O Holy Ghost; make firm, O God, the things that Thou hast wrought in me.

Commemoration of the Living.

O Holy Ghost, Spirit of the Father and the Son, let the might of Thy love be more and more felt in the hearts of men. Let Thy light shine more and more on souls that are wandering in the darkness far away from God. Turn them to the light-giving Heart of Jesus and to the healing streams of His Precious Blood. Strengthen and hearten the souls that love Thee. Perfect in them Thy seven gifts and Thy twelve fruits; and so make them Thy temples here that Thou mayest be adored in them for ever.

At the Hanc igitur.

'It is written that eye hath not seen nor ear heard, neither hath it entered into the heart of man, what things God hath prepared for them that love Him. But to us God hath revealed them by His Spirit; for the Spirit searcheth all things, yea, the deep things of God. For what man knoweth the things of a man but the spirit of a man that is in him? So the things also that are of God no man knoweth but the Spirit of God. Now we have received not the spirit of this world, but the Spirit that is of God, that we may know the things that are given us from God; which things also we speak, not in the learned words of human wisdom, but in the doctrine of the Spirit, comparing spiritual things with spiritual. But the sensual man perceiveth not these things that are of the Spirit of God; for it is foolishness to him, and he cannot understand, because it is spiritually

examined. But the spiritual man judgeth
all things, and he himself is judged by no
man : for who hath known the mind of the
Lord that he may instruct Him ? But we
have the mind of Christ.'

O Spirit of wisdom, enlighten our souls,
and let our mouths be filled with Thy praise.

At the Consecration.

O Holy Ghost, by Thee Jesus offered Himself without spot to God. Being anointed
and sanctified in His manhood by that
substantial holiness which is the Word, He
was also anointed and sanctified by Thee,
O Thou Eternal Spirit. Being holy by the
grace of union, He was holy also by the
created grace which Thou dost give. His
Human Nature is hypostatically united to
the Word, and it is also Thy Temple, O
Spirit of promise. Now the Sacrifice is
offered on the Altar, and this Jesus, whom
we love, is the Lamb slain, who yet dieth no
more. We adore Thee, O Father, and Thee
O Son, and Thee, O Holy Ghost, in this
mystery of Heaven. We adore Thee, the
One God, dwelling in the inaccessible light.
Towards that light our souls are lifted, and
in Thy love they are hidden, O Blessed
Trinity.

O Holy Ghost, loved and loving, who didst overshadow the Mother of God in the splendor of the Incarnation, overshadow now this Altar of Sacrifice, and keep us in the light with Thee. By Thee the spotless Victim is offered to God. Thy love and Thy wisdom and Thy might are seen in these high places of the city of peace. Thou bringest to me the joys of the morning, and the sweetness of the Garden of the King.

At the Commemoration of the Dead.

The Holy souls are Thy temples, Thou gracious Spirit, and Thou dost watch over them, and love them, and help them in their pain. The dimness of their dwelling-place is an abode for Thee, and the brightness of their souls is the kindling of Thy light. They ever taste and know the sweetness of Thy care and the watchful tenderness of Thy love. Dear Spirit, help these loved ones of God. . . .

O Mary, bride of the Holy Ghost, pray for these suffering souls, who are very dear to thy Spouse of light. Pray for them in the piercing keenness of their pain, that they may soon come to the vision of God.

At the Nobis quoque.

Our hearts faint within us, Blessed Spirit, when we think of all the gifts that Thou givest to us sinners. In Thy love Thou dost make us Thy friends. One thing we ask of Thee, that we may be more faithful to Thy light. It is sweet to think of Thee in Thy works. It is very sweet to think of Thy unction in our Lord as man, and of Thy love poured fourth in the Soul of the Holy Child Jesus, whom Thou didst anoint. Thy gifts and fruits are in Him, as in no other created spirit. He is God and man. He was dead, and liveth for evermore, having in His pierced hands the keys of hell and of death. O Jesus, Saviour, King, Judge, anointed with the Holy Ghost, draw me to Thyself, and be to me more and more an everlasting rest.

Our Lady of the Holy Ghost, ask thy Spouse of love to bless me more and more.

O ye seven Spirits who stand before the Face of Jesus, the faithful witness and firstborn of the dead, kindle the fire of God in our souls, and be to us round about like a wall of flame.

Jesus 'hath loved us and washed us from our sins in His own Blood.'

At the Pater noster.

O Holy Ghost, my Lord and my Love, in Thee I say this prayer of my Elder Brother, my Saviour and God. Thou hast given me the spirit of the adoption of a son, and by Thee I cry Abba, Father. Thou dost make me and keep me the child of my Father, who is in Heaven. Once I was a great darkness; now by Thee I am light in the Lord. Give me grace to walk as a child of the light. They who are led by the Spirit of God are the children of God. Give me grace so to be faithful to Thee, that in me the name of God may be hallowed, and that by me the will of God may be done. Thou art the all-wise Love, who dost save us from evil, and dost lead us into light. In Thee, O Holy Ghost, I have hoped; let me not be cast away. In Thy goodness free me and save me, for I love Thee and trust Thee.

At the Agnus Dei.

O ever-loving Spirit, by Thee the holy Baptist, when he saw Jesus coming to him, said, 'Behold the Lamb of God; behold Him who taketh away the sins of the world.' Fill my heart with sorrow for my sins, and lead me to the Fountain of

cleansing.   Thou dost bring me to the
Precious Blood by which we are redeemed
from all peoples and tongues.   By Thee
the holy Baptist said of Jesus, 'He it is
that baptiseth with the Holy Ghost."   O
indwelling Spirit, make me ever more and
more a dwelling of God.   Give me light
to understand better the holiness of His
living temples ; and give me strength to
strive more earnestly to keep myself without spot, blameless to the coming of my
Lord to Jesus Christ.   Now help me, Thy
Servant, that then I may love Thee and
praise Thee and adore Thee for ever in Thy
kingdom.

Our Lady of the Holy Ghost, pray for all
faithful souls.

At the Communion.

'Know you not that you are the temple
of God, and that the Spirit of God dwelleth
in you?   But if any man defile the temple
of God, him will God destroy ; for the temple
of God is holy, which you are.'

'Grieve not the Holy Spirit of God whereby you are sealed to the day of redemption.'

'We in spirit by faith, wait for the hope
of justice.'

'I therefore, a prisoner in the Lord, beseech you that you walk worthy of the vocation in which you are called, with all humility and mildness, with patience, supporting one another in charity, careful to keep the unity of the Spirit in the bond of peace: one body and one Spirit, as you are called in one hope of your calling; one Lord, one faith, one Baptism; one God and Father of all, who is above all and through all and in all.'

'Be renewed in the Spirit of your mind; and put on the new man, who, according to God, is created in justice and holiness of truth.'

'According to the foreknowledge of God the Father, unto the sanctification of the Spirit, unto obedience and sprinkling of the Blood of Jesus Christ, grace unto you, and · peace be multiplied.'

'Purifying your souls in the obedience of charity, with a brotherly love, from a sincere heart, love one another earnestly; being born again not of corruptible seed, but incorruptible, by the Word of God, who liveth and remaineth for ever.'

At the Collects.

O Holy Ghost, Living God, dwell in me, and let the sunshine of Thy love ripen Thy fruits in my soul. May I grow in love, joy, and peace; in patience, kindness, and goodness; in long-suffering, mildness, and faith; in modesty, continence and chastity. Help me to crucify the flesh with its vices and desires. Let me not fail in doing good, that in due time I may reap. Show Thy mercy upon the Israel of God. Hear me quickly, O Lord, for without Thee my spirit faileth, and my life withereth away. Guide me, for Thou art the Spirit of grace; and bring me to my inheritance, for Thou art the Spirit of truth. Make me poor in spirit, that mine may be the kingdom of Heaven.

O Mother of God, sanctified by the Holy Ghost in thy Immaculate Conception, pray for me.

O Mother of God, sanctified by the Holy Ghost in the sweetness and brightness of thy Annunciation, pray for me.

O Mother of God, sanctified by the Holy Ghost in the flames of Pentecost and the fire of thy uncreated Love, pray for me.

O ye Apostles of the Lamb, filled with the Holy Ghost at Pentecost, and crowned with living fire, pray for me.

At the Last Gospel.

'There shall come forth a rod out of the root of Jesse, and a flower shall rise up out of his root; and the Spirit of the Lord shall rest upon Him; the Spirit of wisdom and understanding, the Spirit of counsel and of fortitude, the Spirit of knowledge and of godliness; and He shall be filled with the Spirit of the fear of the Lord."

'Be not deceived, God is not mocked; for what things a man shall sow, those also shall he reap. For he that soweth in his flesh, of the flesh also shall reap corruption. But he that soweth in the Spirit, shall of the Spirit reap life everlasting.'

'The fruit of the light is in all goodness and justice and truth; proving what is well pleasing to God: and have no fellowship with the unfruitful works of darkness, but rather reprove them. For the things that are done by them in secret it is a shame even to speak of. But all things that are reproved are made manifest by the light, for all that is made manifest is light. See, therefore, brethren, how you walk circumspectly; not as unwise, but as wise, redeeming the time because the days are evil. Wherefore become not unwise, but understanding what is the will of God.'

'Put you on the armor of God, that you may be able to stand against the deceits of the devil. For our wrestling is not against flesh and blood; but against principalities and powers, against the rulers of the world of this darkness, against the spirits of wickedness in the high places. Therefore take unto you the armor of God, that you may be able to resist in the evil day, and to stand in all things perfect. Stand, therefore, having your loins girt about with truth, and having on the breastplate of justice; and your feet shod with the preparation of the gospel of peace: in all things taking the shield of faith, wherewith you may be able to extinguish all the fiery darts of the most wicked one; and take unto you the helmet of salvation, and the sword of the Spirit, which is the Word of God.'

O Holy Ghost, most precious, most dearly loved, Thou God of my salvation, I cry to Thee in the daytime, and in the night to Thee I lift up my voice. Thy mercy and Thy truth are built up forever in Heaven. They go before Thy face. Thou art glorified in the assembly of the Saints. Justice and judgment are the preparation of Thy Throne. Let me, Thy Servant, walk in the light of Thy countenance, and rejoice in Thy name. Let Thy hand help me and Thine arm strengthen me. Let my words come in before Thee, and bend down Thine ear to my prayer.

O Holy Ghost, whom my soul loveth, I

bless Thee and thank Thee and praise Thee with all my heart for the help that Thou hast given to me, the unworthiest of Thy Servants, in hearing this Mass. Let its light be in me, all day and all night, like the morning star, like the shining of the sun, like the brightness of seven days. Let it drive far from me every kind of darkness, and every shadow of gloom. May the offering of this Victim of God be strength and light in my soul till the glory of Jesus Crucified again falls on me from the Altar. Give me every day more love for this adorable Sacrifice. Let me be always very glad when I can go to the Altar of my God. Show me every day more and more of the splendor and sweetness of Mass, as the light of Jesus comes to Jerusalem, and the glory of my Lord rises upon me. Give me always silver for iron, O Thou bountiful Spirit, and for brass enrich me with gold. Bring me always to my Redeemer in Sion, that I may inherit the land in which are trees of Thy planting, and harvests of which Thou didst sow the seed. Be to me an everlasting joy, and give to me Thy everlasting light, O Spirit of love and grace. Make me, the least of Thy Servants, an everlasting glory where the sun goeth down no more.

IV

Prayers to the Holy Ghost for Extraordinary Occasions.

To rouse once more in the servants of the Holy Ghost the spirit of devotion and of supplication, we again give as an introduction to this class of prayers another exhortation of Cardinal Manning:

Be devout to the Third Person of the Holy Trinity. To know Him, His presence, personality, and power, His twofold office in the Church and in our own soul, is the condition of the perfect illumination of the intellect. Without this, the intellect may be cultivated, but it will be cold and dim. The errors, low views, fragmentary opinions, distorted judgments, partial statements, ill-sounding propositions, shallow appreciations, of men endowed with great natural gifts, are to be traced to an inadequate realization of the office of the Holy Spirit, and of His relation to their intellect and their will. Their theology is like themselves. A student who is united by the gift of piety to the light of the Holy Spirit will be implicitly a theologian. The degree of his explicit knowledge will still depend on natural gifts, and their due cultivation; and yet there is an infused theology in docile hearts which is seldom at fault, and often transcends the cultivation of the intellectual.

Before and after your studies, ask light from your divine Teacher. Then, with the page before you, preserve a consciousness of your dependence upon Him.

St. Edmund was one day waiting in the schools of Paris for the coming of his scholars. He was about to expound to them the mystery of the Holy Trinity. While they tarried, he fell into a slumber or a rapture; and he saw a Dove descending towards him. It bore in its beak the Sacred Host, and laid It on his lips. When he returned to himself, he began his lecture, and all who heard him wondered at the words of sweetness and of light which proceeded out of his mouth. It was this which gave to all he spoke its energy and power. The few brief writings which remain to us are full of the unction and the fire of the Spirit of God.

(Card. Manning, "The disciples of the Holy Ghost." Sermons on Ecclesiastical subjects, page 338.)

1.

Prayers of the Seven Gifts of the Holy Spirit.

(From the Manual of Rev. Rawes.)

1.

Come, Holy Ghost, Thou Lord of love;
Pour on us from Thy throne above
Thy unction and Thy light.

Come, O Spirit of Wisdom, and teach our hearts how to value and love heavenly things, and how to seek for them always before the things of earth. Show us the way by which we may gain the joys of Heaven, and keep them for ever. Amen.
Our Father. Hail Mary. Glory.

2.

Come, Holy Ghost, Thou Lord of love;
Pour on us from Thy throne above
Thy unction and Thy light.

Come, O Spirit of Understanding, and enlighten our minds, that we may know and believe all the mysteries of salvation; and may merit at last to see the eternal light in Thy light, and in the light of glory to have the clear vision of Thee and the Father and the Son.
Our Father, Hail Mary. Glory.

3.

Come, Holy Ghost, Thou Lord of love ;
Pour on us from Thy throne above
Thy unction and Thy light.

Come, O Spirit of Counsel, and help us
in all the changes of this mortal life. Keép
our minds from what is evil, and turn
them to what is good. Guide us in the
straight way of Thy Commandments to the
wished-for home of everlasting rest.

Our Father. Hail Mary. Glory.

4.

Come, Holy Ghost, Thou Lord of love ;
Pour on us from Thy throne above
Thy unction and Thy light.

Come, O Spirit of Fortitude, and give
fortitude to our souls. Make our hearts
strong in all trials and in all distress,
pouring forth abundantly into them the
gifts of strength, that we may be able to
resist the attacks of the devil. Help us,
Spirit of strength, to win the victory, so
that we may not be cut off from Thee, our
highest good and our God.

Our Father. Hail Mary. Glory.

SPECIAL DEVOTION

5.

Come, Holy Ghost, Thou Lord of love;
Pour on us from Thy throne above
Thy unction and Thy light.

Come, O Spirit of Knowledge; make us understand and despise the emptiness and nothingness of the world. Give us grace to use the world only for Thy glory and the salvation of Thy creatures. May we always be very faithful in choosing Thy rewards before every earthly gift.

Our Father. Hail Mary. Glory.

6.

Come, Holy Ghost, Thou Lord of love;
Pour on us from Thy throne above
Thy unction and Thy light.

Come, O Spirit of Piety, and fill our hearts to overflowing with love of the Lord our God, that we may always seek Him with true devotion, and always find Him in the charity which surpasseth knowledge, and in the peace which the world can neither give nor take away.

Our Father. Hail Mary. Glory.

7.

Come, Holy Ghost, Thou Lord of love;
Pour on us from Thy throne above
Thy unction and Thy light.

Come, O Spirit of the Fear of the Lord, and with holy fear pierce our flesh and our spirit through and through, that we may always keep Thee, the Lord our God, in our hearts, and may always live in Thy sight. Give us grace always to shun with the greatest care everything that may be in the least displeasing to the most pure eyes of Thy majestic Godhead.

Our Father. Hail Mary. Glory.

V. Come, Holy Spirit, fill the hearts of Thy servants:

R. And kindle in them the fire of Thy love.

V. O Lord, hear Thou our prayer:

R. And let our cry come to Thee.

Let us pray.

Mercifully pour forth into our hearts, we beseech Thee, O Lord, Thy Holy Spirit, by whose wisdom we have been made, and by whose providence we are governed; through our Lord Jesus Christ.

V. May the help of God be always with us.

R. Amen.

2.

Acts of Adoration.

(From Father Rawes' Manual.)

1.

1. I adore Thee, Eternal Spirit of God, giving graces to the heathen and to unbelievers.

2. I adore Thee, Eternal Spirit of God, converting souls from mortal sin.

3. I adore Thee, Eternal Spirit of God, quickening to sorrow the souls that do penance.

4. I adore Thee, Eternal Spirit of God, who dost dwell in my own soul and dost sanctify it.

5. I adore Thee, Eternal Spirit of God, burning up in souls all affection to venial sin.

6. I adore Thee, Eternal Spirit of God, filling souls with light and love and strength; leading them on to perfection; giving them grace to have their lives always hidden with Christ in God.

7. I adore Thee, Eternal Spirit of God, giving to souls the grace of final perseverance, and crowning them in the judgment of the Son.

2.

1. I adore Thee, Spirit of the Father and the Son, in the Holy Angels, and especially in the Seven Princes who stand before the Face of God.

2. I adore Thee, Spirit of the Father and the Son, in the Twenty-four Ancients, and the Four Living Creatures; in the Choir of the Virgin-Martyrs, and in the Hierarchy of the Incarnation.

3. I adore Thee, Spirit of the Father and the Son, in the great multitude which no man can number, of all nations and tribes and peoples and tongues; standing before the Throne and in sight of the Lamb; clothed with white robes, and palms in their hand; crying with a loud voice and saying, Salvation to our God who sitteth on the Throne and to the Lamb.

4. I adore Thee, Spirit of the Father and the Son, in the hundred and forty and four thousand, standing with the Lamb on Mount Sion; having His name and the name of His Father written in their foreheads; the first-fruits to God and the Lamb; who follow the Lamb whithersoever He goeth, and are without spot before the Throne of God.

5. I adore Thee, Spirit of the Father and the Son, in the Immaculate Heart of Mary,

the elect Daughter of the Eternal Father.

6. I adore Thee, Spirit of the Father and the Son, in the Sovereignty of Mary, the elect Virgin-Mother of the Incarnate Word.

7. I adore Thee, Spirit of the Father and the Son, in the twelve-starred crown of Mary, Thine elect Bride.

3.

1. I adore Thee, Spirit of the Living God, in the infallible Scriptures of truth, which Thou hast revealed.

2. I adore Thee, Spirit of the Living God, in the Sacraments of the dead, and in the Sacraments of the living.

3. I adore Thee, Spirit of the Living God, in the suffering and the joy and the waiting of the souls in Purgatory.

4. I adore Thee, Spirit of the Living God, in the light of infallible truth shining from the throne of Peter, the first Vicar of our Lord.

5. I adore Thee, Spirit of the Living God, in the Passion of Jesus, in His Precious Blood, and in the Holy Sacrifice of the Mass.

6. I adore Thee, Spirit of the Living God, in the Heart of Jesus, hidden in the Tabernacle, and in the Heart of Jesus, given in Communion.

7. I adore Thee, Spirit of the Living God, in the Heart of Jesus, the King in His beauty, the Desired of all nation, the Desire of the everlasting Hills, on the saphire Throne of the Ancient of days.

3.

Little Office of the Holy Ghost.

(From the Manual of Rev. Rawes.)

THE OFFICE OF THE HOLY GHOST.

At Matins.

May the grace of the Holy Ghost enlighten our minds and our hearts. Amen.

V. O Lord, open Thou our lips:

R. And our mouth shall show forth Thy praise.

V. O God, make speed to save us.

R. O Lord, make haste to help us.

Glory. Alleluia.

From Septuagesima to Holy Thursday, instead of Alleluia, is said, Praise be to Thee, O Lord, Thou King of everlasting glory.

Hymn.

From the rippling of the river,
　From the waving Tree of life,
Gabriel came, a fiery splendor,
　Came from God to Joseph's wife.

When with spirit, strong and tender,
　Low he knelt in Mary's cell,
In the wondrous work of ages
　Jesus came with us to dwell.

Ant. Come, Holy Ghost, fill the hearts of Thy faithful ones, and kindle in them the fire of Thy love.

V. Send forth Thy Spirit, and they shall be made:

R. And Thou shalt renew the face of the earth.

Prayer.

May the power of the Holy Ghost be ever with us, we beseech Thee, O God; and may He in His mercy cleanse our hearts and save us from all dangers; through our Lord Jesus Christ, who with Thee and the same Holy Ghost liveth and reigneth, one God, world without end. Amen.

At Lauds.

May the grace of the Holy Ghost enlighten our minds and our hearts. Amen.

V. O God, make speed to save us.
R. O Lord, make haste to help us.
Glory.   Alleluia.

Hymn.

Angels, kneeling by the Manger,
Gazed upon the kingly Child;
Jesus, born of Virgin-Mother,
Looked up in her face and smiled.

Through long years He dwelt with Mary
In the Holy Home unseen;
Waiting for the time appointed
Lived the lowly Nazarene.

Ant. Come, Holy Ghost, &c., with the prayer as before.

———

At Prime.

May the grace of the Holy Ghost enlighten our minds and our hearts.   Amen.
V. O God, make speed to save us.
R. O Lord, make haste to help us.
Glory.   Alleluia.

Hymn.

On He went with blessings laden
In His sweetness and His might;
And the souls that lay in darkness
Saw the shining of His light.

> Crucified and dead, He slumbered
>   Sweetly in His Garden grave :
> In His risen light ascending
>   Blessings to His own He gave.

Ant. Come, Holy Ghost, &c., with the prayer as before.

At Terce.

May the grace of the Holy Ghost enlighten our minds and our hearts.   Amen.

V. O God, make speed to save us.

R. O Lord, make haste to help us.

Glory.   Alleluia.

Hymn.

> After ten long days of waiting
>   Came the Spirit from above ;
> For He would not leave them orphans,
>   And He brought them gifts of love.

> Fount of truth and light and healing,
>   With His gifts that Spirit came ;
> Then the tongues of cloven brightness
>   Swiftly set their hearts on flame.

Ant. Come, Holy Ghost, &c., with the prayer as before.

At Sext.

May the grace of the Holy Ghost enlighten our minds and our hearts.   Amen.

V. O God, make speed to save us.

R. O Lord, make haste to help us.
Glory. Alleluia.

Hymn.

Then the sevenfold grace descended ;
  With it all their souls were filled ;
And they gave their Master's message,
  Speaking as the Spirit willed.

Forth they went, in light and gladness,
  Never ceasing, never dim ;
Leaving every love for Jesus,
  Giving every love to Him.

Ant. Come, Holy Ghost, &c., with the prayer as before.

At Nones.

May the grace of the Holy Ghost enlighten our minds and our hearts. Amen.
V. O God, make speed to save us.
R. O Lord, make haste to help us.
Glory. Alleluia.

Hymn.

Reigneth over all the Spirit
  Of the Father and the Son ;
Yet in lowly hearts He dwelleth
  Till the work of God be done.

Balsam of the true Physician,
  Always, Holy Ghost, Thou art ;
Healing every pain and sorrow,
  Giving joy to every heart.

Ant. Come, Holy Ghost, &c., with the prayer as before.

———

At Vespers.

May the grace or the Holy Ghost enlighten our minds and our hearts. Amen.
V. O God, make speed to save us.
R. O Lord, make haste to help us.
Glory. Alleluia.

Hymn.

Now the shades of evening deepen,
  Now the night comes on apace ;
Holy Spirit, give Thy servants
  Thoughts of fire and gifts of grace.

Thou dost shine on those who love Thee,
  Through the darkness of the night ;
Holy Spirit, be our Helper,
  Be our Everlasting Light.

Ant. Come, Holy Ghost, &c., with the prayer as before.

———

At Compline.

May the grace of the Holy Ghost enlighten our minds and our hearts. Amen.
V. Convert us, O God, our salvation.
R. And turn away Thy anger from us.

V. O God, make speed to save us.
R. O Lord, make haste to help us.
Glory.   Alleluia.

Hymn.

May the Spirit, dwelling in us,
  As the noonday, bright and clear,
Fill the souls of all His servants
  Full of love and holy fear.

So when Jesus comes to judgment,
  And before His throne we stand,
Words of gracious love will bring us
  Safely to the Promised Land.

Ant. Come, Holy Ghost, &c., with the prayer as Before.

Commendation.

These prayers, Eternal Spirit, I have offered to Thee, loving Thee and praising Thee and adoring Thee, in Thy beauty and Thy majesty, in Thy light and in Thy strength.   I pray, Divine Spirit, that Thou wilt always visit us with Thy inspirations and guide us by thy counsel, that one day we may dwell with Thee for ever in the Heavenly Kingdom.   Amen.

4.

Litany of the Holy Ghost.

(Taken from the Manual.)

A LITANY OF THE HOLY GHOST.

Lord, have mercy.

Christ, have mercy.

Lord, have mercy.

Holy Spirit, proceeding from the Father and the Son, *Have mercy upon us.*

Spirit, by whom the Holy Child Jesus was annointed,

Spirit, by whom Jesus, before He was taken up to Heaven, gave commandments to the Apostles whom He had chosen,

Spirit, that fell on all who heard the word when St. Peter was preaching,

Spirit of the Lord, the God of Israel,

Lord of men, who fillest the whole world and hast all power,

Thou who adornest the Heavens in Thy eternity, and seest all things, and workest all things that are good,

Spirit of truth, infallible Teacher, dividing gifts to all,

Spirit of wisdom and understanding,

Spirit of counsel and knowledge,

Have mercy upon us.

Spirit of fortitude and piety,
Spirit of the fear of the Lord,
Spirit, by whom the holy men of God
ever spoke,
Spirit, who didst tell in prophecy the
things to come,
Thou gift and promise of the Father,
Spirit, the Holy Paraclete, reproving the
world,
Spirit, by whom devils are cast out,
Spirit, by whom we are born again,
Spirit, by whom the love of God is shed
abroad in our hearts,
Spirit of the adoption of the sons of
God.
Spirit of grace and mercy,
Spirit, who helpest our infirmities and
givest testimony to our spirit that we
are the children of God,
Spirit, compassionate and kind, sweeter
than honey and the honeycomb,
Spirit, pledge of our inheritance, bringing
us to the land of life,
Spirit who art the beginning and the end,
giving life and strength and victory,
Spirit of judgment and salvation and joy,
Spirit of faith and hope, of peace and fer-
vor,
Spirit of humility and charity and chas-
tity,

Have mercy upon us.

Spirit of kindness and goodness, of long-suffering and gentleness.

Spirit of meekness and truth, of unity and comfort,

Spirit of sorrow for sin and of penance, of renewal and sanctification,

Spirit of patience and purity, of modesty and brotherly love,

Spirit of life.

Be propitious to us, *Spare us O Holy Ghost.*

Be propitious to us, *Hear us, O Holy Ghost.*

Be propitious to us, *Help us, O Holy Ghost.*

From the spirit of error and unbelief *Save us, O Spirit of the living God.*

From the spirit of uncleanness and lawlessness,

From the spirit of superstition and blasphemy,

From all falsehood and false dealing and lying.

From all despair and rebellious thoughts,

From vainglory and neglect of grace,

From all presumption and denial of the truth,

From pride, anger, and evil-speaking.

From all malice and darkness of soul,

From avarice and hardness of heart,

From all envy, jealousy, and hatred,

From slothfulness and gluttony,

Have mercy upon us.

Save us, O Spirit of the living God.

From all scruples and all distrust of Thy justice and Thy love,

By Thine Eternal Procession from the Father and the Son,

By the might of Thy invisible Unction,

By the sweetness of Thy name,

By the fire of Thy love,

By the fulness of graces in which Thou didst always possess the soul of the most blessed Virgin Mary,

By the overflowing depths of holiness wherein Thou didst flood with grace the soul of the Mother of God, in the Conception of the Word,

By the glory which Thou hast given in Heaven to Mary, Thy Spouse,

By Thy holy appearance, as a Dove, in the Baptism of our Lord.

By Thy holy appearance, as a white Cloud, in His Transfiguration,

By Thy holy appearance, at Pentecost, in cloven tongues of fire, on Mary, the Mother of God, and on the Apostles of the Lamb,

By Thy strength in the white-robed army of Martys,

By Thy light in Prophets and Doctors of the Church,

By Thy purity in Confessors and Virgins, in Priests and Bishops, and in all Thy ser-

Save us, O Spirit of the living God.

vants, both in religion and in the world,
Save us, O Spirit of the living God.

By the unspeakable goodness in which Thou
dost guide the Vicar of Christ, and which
Thou dost teach and govern the Church,
Save us, O Spirit of the living God.

We sinners beseech Thee to hear us,

That we may walk in the spirit, and not
fulfil the lusts of the flesh,

That we may never grieve Thee,

That Thou wouldest keep all religious Orders in charity and fervor, and guide
them in the true spirit of their Founders,

That Thou wouldest give to all Christian
people one heart and one soul,

That Thou wouldest perfect us in all virtues,

That Thou wouldest always listen to our
prayers,

We beseech Thee to hear us.

Spirit of the Father and the Son,

Spirit of Almighty God,

Lamb of God, who takest away the sins of
the world, pour upon us Thy Holy Spirit.

Lamb of God, who takest away the sins of
the world, pour upon us the Spirit, the
promise of Thy Father.

Lamb of God, who takest away the sins of
the world, pour upon us Thy most Holy
Spirit,

V. The Spirit of the Lord hath filled the whole earth :

R. And that which containeth all things hath knowledge of the Voice.

V. The voice of the Lord breaketh the cedars of Libanus.

R. The voice of the Lord divideth the flame of fire.

Prayer.

May the power of the Holy Ghost be ever with us, we beseech Thee, O God; and may He in His mercy cleanse our hearts and save us from all dangers; through our Lord Jesus Christ, who with Thee and the same Holy Ghost liveth and reigneth, one Tod, world without end.   Amen.

5.

A Prayer for Our Country.*)

We pray Thee, O God of might, wisdom, and justice, through Whom authority is rightly administered, laws are enacted and judgment decreed, assist *with Thy Holy Spirit of counsel and fortitude* the President of these United States, that his Administration may be conducted in righteousness, and be eminently useful to Thy people over whom he presides, by encouraging due respect for virtue and religion by a faithful execution of the laws in justice and mercy, and by restraining vice and immorality. Let the light of Thy divine wisdom direct the deliberation of Congress and shine forth in all their proceedings and laws framed for our rule and government, so that they may tend to the preservation of peace, the promotion of national happiness, the increase of industry, sobriety and useful knowledge, and may perpetuate to us the blessings of equal

---

*) This Prayer is said to have been composed by the Patriarch of the Rom. Catholic Hierarchy, Archbishop *John Carroll, of Baltimore.* It was solemnly recited by His Eminence, *Card. Gibbons,* at the Centennial Celebration of our Constitution in *Philadelphia,* in September 1887. As it contains a *direct* invocation of the Holy Spirit and we showed this Devotion to be the devotion of *"our country,"* we saw it fit to insert this oration.

liberty. We pray Thee for all judges, magistrates and other officers who are appointed to guard our political welfare, that they may be enabled by Thy powerful protection to discharge the duties of their respective stations with honesty and ability. We pray Thee especially for the Judges of our Supreme Court that they may interpret the laws with evenhanded justice. May they ever be the faithful guardians of the temple of the Constitution, whose construction and solemn dedication to our country's liberties we commemorate to-day. May they stand as watchful and incorruptible sentinels at the portals of this temple, shielding it from profanity and hostile invasion. May this glorious charter of our civil rights be deeply imprinted in the hearts and memories of our people. May it foster in them a spirit of patriotism. May it weld together and assimilate in national brotherhood the diverse races that come to seek a home among us. May the reverence paid to it conduce to the promotion of social stability and order, and may it hold the Ægis of its protection over us and generations yet unborn, so that the temporal blessings which we enjoy may be perpetuated. Grant, O Lord, that our republic, unexampled in the history of the world in material prosperity and growth of population, may be also under Thy overruling Providence a model to all nations in upholding liberty without license and in wielding authority without despotism. Finally, we recommend to Thy unbounded mercy all our brethren and fellow-citizens throughout the United States, that they may be blessed in knowledge and sanctified in the observance of Thy most holy law; that they may be preserved in union and in that peace which the world cannot give, and after enjoying the blessings of this life be admitted to those which are eternal. Our Father, who art in heaven, hallowed be Thy name; Thy kingdom come; Thy will be done on earth as it is in heaven. Give us this day our daily bread, and forgive us our trespasses as we forgive those who trespass against us; and lead us not into temptation, but deliver us from evil. Amen.

May the blessing of Almighty God, Father, Son, and Holy Ghost, descend upon our beloved country and upon all her people, and abide with them forever. Amen.

V.

Hymns to the Holy Ghost.

The following Hymns with the exception of the *first two* taken from the Manual of the late Very Rev. Father Rawes, D. D., and composed by the saintly deceased founder of the Confraternity, are mostly taken from a Collection of "Songs of the Spirit," giving a translation of nearly all the beautiful Latin Hymns to the Holy Ghost. We have reserved, however, all Hymns, referring to Pentecost for our next volume.

1.

To the Holy Ghost; God Over All, Blessed for Ever.

1.

O Paraclete, whom Jesus sent to me,
Who, one with Him, didst give Thyself to me,
Thou Love of God most High, who lovest me,
Thou King and Lord, who sweetly drawest me,
For life and light and love I come to Thee.

2.

From Father and from Son proceedest Thou ;
Of Father and of Son the love art Thou ;
Their Kiss of everlasting peace art Thou ;
The Bond unbroken of their rest art Thou ;
One God with Father and with Son art Thou.

3.

My soul is dark and hopeless without Thee ;
My heart is weak and withered without Thee ;
My life is burnt, like stubble, without Thee ;
I cannot say ' My Jesus ' without Thee :
O Loved One, pour Thy living light on me.

4.

I come to Thee, Almighty, Living One,
In poverty of soul, O Living One,
In sinfulness and death, O Living One ;
O make my spirit Thine, Thou Living One,
And be Thou mine, Thou Ever-Living One.

5.

For sorrow for my sins, I come to Thee ;
For confidence in God, I come to Thee ;
For faithfulness to grace, I come to Thee ;
To keep, O Love, my promises to Thee,
And walk in white with Jesus and with Thee.

6.

A Wind rain-laden from the South art Thou :
The Dew that falleth in the light art Thou ;
A Fountain in a desert land art Thou ;
A flame-girt Citadel of strength art Thou ;
The fiery Furnace of God's love art Thou.

7.

O Spirit of my Lord, who lightest me,
Thou, who didst come at Pentecost for me,
Thou Love, who seekest thirstingly for me,
Burn up all evil and all death in me,
And make my heart a holiness to Thee.

8.

O Gift of Jesus Crucified ; O Love ;
Send down Thy showers upon Thy fields, O Love;
Fill all the valleys with Thy corn, O Love ;
And girdle all the hills with joy, O Love ;
O First and Last; O uncreated Love.

9.

Thou stoopest in Thy deathless love to me,
Thou fillest at the House of God for me,
Thou crownest all the years with grace for me ;
Long-suffering Spirit, how I cling to Thee,
And love and bless and praise and worship Thee.

10.

My Jesus gave Himself in death by Thee,
A spotless Sacrifice to God by Thee :
O perfect all Thy gifts and fruits in me,
That, crowned and sceptred, I may dwell in Thee,
White-robed, palm-bearing in the light with Thee.

2.

A Hymn of the Servants of the Holy Ghost to their Loved One.

O Holy Ghost, Eternal God, Spirit of truth and grace and light, I adore Thee with a great adoration, and praise Thee with a great praise, and love Thee with a great love, as Thou art now proceeding from the Father and the Son, in Thy unbeginning life. The very thought of Thy procession of

love is to me a deathless joy, filling my heart
with tears. Thou art Lord God, Almighty.
From Thee I come: in Thee I live: to
Thee I go. Amid the prayers of St. Michael
and the Mother of Jesus I draw near to Thy
footstool, for they are very dear to Thee.

In the soul of St. Michael Thou didst pour
forth Thy grace when the might of his spirit
flashed, like a gleam of the brightness of
God, on the faces of the rebel-angels. By
Thee, O Spirit of truth, he was clothed with
beauty and girded with strength, in the
righteousness of his anger. By Thee he
was faithful as he stood with his flaming
sword on the battlements of Heaven, sceptred and crowned. His raiment was like
the sea in the morning light, as he cast his
diadem of gold before Him who liveth and
sitteth on His throne.

In the soul of Mary Thou didst pour forth
Thy grace, when without a sword she slew
the dragon. Then in her strength she trod
the proud ones in the dust; and the sweetness of her spirit went forth to the four
winds of Heaven. The fragrance of her
raiment was carried by the north wind and
the south wind through the garden of the
Spouse, like myrrh and stacte and cassia
from the ivory palaces of the King. The
brightness of her soul lighted up the sinless

kingdom, and shed its bloom of healing on the wanderers in the shadow of death.

The Mother of God arose and uttered her song. Her Son, the Son of God, arose; and turned the captivity of Sion. He, the Lord, fought among the valiant ones; at His feet they fell; and where they fell they lay stricken and dead. Then the remnant of the people was saved.

It was by Thee, O Spirit of grace, that Mary was thus made the Mother in Israel, when the gates of the enemy were overthrown. By Thee she put her hand to the nail, and her right hand to the workman's hammer. By Thee her soul was ever a brighter flame as she drew nearer to the King; and her raiment was like the noontide sun as she cast the splendor of her crown on the crystal-gold of the pavement that is beneath the feet of God.

In the rock-built city of the eternal years there standeth, high and lifted up, the great white Throne. Round it there clingeth a sapphire light; it is enfolded by a brilliance of fire. An amber-glory is its girdle of praise; and over it is the gleaming of a rainbow, 'in sight like unto an emerald.'

On that Throne, O Holy Ghost, Thou reignest for evermore, being God and Lord in Thy uncreated life. Before Thee the

living creatures ever stand in the might of
their beauty and the throbbing of their
love. Looking on Thee, they rest not day
and night saying, 'Holy, holy, holy, Lord
God Almighty, who was, and who is, and
who is to come.'

With unwearied longing, O Spirit of love,
Thou didst long for the salvation of the
lost. With unwearied patience Thou didst
wait for them. Lavishly Thou didst always
pour forth Thy graces on them, as they
spurned Thy counsel and cast away Thy
gifts and made themselves deaf to Thy
words and refused to obey Thy laws and
blinded themselves to Thy light and hardened their hearts. Through all Thy plead-
ing, and despite all Thy grace, they made
themselves a wilderness of fruitless trees,
without the sunshine, without water, without dew. Therefore they are cursed with
the deathless curse of God. They are like
the barren fig-tree; and no man can find
fruit on them for evermore, as they wither
in the breath of the unquenchable fire.

With boundless longing, O Spirit of
brightness, Thou didst long for the salvation of the saved; and wast ever adorable
in the patience of Thy love. Most lavishly
Thou didst pour forth Thy graces on them.
They listened to Thy words, and kept Thy

commandments, and walked in Thy ways, and took delight in Thy law. They loved Thy light, and were ever cleansed by Thy fire, and lived by Thy dew. Thou didst make them well-watered gardens, with unfailing springs and wealthiness of blossom and heavy-laden branches of fruit. The white lilies were fragrant with the sweetness of Thy love; and the scarlet blossoms of the pomegranates gleamed with a dewy radiance, brighter than the precious stones of Paradise, in the splendor of Thy light. Therefore when the Spouse came, day by day, to walk in His garden and to gather lilies, He gathered for Himself flowers of Thy planting and Thy watering. He held them in His pierced Hands, and took delight in their sweetness and their loveliness, as He looked upon them. Then He bore them on His Heart to the garden of the second spring. There, by the river of the water of life, they grow in the fadelessness of their beauty, filling Heaven with sweetness, for ever fair, for ever fragrant, for ever unwithered, in the dew of the light, in the day-spring of the Most High, in the glory of the Paradise of God.

With unwearied longing, O Spirit of compassion and pity, Thou art now seeking to save souls, in this accepted time, in this day of salvation, before the night cometh in which no man can work.

There are many who spurn Thy pleadings of love, and blind themselves with evil wiles, and choose the darkness. They will not listen to the voice of the charmer, charm he never so wisely; not even to Thy voice, O Thou wisest charmer of all. With unwearied patience Thou dost wait for them; and with love that knows no bounds Thou dost forgive them till seventy times seven times; for Thou art long-suffering, gracious, merciful, very pitiful, very full of compassion, very loving, very ready to forgive. A time comes when they repent no more. The light in them is quenched for ever. They choose to be lost, and their sins are not forgiven again.

There are many who love Thee and seek for Thy gifts, reckoning them far more precious than gold, and far dearer than life. In weakness and in trembling, with many falls, they follow whither Thou dost lead; for Thou art ever to them in the daytime a pillar of cloud, and in the nighttime a pillar of fire. They use Thy gifts according to Thy will. That which is weak Thou dost strenghten; that which is dry Thou dost water; that which is wounded Thou dost heal; that which is barren Thou dost make fruitful; that which is filthy Thou dost cleanse; that which is dark Thou dost lighten; that which is dead Thou dost make alive. Thou desirest not the death of a sinner; and therefore to sinners Thou givest new hearts and new spirits, that they may live to Thee, O Thou Spirit of love and grace. A time comes, when having been faithful to the end, they sin no more. They hear the words of acceptance, and the welcome of Jesus. Then the flame of Thy love burns in them ever bright and high, where Thy Servants serve Thee, and see Thy face, and have Thy name in their foreheads.

With boundless love, O Spirit of the living God, Thou dost hold me in Thy everlasting arms; in pity Thou dost stoop to me; in patience Thou dost bear with me; in loving-kindness Thou dost draw me to Thyself. With the longing of God, Thou dost ever 'thirst to be thirsted after;' and with great desire Thou desirest to save me from the blackness of the everlasting death. Thou pourest on my soul the former rain of grace; and the latter rain of salvation will come to me from Thee. Thou dost call me, and then waitest for my answer. Thou dost speak, and then waitest in Thy patience of love. Waiting, Thou dost call me again with the piercing sweetness of Thy voice. In my soul there is the thrillingness of Thy touch. Thou holdest me to Thyself in a clinging grasp of love, which nothing but my own wilful sin can loosen. In my heart Thou kindlest a fire, which no floods of pain or sorrow can quench. Give me grace, O loving Spirit, to follow always where Thou dost lead; and to turn back always when Thou forbiddest. This thing I have asked of Thee, O uncreated Love; and this is the longing of my soul.

As the days and the years go by, let me ever have in my heart more faithfulness to Thee. Be with me in the spring-time and in the harvest; in summer and in winter; by day and night.

The brightness of Thy hand is seen in the sparkling of the rhime and the glittering of the winter ice; in the frost-laden winds and the feathery flakes of snow. Thou givest snow like wool. Thou sendest forth the ice in crystals. I adore Thee, O Holy Ghost, the giver of cold.

The young strength of the year passes over the world like a fruitful flame. The sleeping seeds are stirred; and a new life clothes the leaflessness of the trees. A ripple of light passes over mountain and forest and meadow, in leaf and bud and blossom. The world sings before Thee, according to the days of her youth, and her coming up from the winter-darkness. I adore Thee, O Holy Ghost, the giver of life.

Then summer comes from Thee, clothed in her scented apparel, in the raiment of her glory. She has a sapphire crown which Thou hast set upon her head, and sandals of violet which Thou hast given her for her feet. She sets her foot on the rose-covered plain; and walks through the orchards and the vineyards and the fields of corn; all of them bright with Thy blessing; all of them overflowing from Thy fruitful hand. I adore Thee, O Holy Ghost, the giver of sunshine.

Autumn passes on with baskets of fruit and ears of corn; signs of the abundance of Thy life; gifts of Thy love to the children of men. Her crown is yellow, like the sheaves in the harvest-fields; and her feet are reddened with stains of the wine-press in the treading of grapes. Her sickle is bright. She is the bearer of corn and wine; the dispenser of the hospitality of God. I adore Thee, O Holy Ghost, the giver of food on earth and in Heaven.

Through all this beauty of the seasons, as I go onward to my grave, O maker of all things, let my love be stronger for Thee;

and let Thy graciousness be to me more and
more like rivers of water, and like the
shadow of a rock.

O Holy Ghost, uncreated Love, Thou art
God.   Thou sittest above the water-floods,
and before Thee the Cherubim cover their
faces.   Seraphim and Thrones veil their
eyes in the brightness of Thy light.   Yet I
will speak to Thee, my Tord, though I am
dust and ashes.   To Thee, O Spirit of life,
I lift up my hands as the deep of my sorrow crieth out to the deep of Thy love.
My soul is athirst for Thee.   Day by day I
long more to drink of Thy sweetness, O my
God and my love.   My spirit is fainting for
Thee and is waiting for Thee, till my change
comes and till Thy glory shall be seen.
Wash my heart with Thy dew of the light;
purify my heart with Thy flame of Heaven;
speak to my heart in the wilderness.   Teach
me to understand the piercingness of Thy
voice.   O Spirit of burning, Thy flames en-
fold me.   Thou steepest my heart in fire.
O Spirit of love, my heart leaps up to
Thee; as Thou givest Thyself to me; as
my lips ever taste the honey from the rock.
Thou steepest my soul in dew.   My spirit
stretches forth her arms to Thee; my
ears listen for Thee; my eyes look wist-
fully for Thee.   Through the night-watches

I look for the coming of Thy morning-light. Without Thee, my heart and my soul are like the earth when it is without water and without the sun. Waiting, I wait for Thee, O sweetest Sanctifier, whom my soul loveth, till the breaking of the day, till the resurrection of the flesh, till the spring-tide of sapphire-light in which the shadows flee away for ever. I shall be satisfied when Thy glory shall be seen.

O Holy Ghost, Thou Life-giver, let me be Thine for ever, and do Thou forever be mine. Let my soul be for ever bathed in Thy dewy splendors; and let it lie for ever, thrilling with love, stilled and adoring, on Thy uncreated Heart, in Thy embrace of fire. There let my spirit cling to Thee, O Thou Spirit of God. Make me faithful, O Holy Ghost, Thou living Fire; make me faithful in every thought to Thee. Fold me to Thy Heart, O undying Sweetness, and keep me there. After the winter and rain, do Thou O Lord of life, be mine for ever; and let me, Thy Servant, O Lord of love, for ever be Thine.

Glory be to the Holy Ghost for ever and ever.
Glory be to the Comforter for ever and ever
Glory be to the Spirit of truth for ever and ever.
Glory be to the Spirit of grace and prayers for ever and ever.
Glory be to the Spirit of Jesus for ever and ever.

Glory be to the Spirit of Father and of Son for ever and ever.
Glory be to the Third Person of the Adorable Trinity for ever and ever.

3.

Nunc Sancte Nobis Spiritus.

Wackernagel ascribes this to St. Ambrose, who died, A. D. 397.   Daniel in his first volume calls it Ambrosian (a term applied to a mass of hymns resembling those of Ambrose in style and structure, though of later date); and in his fifth volume refers its first appearance to the 7th or 8th century. The earliest MS. of it is at Darmstadt, and of the 8th century. It has always been used at Terce (the third hour).   The doxolgy is of later addition.   Translation by the famous Dr. John Henry Newman, 1836, from one of the *Tracts for the Times*.   He has since rewritten it.

Come, Holy Ghost, who ever One,
Art with the Father and the Son:
Come, Holy Ghost, our souls possess
With Thy full flood of holiness.

Let mouth and heart and flesh combine
To herald forth our creed divine;
And Love so wrap our mortal frame,
Others may catch the living flame.

Thou ever-blessed Three in One,
O Father and coequal Son,
O Holy Ghost, the Comforter,
Thy Grace on Thy redeemed confer.

4.

O fons Amoris Spiritus.

Of unknown origin. John Chandler. 1837.

O Holy Spirit, Lord of grace,
Eternal source of Love,
Inflame, we pray, our inmost hearts
With fire from Heaven above.

As Thou dost join with holiest bonds
The Father and the Son,
So fill Thy saints with mutual love
And link their hearts in one.

To God the Father, God the Son,
And God the Holy Ghost,
Eternal glory be from man,
And from the angel-host.

5.

Sancti Spiritus Adsit Nobis Gratia.

By Notker, a monk of St. Gall: died about 912: author of the famous hymn, "In the midst of life we are in death," and introducer of a new style of sacred poetry. This sequence, says the translator. "was in use all over Europe, even in those countries, like Italy and Spain, which usually rejected sequences. In the Missal of Palencia the priest is ordered to hold a white dove in his hand while intoning the first syllables, and then to let it go."— Prose version by Dr. John Mason Neale, in his *Mediaeval Hymns and Sequences*, second edition 1863.

The Grace of the Holy Ghost be present with
us;
And make our hearts a dwelling-place to Itself.

And expel from them all spiritual wicked-
ness, merciful Spirit, Illuminator of men.
Purge the fearful shades of our mind.
O holy Lover of thoughts that are ever wise,
Of Thy mercy pour forth Thine Anointing
into our senses.
Thou Purifier of all iniquities, O Spirit,
Purify the eye of our inner man,
To the end that the Father of all things may
be seen by us;
He, whom the eyes of none save the pure in
heart can behold,
Thou didst inspire the Prophets to chant
aforehand their glorious heralding of
Christ.
Thou didst confirm the Apostles, so that
they shall bear Christ's glorious trophy
through the whole world.
When, by His Word, God made the system
of heaven, earth, seas;
Thou didst stretch out Thy Godhead over the
waters, and didst cherish them, O Spirit!
Thou dost give virtue to the waters to
quicken souls;
Thou, by Thine inspiration, grantest to men
to be spiritual;
Thou didst unite the world, divided both in
tongues and rites, O Lord!
Thou recallest idolaters to the worship of
God, Best of masters!

Wherefore of Thy mercy hear us who call
 upon Thee, Holy Ghost,
Without Whom, as the faith teaches, all
 our prayers are in vain, and unworthy of
 the ears of God.
Thou, O Spirit, who by embracing the saints
 of all ages, dost teach them by the impulse of Thy Divinity ;
Thyself, by bestowing on the Apostles of
 Christ a Gift immortal, and unheard of
 from all ages,
Hast made this day glorious.

A Metrical Version.

By Erastus C. Benedict, LL. D., of the New York Bar,
translator of *The Hymns of Hildebert, and other Mediaeval
Hymns.*

Come Holy Spirit, with Thy Grace,
And make our hearts Thy dwelling-place,
 Our vices all expelling.
Thou only Source of light divine,
Come, chase away, with beams of Thine,
 The darkness in us dwelling.

Lover of thoughts, forever wise,
Do Thou our senses exercise,
 Thine unction on them pouring.
Spirit that cleanseth every Sin,
Come, purify our eye within,
 The soul to sight restoring.

For then, Almighty Maker, we
May face to face look up to Thee,
　The sacred precept showing.
That none, except the pure in heart,
Can ever see Thee as Thou art,
　Thy presence ever knowing.

When by His Word, God called to birth,
The frame of sea and skies and earth,
　Thou on the waters moving,
With gracious goodness didst incline
To cherish them with power divine,
　The Spirit's Godhead proving.

Thou dost the waters fructify,
And there the gift of life supply,
　Thy breath the gift bestowing.
Thou Spirit, breathing on the soul,
Dost bring it in Thine own control,
　Like Thee in spirit growing.

Thou, holy prophets didst impel
The coming Saviour to foretel,
　By inspiration teaching.
Thou strengthenedst His Apostles too,
To bear the cross the nations through,
　His blessed Gospel preaching.

And Thou this day hast glorious made;
And here, Thy wondrous power displayed
　The spread of truth presages,
The Apostles' faith Thou didst restore,
By gifts to them unknown before,
　Unheard in all the ages.

And here in one Thy power unites
The world, which many tongues and rites
　In former times divided.

Thou Best of masters, by Thy Grace,
Idolaters in every place
  To worship God are guided.

Then, Holy Ghost, with willing ear
We pray Thee now our prayers to hear,
  Without Thee unavailing.
Thou who Thy saints hast always taught,
To Thy embrace they must be brought:
Now make our prayers prevailing.

6.

O Ignis Spiritus Paracliti.

This lovely sequence is ascribed to St. Hildegarde, Abbess of the Cloister Rupertsburg, near Bingen; died 1179 or 1197. It was printed by Mone, I. 234: here is his account of it. "A MS. of the 12th century at Wiesbaden, containing the letters of Hildegarde gives this hymn with the music: the hymn was probably written by her. In the several parts, assonances and even rhymes are noticeable but there is no regular division into correspondent verses, as in the tropes and sequences. Hildegarde appears no longer to have recognized the rules of Notker's sequences, and probably held them to be unmetrical hymns, like the Latin psalms."

O Fire of God, the Comforter, O Life of all that
  live,
Holy art Thou to quicken us, and holy, strenght to
  give:
To heal the broken-hearted ones, their sorest
  wounds to bind,

O Spirit of all holiness, O Lover of mankind!
O sweetest taste within the breast, O Grace upon
    us poured,
That saintly hearts may give again their perfume
    to the Lord.
O purest Fountain! we can see, clear mirrored in
    Thy streams,
That God brings home the wanderers, that God the
    lost redeems.
O Breastplate strong to guard our life, O Bond of
    unity,
O Dwellingplace of Righteousness, save all who
    trust in Thee:
Defend those who in dungeon dark are prisoned by
    the foe,
And, for Thy will is aye to save, let Thou the
    captives go.
O surest Way, that through the height and through
    the lowest deep
And through the earth dost pass, and all in firmest
    union keep;
From Thee the cloulds and ether move, from Thee
    the moisture flows,
From Thee the waters draw their rills, and earth
    with verdure glows,
And Thou dost ever teach the wise, and freely on
    them pour
The inspiration of Thy gifts, the gladness of Thy
    lore.
All praise Thee, O Joy of life, O Hope and
    Strength, we raise,
Who givest us the prize of Light, who art Thyself
    all Praise.

7.

Amor Patris et filii.

From the Missal of Liege, 13th century: author unknown.
Dr. Neale calls it "A very admirable sequence: it seems as if
the poet had the *Veni Creator* before his eyes when writing it.
In some respects it resembles the Notkerian, in others the
Victorine sequences."

Love of Father and of Son,
True and glorious helping One,
  Comforter and hope of all :
Of the saints' unfading Light,
Prize of those that do aright,
  Lifter up of them that fall :
Giver of all holiness,
Fortitude and blessedness,
Lover of all righteousness,
Gracious and of perfect might,
Merciful and infinite
    Ever dearest, purest,
    Wisest, strongest, surest,
    Ever most unfailing Trust,
    Ever tender, ever just ;
Lightener of hearts, through whom the Father and
  the Son we find,
Spirit of counsel, Balm for sin, Giver of joy, and
  Source of mind,
    Unchanging, gentle, lowly,
    Unconquered, noble, holy,
    Ever loving, ever swift,
    Most divine and chosen Gift ;
    Understanding clear bestowing,
    Giver of affection glowing,
    Truth in Love forever showing:
      The Spirit of the Father,
      The Spirit of the Word,

The Comforter who quickeneth,
The finger of the Lord ;
Highest, sweetest, kindest, best,
Bountiful and lowliest ;
Who as He wills, and when He wills,
And where He wills, His Grace instils,
Teaches, fills, and lifts,
Enriches with His gifts :
To gladen the Apostles, to take their grief away,
The Spirit of all knowledge, He comes to earth
to-day :
He comes in all His fulness, the everlasting Lord,
And the Fount of perfect Wisdom upon their souls
is poured.

8.

Veni Creator Spiritus, Spiritus Recreator.

Adam of St. Victor, the most prolific, and probably the greatest, of the mediaeval hymnists. Born either in England or Brittany, he studied at Paris, and about A. D. 1130 entered the monastery. whence his name is taken, in the suburbs of that city. He died "somewhere between 1172 and 1192." The majority of his hymns, which had been lost, were recently discovered by M. Gautier. and the whole, amounting to 106, published at Paris in 1858.

Come, Creator Spirit high
Recreating ever ;
Given and giving from the sky,
Thou the Gift and Giver.
Thou the Law within us writ,
Finger Thou that writest it,
Inspired and Inspirer !

With Thy sevenfold graces good
  Sevenfold gifts be given,
For sevenfold beatitude
  And petitions seven.
Thou the pure unstained Snow,
That shall never sullied flow;
Fire, that burns not though it glow;
Wrestler, ne'er defeat to know,
  Giving words of wisdom.

Kindle Thou Thyself in us,
  Thou both Light and Fire;
Thou Thyself still into us,
  Breath of Life, inspire!
Thou the Ray and Thou the Sun,
Sent and Sender. Thee we own:
Of the blessed Three in One,
Thee we suppliant call upon,
  Save us now and ever.

9.

Veni, Summe Consolator.

Adam of St. Victor. Trench calls this "a very grand hymn:" it was first published by Gautier, 1858. The rendering (which we do not give entire) is by William John Blew, in *Lyra Mystica*, 1865. It is there headed, "After Adam of St. Victor," and is a paraphrase, or original poem founded on the Latin, rather than a translation. The ideas however are Adam's.

Health of the helpless, Crown of consolation,
Giver of Life, sweet Hope of man's salvation,
  Come with Thy Grace, O come,

Sun of the soul, and let Thy sunlight shine,
And warm with Love's soft glow the hearts of
   Thine;
And o'er the freshening field of Christendom
   Drop fatness, Dew divine;
   Till day by day, and hour by hour,
   Fed with the fulness of Thy power,
   Every woodland, every bower,
   Burst into leaf and fruit and flower,
      Filled with true Life's best food
   From thee, the Fountain of all good.

Thou hearest the Dew fall on earth, where it lies,
From the River Thou hearest the Vapor arise,
And the scent of sweet Odor Thou knowest,
   whereby
Thy faith can the presence of Godhead descry:
   Dew, that from the Godhead bursts,
   Whereof who deepest drinks the more he thirsts;
   Thirsting ever with a glow
   Quenchless as the Spirit's flow.
   Flowing alway, alway blessing:
   Thirst that knoweth no repressing.
   By Him the wave is consecrate
Where for new birth the holy people wait.
   The water on whose face was borne
   God's Spirit at Creation's morn.
   Fount, of all holiness the Spring,
      Whence flows true love abroad,
   Clear Fount that cleanseth from all sin,
      Fount from the font of God;
   Great Fount, all fountains hallowing,
Without all blessings and all God within.

   Fire of flint, with naught of wood,
   Faring forth in mystic flood,
   Kid consuming, Fire of Heaven,
   Feeding on the dread unleaven,
   Fire, all earthly fire unlike,
      On the altar of our heart

Strike the spark of light, O strike
The flame there still to burn and never thence
  depart.

Shadow of the maidens seven,
  Seven that compassed the One;
Type of the very Truth of Heaven
  That through all things dost run;
All-quickner, that with Life the world dost warm,
  O Spirit septiform;
In several shape outlined,
Yet varying not in kind,
Forefend it ever, that we say
  Of Thee, the almigthy Mind,
That Thou dost form obey,
  To form and shape confined.

Fire of Life, Life-giving Spring,
  Cleanse our hearts, and thither bring
Thy gifts of Grace, to enrich them and to bless;
    That kindled by the flame of charity,
  Meet offering we become to Thee
    Of love and holiness.
Breath of the Father and of the Son, Thou best
  Leech of the sinful, Solace of the sad,
Strength of the weak, the worn wayfarer's Rest,
  Health of the sick, make Thou the mourner glad,
Holy Love, like virgin's chaste,
  Fire of soul, yet maiden-pure,
Those whom evil passions waste
  May Thine hallowed untion cure.

    Voice of voices manifold,
    Subtle Voice, by sound untold,
    In the ear, and in the breast,
    Voice to each that whisperest :
    Voice enbreathed into the blest;
    Stilly Voice and secret-Voice
    Making men of peace rejoice,

Voice of sweetness, Voice of bliss,
Voice of voices, ours be this
Sounding through our inmost heart.

Light that bidst all lies depart,
Light that falsehood's router art,
Light that drawest unto Thee
Faith and Truth and Verity;
Light, vouchsafe to us, to all,
Life and health and wealth, that we,
Lit with Light perennial,
Live in sunshine that shall be
Brightening everlastingly.

10.

Simplex in Essentia.

Adam of St. Victor. The first half of this hymn (after the opening stanza), says Archbishop Trench, is ' in the true spirit of St. Paul and St Augustine, and hardly to be fully understood without reference to the writings of the latter, above all to his Anti-pelagian tracts; wherein he continually contrasts, as Adam does here, the killing letter of the Old, and the quickening spirit of the New Covenant. A few chapters of his treatise *De Spiritu et Litera*, c. 13—17, would furnish the best commentary on these lines.

Thou, who One in Essence livest
Sevenfold in the Grace Thou givest,
  Holy Spirit, on us shine!
All the shadows o'er us brooding,
All the snares our flesh deluding,
  Lighten by Thy beam divine.

Clad in fear, in darkness clouded,
Came the Law in figure shrouded :
  Now behold the Gospel ray,
Now the Spirit's wisdom better,
Hidden by the leafy letter,
  Open into perfect day.

'Neath the mount the people trembled:
In the upper room assembled,
  Heard a few the word of Grace :
Nobler law than Sinai telling,
Newer precepts, gifts excelling,
  Learn we in that holy place.

Trumpet clang and fiery wonder,
Midnight and the muttering thunder,
  Bickering lamps and sounds of dread,
Shook the Hebrew, conscience-stricken;
But the love it could not quicken,
  But the Oil of gladness shed.

See the fathers, fore-appointed,
God's embassadors anointed,
  Break the chains of human ill :
Raining truth, and judgment pealing,
With new tongues and doctrines healing,
  Heavenly signs attend them still.

See, the sick they kindly cherish :
Man's lost nature, nigh to perish,
  Love divine will seek, will find :
But the guilty, past repentance,
Scourge they will pursuing sentence ;
  Theirs to loose, and theirs to bind.

This the time to by-gone ages,
If you search the mystic pages,

In the Jubilee foreshowed;
Lo! the long described fulfilling,
When three thousand converts willing
  Bloomed within the Church of God.

Jubilee! the glorious token,
When the captive's bonds were broken,
  Rose anew Redemption's morn;
So from sin's dark, hapless prison,
By the law of love new risen,
  Sons of God are we freeborn.

11.

Part of a Hymn of Adam of St. Victor.

Translated in Edward Caswall's *Poems*, 1858.

O inexhaustive Fount of Light!
How does Thy radiance put to flight
  The darkness of the mind!
The pure are only pure through Thee;
Thou only dost the guilty free,
  And cheer with light the blind.

Thou to the lowly dost display
The beautiful and perfect way
  Of justice and of peace:
Shunning the proud and stubborn heart,
Thou to the simple dost impart
  True wisdom's rich increase.

Thou teaching, naught remains obscure:
Thou present every thought impure
  Is banished from the breast;
And full of cheerfulness serene
The conscience, sanctified and clean,
  Enjoys a perfect rest.

Dear Soother of the troubled heart!
At Thine approach all cares depart,
  And melancholy grief:
More balmy than the summer breeze,
Thy presence lulls all agonies,
  And lends a sweet relief.

Thy Grace eternal truth instils,
The ignorant with knowledge fills,
  Awakens those who sleep;
Inspires the tongue, informs the eye,
Expands the heart with charity,
  And comforts all who weep.

O Thou the weary pilgrim's Rest!
Solace of all that are opprest,
  Befriender of the poor:
O Thou in whom the wretched find
A sweet Consoler ever kind,
  A Refuge ever sure!

Teach us to aim at Heaven's high prize.
And for its glory to despise
  The world and all below:
Cleanse us from sin; direct us right;
Illuminate us with Thy Light;
  Thy peace on us bestow.

And as Thou didst in days of old
On the first Shepherds of the Fold
  In tongues of flame descend,

Now also on its pastors shine,
And flood with fire of Grace divine
  The world from end to end !

Lord of all sanctity and might,
Immense, immortal, infinite,
  The Life of Earth and Heaven !
Be, through eternal length of days,
All honor, glory, blessing, praise,
  And Adoration given.

12.

Spiritus Sancte Pie Paraclite.

Hildebert, Bishop of Mans (1097), and Archbishop of Tours (1125), died 1133. This fine hymn, is of very irregular and complicated structure, full of alliteration and interlaced rhymes.

O pious Paraclete! O Holy Spirit!
  Love of the Father and the blessed Son!
Goodness of each, the Heart of their twin-Being,
  Kindness Thou art, Sweetness and Joy in one.

O Chain, the highest God with man allying,
  Strength, man uplifted to the Power divine,
Meek, lowly, pure, the vain world purifying;
  All worship due, all honor true be Thine!

Voice, sweetly singing to the exiles lonely,
  Music, still ringing 'mid the city's mirth;

For those in tell despair their Solace only,
  For these a prayer for joys beyond the earth.

Inspirer of the good, Consoler, Healer
  Of all who mourn, Enligtener of the blind,
Purger of every lie, and the Revealer
  Of mysteries that try the groping mind.

Thou holdest up the weak; all those, who perish
  Dost kindly seek, dost gather all that stray;
The fainting and the fallen ever cherish,
  And tread before us in our toilsome way.

Ripening our early love, the soul perfected
  Thou drawest above from slimy pools of sin,
Into the happy road of peace directed,
  Fair Wisdom's hall through cloud it enters in.

Pillar of the sanctity, and Bread of chasteness!
  Gem of all gentleness, in want our Balm,
Increase of generous wealth, the upright's Fastness,
  The wretched's Port of health, the captive's Arm.

Spirit of Truth, all brother-hearts embracing.
  Judge of the world, as once Thou didst create,
With honors glad the worthy alway gracing ;
  Shaming the bad with his self-chosen fate.

Thou blowest where Thou listest ; out of error
  Dost lead the doubting, and with knowledge fill :
Thy might our weakness stays in sudden terror ;
  Thou rulest in sure ways of wisdom still.

Order that beauty to each creature giveth,
  Beauty that ordereth each with grace from Thee;

In word, in deed, in thought, in all things liveth,
  Words sooth, deeds truth, thoughts of Thy
    purity.

Good Gift and perfect God! Thine every motion
  Of intellect, of heart, on each endeavor
Thy Spirit waits; shapes, guides our true devotion,
  And at Heaven's gates crowneth the blest for-
    ever.

CORRIGENDA.

On page 68, line 14, read "motives" instead of "notices."

On page 92, line 12, read "he who knows" instead of "he knows."

On page 93, line 8, read "Cor unum et anima una" instead of "Cor meum et anima mea."

    line 12, read "Cor unum" instead of "Cor meum."

    line 14, read "Anima una" instead of "Anima mea."

On page 115, line 2, read "propagation" instead of "prerogative."

On page 119, line 20, before "XVI, 18" insert "Matth."

On page 177, line 3, read "American" instead of "Amrican."

On page 178, line 14, read "without" instead of "in the out."

On page 189, line 15, read "justification" instead of "satisfaction."

On page 210, line 3, read "Himself" instead of "himself."

On page 215, line 14, read "than" instead of "then."

    line 18, read "perfection" instead of "profession"

On page 218, line 11, read "spirit" instead of "Spirit."

    line 18, read "Israelites" instead of "Israelities."

    line 19, read "testament" instead of "treatment."

On page 220, line 29, insert "the" before "promise."

On page 224, line 7, read "flower" instead of "flowers."

On page 228, line 17, read "revering" instead of "reserving."

On page 230, line 25, read "before" instead of "afterwards."

On page 242, line 9, read "as" instead of "than."

On page 244, lines 9 and 10, read "founded" instead of "found."

On page 247, line 25, read "there to be made" instead of "make partakers of."

On page 248, line 19, insert "by" before "my."

On page 264, line 22, read "proclaimed of" instead of "proclaimed to."

On page 265, line 21, read "she" instead of "He."

On page 275, line 12, read "merely" instead of "nearly."

On page 276, line 9, read "their operation" instead of "the operation."

    line 13, insert "to" after "so."

    line 29, read "he" instead of "He."

On page 277, line 1, read "be" instead of "He."

On page 279, line 13, read "in a word" instead of "in a work."

On page 288, line 11, read "prophecy" instead of "prophesy."

On page 299, line 34, insert "procession of the" before "Holy Ghost."

On page 304, line 12, read "darkness" instead of "action."

Made in the USA
Lexington, KY
28 June 2018